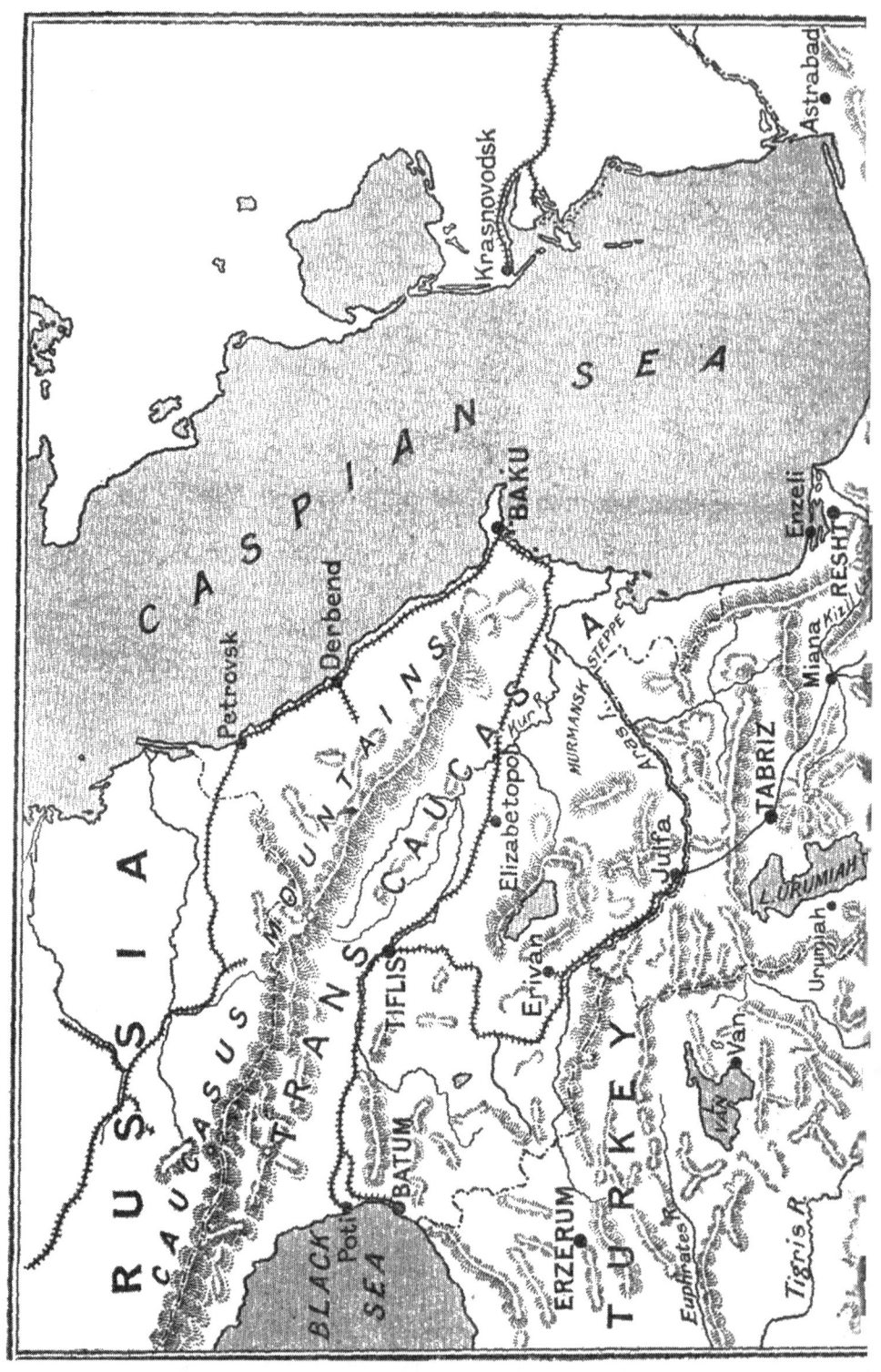

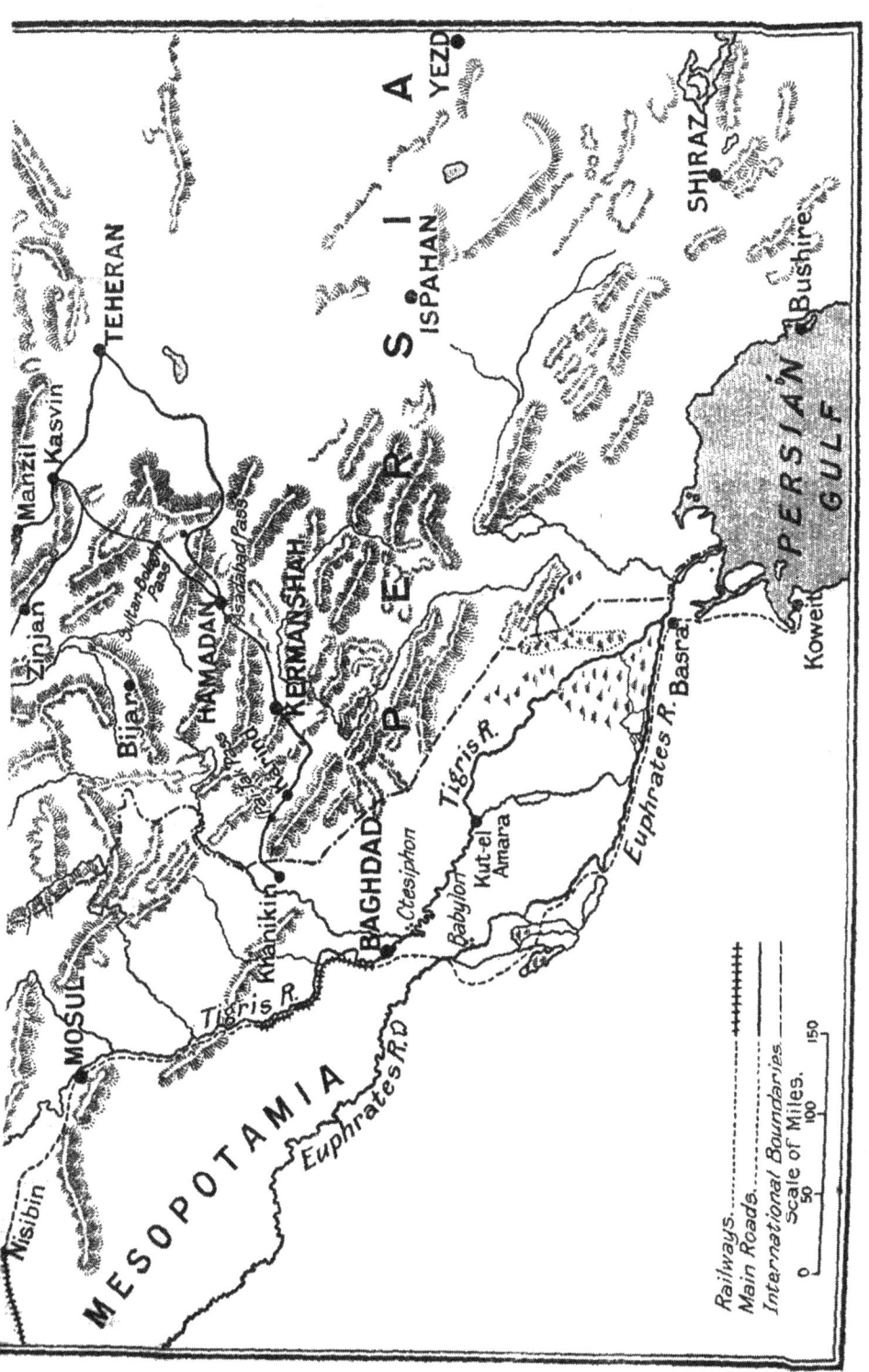

THE ADVENTURES OF DUNSTERFORCE

Major-General L. C. Dunsterville.
C.B., C.S.I.

LONDON, EDWARD ARNOLD

THE ADVENTURES OF DUNSTERFORCE

THE ADVENTURES OF DUNSTERFORCE

Major-General L. C. Dunsterville, C.B., C.S.I.

The Naval & Military Press Ltd

Reproduced by kind permission of the Central Library, Royal Military Academy, Sandhurst

Published by
The Naval & Military Press Ltd
Unit 10, Ridgewood Industrial Park,
Uckfield, East Sussex,
TN22 5QE England
Tel: +44 (0) 1825 749494
Fax: +44 (0) 1825 765701
www.naval-military-press.com
www.military-genealogy.com

© The Naval & Military Press Ltd 2007

The Naval & Military Press ...

...offer specialist books for the serious student of conflict. The range of titles stocked covers the whole spectrum of military history with titles on uniforms, battles, official histories, specialist works containing Medal Rolls and Casualties Lists, and numismatic titles for medal collectors and researchers.

The innovative approach they have to military bookselling and their commitment to publishing have made them Britain's leading independent military bookseller.

In reprinting in facsimile from the original, any imperfections are inevitably reproduced and the quality may fall short of modern type and cartographic standards.

Printed and bound by Antony Rowe Ltd, Eastbourne

PREFACE

THIS book is not intended to form a precise record of military operations and will be of small value to the student of strategy and tactics; it is written solely with the design of interesting the general reader. Stories of the Hush-Hush Army, which bear no relation to facts, have been for a long time current, and it may be as well, therefore, to give an account of the actual occurrences. It would be impossible for any one member of my force to give a truthful account of anything but the actual operations in which he was personally engaged, and this would give no idea at all of the undertakings and achievements of the mission as a whole; the task, therefore, devolves on myself. This account is written from memory with only the assistance of a rough private diary. I can, therefore, only guarantee the facts while leaving numbers "round" and figures "approximate."

To attempt a detailed account of the various operations undertaken by detachments of the Force would be quite beyond the scope of the present volume, and such accounts to be of real value should be written by those who led the several expeditions. Thus Major Wagstaff would tell of the Zinjan-Mianeh venture among the Shah-Savans, Major Starnes of the dealings round Bijar with the Kurdish tribes, Major Macarthy of the Persian levies, Colonel

Matthews of the fighting round Resht, Colonel Keyworth of the Baku fighting, and Colonel Stokes of Staff work in a revolutionary army.

In recounting the various episodes, it is not possible always to give full recognition to those officers who contributed on each occasion to the success of certain enterprises or to whose ingenuity and suggestions certain plans were due. Such recognition is found in the official records, and the reader will understand that when a General is writing an account of the achievements of a force under his command, it is not possible for him entirely to eliminate the first person and say " I and my Staff," or to add in each case the name of any officer who may have furnished the brilliant idea.

I was particularly well served not only by my Staff, but by all the officers to whom various tasks were entrusted, and to whom I desire to record my deep sense of gratitude.

L. C. DUNSTERVILLE.

AGRA.

CONTENTS

CHAPTER		PAGE
I.	THE GATES AJAR	1
II.	A PLEASURE TRIP ON RECONNAISSANCE	11
III.	"THE SEA! THE SEA!"	31
IV.	WE FALL BACK TO HAMADAN	50
V.	AN ALLIANCE OF PHANTOMS	68
VI.	WE GET TO KNOW OUR HOSTS	85
VII.	FAMINE	102
VIII.	A PAUSE AT HAMADAN	118
IX.	A STEP IN ADVANCE	139
X.	THE LAST STAGE TO THE SEA	155
XI.	TURKS, INFIDELS AND HERETICS	175
XII.	IN TOUCH WITH BAKU	195
XIII.	WE MAN THE BAKU LINE	218
XIV.	SHORT OF EVERYTHING	239
XV.	THE ENEMY WITHIN THE GATES	263
XVI.	THE SHADOW OF COMING EVENTS	279
XVII.	THE WITHDRAWAL	297
	INDEX	319

LIST OF ILLUSTRATIONS

PORTRAIT OF THE AUTHOR	*Frontispiece*
	TO FACE PAGE
"COLONEL DUNCAN AND MYSELF SET OFF IN THE EARLY MORNING"	24
THE KASVIN–RESHT ROAD	32
LIEUTENANT SINGER IN THE ARMOURED CAR	36
"A MOUNTAIN STREAM PROVIDES WATER AND A DRAINAGE CHANNEL"	58
GENERAL BARATOV	70
COSSACKS HOMEWARD BOUND	86
A COURTYARD IN THE BAZAAR, HAMADAN	112
RESHT, CLOSE TO THE CONSULATE	164
A BRANCH OF THE SEFID-RUD AT RESHT	172
MIRZA KUCHIK KHAN: RETURNED TO CIVIL LIFE	190
"A MAZE OF NARROW AND TORTUOUS STREETS"	202
OIL WELLS AT BIBI-EIBAT	226
"THE QUAYS IN THE NEIGHBOURHOOD OF OUR WHARF"	232
MAJOR-GENERAL DUNSTERVILLE AND COLONEL ARATUNOV	256
"REFUGEES ESCAPING FROM THE WRATH TO COME"	260
AFTER THE EVACUATION. THE 39TH INFANTRY BRIGADE AT ENZELI	314

LIST OF MAPS

GENERAL OUTLINE MAP OF MESOPOTAMIA, PERSIA AND TRANSCAUCASIA . . . *Inside front cover*

THE ENVIRONS OF BAKU . . . . *Facing page* 220

THE BAKU PENINSULA . . . . . *At end*

THE ADVENTURES OF DUNSTERFORCE

CHAPTER I

THE GATES AJAR

THE history of these adventures, which cover the whole stretch of country lying between Baghdad and Baku, deals with a problem which by a curious coincidence abounds in unavoidable alliterations, the letter B standing for Berlin, Batoum, Baku, Bokhara and Baghdad, and if one wanted to run the alliteration to death, one might add Byzantium for Constantinople. Thus the object of the mission with which I was ordered to proceed to the Caucasus at the end of 1917, as well as the enemy plans that led to the dispatch of the mission, can best be set forth briefly under this letter of the alphabet.

One of the big items in the deep-laid pre-war schemes of Germany for world-domination was the absorption of Asia Minor and the penetration into further Asia by means of the Berlin–Baghdad railway. When Baghdad was taken by the British in March 1917, and the prospect of its recapture by the Turks appeared very remote, the scheme for German penetration into Asia had to be shifted further north and took the obvious line BERLIN–BAKU–BOKHARA.

In this latter scheme it was evident that the Southern Caucasus, Baku and the Caspian Sea would play a large

2 THE ADVENTURES OF DUNSTERFORCE

part; and the object of my mission was to prevent German and Turkish penetration in this area.

Fate ordained that, just at the time that the British thwarted the more southern German scheme by the capture of Baghdad, the Russian breakdown opened the northern route to the unopposed enterprise of the Germans. Until the summer of 1917 the Russian troops held firm, though it was obvious that the process of disintegration could not long be delayed. Their line extended from South Russia, through the Caucasus, across the Caspian, through North-West Persia until its left joined up with the British right on the frontier of Persia and Mesopotamia, east of Baghdad. By the autumn of 1917 this line was melting away, troops deserted *en masse* and the entire army announced its intention of withdrawing from the struggle and proceeding home.

Thus in the neighbourhood of Erzerum the Turkish Army, acting unconsciously as the Advanced Guard of German aims, found nothing between it and the long-coveted possession of the Southern Caucasus, with the exception of a few Armenian troops, disorganized, without cohesion and equally impregnated with the spirit of the revolution. But, as the line of the Turkish advance lay through their homes, they were compelled to offer resistance. Tiflis, the capital of the Southern Caucasus, was likely to fall without serious resistance into the hands of the enemy, and the capture of this town would give the Turko-German armies control of the railway line between Batoum on the Black Sea and Baku on the Caspian, the enormously valuable oilfields of Baku, the indispensable minerals of the Caucasus Mountains, and the vast supplies of grain and cotton from the shores of the Caspian Sea.

The scene of conflict being too far removed from any of the main areas of the war—Baghdad to Baku is 800 miles—it was quite impossible to send sufficient troops to meet the situation.

The only possible plan, and it was a very sound one, was to send a British mission to Tiflis. This mission, on reaching its destination, would set to work to re-organize the broken units of Russian, Georgian and Armenian soldiery, and restore the battle-line against the Turkish invasion. The prospects were considerable, and success would be out of all proportion to the numbers employed or the cost involved. It was attractive and practical.

The honour of command fell to my lot, and I set forth from Baghdad with the leading party in January 1918.

Let me state at the outset that it entirely failed to achieve its original object, and never even reached Tiflis ! But the story I propose to tell is of its endeavours to reach that spot, of the other tasks that fell incidentally to its lot, and of its minor achievements, which I am convinced were of great value to the Allied cause.

It will be left to the reader to deduce from the general narrative the value of these achievements, but I may draw attention to the one immediately following the abandonment of the Tiflis scheme, to wit, that by a kind of moral camouflage, the original first party of twelve officers and forty-one men filled the gap left in North Persia by the evacuating Russians on 300 miles of road, and entirely checked all enemy enterprise on this line, though hampered by the threatening hostility of the neutral Persians.

Before beginning the narrative of the adventures of the mission, it may be interesting to survey very briefly the Tiflis scheme.

From the enemy's point of view, the Turk would undoubtedly be actuated by an intense desire to gain possession of valuable territory in the only theatre of war where victories fell like ripe plums into his lap, he could indulge his long-standing hatred of the Armenian to its fullest extent, and the individual soldier would be tempted

4 THE ADVENTURES OF DUNSTERFORCE

by the rich loot which the larger cities would afford. But on the other hand the Turkish Army as a whole was no longer the well-organized machine of 1916. The troops were tired, and their leaders were no longer inspired by the certainty of ultimate victory, but rather were depressed by the extreme probability of the contrary result. Against such an army it should be easy to reorganize the large numbers of Georgian and Armenian troops, whose fighting spirit would be multiplied a hundredfold by their determination to keep the hated invader out of their homes.

This last proposition seems so obvious that it might well be taken as a foregone conclusion. Unfortunately the event proved the exact reverse! The revolution had so taken the heart out of the men, that this primitive spirit of the defence of hearth and home, one of the strongest instincts the human being possesses, was entirely absent in the case of the South Caucasians.

The only possible line of success for the mission would have been to have worked on this feeling of patriotism and love of home. It may seem incredible, but it is certain that such a feeling did not exist, and plans based upon it would have been foredoomed to failure; but to make the assertion is surely not to be laid to the blame of those who counted on the existence of such a feeling.

The truth of the matter is that Tiflis, long before the war, had what the Russians call a German "orientation."

In their deep preparation for this great war the German left no stone unturned, and the Caucasus, north and south, had been thoroughly exploited by them in view of possible eventualities.

The inhabitants of Tiflis read their Reuters and compared them with the glorious revelations of the German wireless: Obviously Germany was going to win the war. "Therefore why should we have the British here to prolong matters ? Let the Turks take the country : we look to a victorious and magnanimous Germany to protect us from Turkish excesses and to turn them out again when the war is over. The Turkish invasion is only a temporary inconvenience from which the Germans will later relieve us." Such was undoubtedly the Tiflis train of thought, especially among the Georgian population. At the back of the Armenian mind always lay the terror of impending massacre.

This lack of national spirit is an example of the terrible uncertainty with which those are confronted who are called on to deal with military problems. The one factor that may fairly be regarded as certain turns out exactly contrary. When this story reaches the final stage of the defence of Baku against the Turks, it will be seen that in the eleventh hour, with their beloved city, their private wealth, their wives and children, in hourly danger of falling into the hands of the enemy, and firmly believing in the certainty of a general massacre—even at such a moment as this, the spirit on which a successful defence could alone be based was never evoked. There is no doubt that this lack of heart must be attributed to the revolution. All the factors that go to make up what we call " bravery " are shivered to pieces in a revolution, and their place is taken by a dull apathy that meets all situations with the hopeless query, " What is the use of anything ? "

So much for the South Caucasus. Now as to Persia.

Although Persia was declared neutral, her territory had been used from the commencement of the war, both by the Russians and the Turks, who fought each other up and down the road from Kasvin to Kermanshah, until our capture of Baghdad left the Russians in undisputed possession. In 1917, therefore, the Russians were holding the road running north-east from the Perso-Mesopotamian frontier to the Caspian Sea. The Turks, though not showing any intention of attacking on that line, still kept a sufficient number of troops on a line parallel to and north-west of the Russian line to necessitate a constant look-out in that direction.

When, with the advent of the Bolsheviks to power in November 1917, the Russian troops in North Persia began to break away, it became obvious that a gap of some 450 miles would be left open on the right flank of the British Mesopotamian army, through which Turkish and German agents and troops could flood Central Asia unopposed.

It was hoped to stop this gap by re-enlisting, under the British flag, a sufficient number of well-paid volunteers from the ranks of the retreating Russians.

The efforts made in this direction were a complete failure.

The reasons for the failure were mainly those narrated above—revolutionaries will kill, but they won't fight. The few men enlisted were quite worthless, and the revolutionary Committees proclaimed sentence of death on any one supporting the movement; so it had to be abandoned. As a matter of fact, the gap created in this portion of the line was actually filled by the officers and N.C.O.'s of the mission, under circumstances which will be narrated farther on.

It only remains now to give a very short description of the geography of the terrain.

Leaving Baghdad in an easterly direction, the monotonous flat country of Mesopotamia continues for about 80 miles as the crow flies, until the Persian frontier, which practically coincides with the foot of the mountains, is reached. The approach to the hills is gradual, commencing with the usual Jebels, or foothills, which begin to break the level of the dead flat ground at about 20 miles before we come to the actual frontier.

From this point on to the Caspian Sea, 400 miles in

a straight line, the country consists of a succession of barren hills and fertile valleys, the line of the parallel ranges running N.W. to S.E., while the road runs N.E., thus taking each range at right angles. The passes run to between 5,000 and 8,000 feet above sea-level, and the general level of the country lies between 3,000 and 7,000 feet.

On the Taq-i-Giri Pass, by which travellers from Mesopotamia enter the Persian uplands, there are a few stunted oaks on the hillsides; these are practically the only wild trees seen until we come to the Elburz mountains, which skirt the southern shores of the Caspian Sea. Passing through this mountain range at Menjil, the last 70 miles down to the sea display an example of the vivid contrasts that only Asia affords. After more than 300 miles of hills as barren as the rocks of Aden, a country is suddenly entered which is clothed in the very thickest of forest, producing an effect as striking as a sudden transition from one planet to another. The last 20 miles of this road down to the Russian Concession Port of Kazian (or Enzeli) lies on the flat among low dunes, and represents the portion of the sea that has gradually been silted up in the course of centuries by the mud brought down from the Elburz range and the sand blown in from the sea by the northerly gales.

The Caspian basin encloses every sort of climate and temperature, the shores display every variety of country, inhabited by numberless races, the fragments of submerged great races of the past. As regards climate, the port of Astrakhan at the mouth of the Volga in the extreme North is icebound in winter, while the country round Enzeli is rice-growing; plantains and palms flourish in the open, and the winter is chiefly characterized by warm drizzling rain.

The country on the north-west, north and most of the eastern shores is flat, either grass-growing steppe or

8 THE ADVENTURES OF DUNSTERFORCE

sandy desert ; on the west and south tower the offshoots of the Caucasus range and the magnificent range of the Elburz Mountains.

The principal races inhabiting the shores are Russians and Cossacks in the northern area, Turcomans to the east, Persians and Gilanis to the south, Tartars, Georgians, Armenians and Daghestanis on the west.

With the exception of the southern shore, which is Persian territory, the entire sea lies within the Russian zone, and on this southern shore, a veritable Naboth's vineyard, the chief port and the fisheries form a Russian concession—and a very valuable concession it is. The road from the port to Teheran and to Hamadan is equally a Russian property.

The traffic on the sea is very considerable, as it forms a sort of exchange market for the caviare and frozen fish of the Russian fisheries, the rice of Gilan and the wheat and cotton of Turkestan, against the oil of Baku and the cotton fabrics and other European commodities that are brought down the Volga to Astrakhan. Where oil fuel is so cheap, and fierce storms so frequent, there is not much scope for sailing ships, and the fleet of steamships is large for so small an area. Without having access to official figures we calculated on a mercantile fleet on the Caspian of something like 250 ships, running from 200 tons to over 1,000, some, built in England, having reached the Caspian viâ the Volga on their own bottoms.

A small fleet of three very diminutive gunboats, the *Kars*, the *Ardaghan* and the *Geok Tepe*, rules the waves in this inland sea, and are sufficient to keep order where there can be no opposition. This fleet has naturally had a good deal to say in politics since the revolution started, mainly with a view to the financial advantage of the sailors. It is remarkable how willingly a revolutionary government listens to the demands of the fleet when the seat of government is on the seashore and the guns of the ships are trained on vital spots.

The foregoing very rough outline of the political events leading up to the determination to dispatch the mission to Tiflis, and of the general nature of the country traversed in the course of operations, will suffice, I hope, to give the reader a sufficient notion of the setting of the scene.

One other point requires to be dealt with—the composition of the mission.

In view of the special nature of the task with which it was to deal, actual troops would not be required. A nucleus of some 200 officers, and a similar number of N.C.O.'s, would take the place of leaders and instructors in the reorganized units.

These officers and N.C.O.'s were chosen from all the units in the various theatres of the war, from France, Salonika, Egypt and Mesopotamia. They were chiefly from the Canadian, Australian, New Zealand and South African contingents. All were chosen for special ability, and all were men who had already distinguished themselves in the field. It is certain that a finer body of men have never been brought together, and the command was one of which any man might well be proud.

But the assembling of the force was a difficult task. If time had not been an important factor, it would have been a great advantage to have first assembled it at some point, and then set forth on our quest. This, however, was quite impossible. Time was the chief factor in the problem, and I had to push off personally as soon as I could get together an advance party of a few officers.

The remainder of the force arrived in batches during the next two months. In its entirety it was never collected in one place, owing to the varying nature of the duties and the huge area in which it was operating. This, in itself, was a great handicap, but quite unavoidable.

My own knowledge of the Russian language and known sympathy with Russia had probably a good deal to do with my selection for the task, but it was not to be expected that the officers of my force would, as a general rule, be linguists : and they were not.

There were, however, a few who could manage a little Russian as a result of lessons taken on board ship on the way out, and here and there one or two who could manage intelligible French. The officers originally selected for Staff work were admirably chosen and included several who could speak both Russian and French.

Others from the remoter corners of the earth were acquainted with the languages of the tribes they were accustomed to deal with, but such languages would obviously bear little affinity to those of Asia or Europe. On one occasion I had to explain that the Zulu " clicks " would be of no assistance in mastering Persian !

To this body of British officers were added a splendid batch of Russian officers sent out from London, and various other Russians, refugees from the revolution who joined me later, and whose services were of the greatest value.

This, then, will suffice for a general introduction. I have endeavoured to make clear the strategic and political situation that resulted in the sending of the mission : I have given a rough description of the country over which the mission was to seek its adventures, and I have introduced the characters who are to take part in these adventures.

CHAPTER II

A PLEASURE TRIP ON RECONNAISSANCE

ON December 24, 1917, while in command of the 1st Infantry Brigade on the North-West Frontier of India, I received secret orders to report at Army Head Quarters at Delhi, with a view to proceeding overseas on special work.

The Frontier Tribes, who in the previous year had made things quite lively for us, had been lulled to rest by the various ingenuities of frightfulness that accompany modern war—aeroplanes and armoured cars having quite taken the heart out of them.

Things were distinctly dull, and one was beginning to feel that one had drifted into a backwater, when the welcome orders came bringing the longed-for opportunity of plunging once more into the tide.

Arrangements for departure occupied the shortest possible time, and after a brief stay at Army Head Quarters in Delhi for the purpose of conference and selection of Staff, I embarked at Karachi on January 6, 1918, reaching Basra—the new Basra, with its wonderful development and miles of wharves—on January 12th.

On the morning of January 18th I arrived in Baghdad and reported to General Head Quarters.

So far, I was the single representative of my force, and though impatient of delay, it was obviously necessary for me to await my officers there. Even had they been at once available, a certain amount of delay would have been inevitable. There were plans to be considered, experts to be consulted, office arrangements to be perfected and the thousand and one things to be attended to that must crop up on such occasions.

In the first place it was desirable to appreciate the situation and to realize what difficulties would have to be overcome. For this purpose it was necessary to study maps and get in touch with the latest intelligence from the regions in which we would be operating. In this matter I was greatly helped by Major Sir Walter Barttelot, D.S.O., of the Coldstream Guards, who had recently traversed the whole route while the Russians were holding it and before their line had broken away. At this time, Captain G. Goldsmith arrived from England on a special mission which was to link up with mine, and I decided to send both these officers through in motor-cars a few days in advance of my party, to ensure petrol supply at certain points *en route*.

I calculated that I should be able to start in a few days with ten or twelve officers travelling in Ford touring cars and vans.

For the party of twelve officers and two clerks which eventually composed the advanced party, it was necessary to have four touring cars and thirty-six vans—a liberal amount of transport, it may be thought, for so small a party. But the vans are very small and light, and from the space available in each must be deducted the requirements of the driver, including liberal bedding in view of the climatic conditions anticipated. Then there was a considerable weight of money in Persian silver and English gold, an office establishment, medical stores, reserve rations and other impedimenta inseparable from an undertaking of this sort.

In appreciating the situation, the following unfavourable factors constituted a rather formidable list:

A PLEASURE TRIP ON RECONNAISSANCE

(*a*) Road difficulties.
(*b*) Winter storms.
(*c*) Question of Persian neutrality—a very doubtful factor at this period.
(*d*) Hostility of Kurds.
(*e*) Possible difficulties with revolutionary Russians, especially with Bolsheviks.
(*f*) Declared hostility of the Jangalis of Gilan on the South Caspian shore.
(*g*) Supplies of food.
(*h*) Supplies of petrol.

To take these in turn : The road from Baghdad to Khanikin, 94 miles, over the ordinary hard clay soil, was reported quite good in dry weather ; from Khanikin to Hamadan, 240 miles, a very doubtful road, improved and made passable for motors by the Russians, difficult in good weather, impassable in bad ; from Hamadan to Enzeli (Kazian), 267 miles, a first-rate road made by the Russian Road Company many years ago, and now sadly in need of repair.

Snowstorms were reported to be frequent at this time of year, possibly blocking the passes.

Possible hostility of Persians ; it was hard to feel certain on this point. The known factors were that the inhabitants were well armed and strongly resented our intrusion. At the same time a study of Persian character in the world-famous book of "Haji Baba of Ispahan" led one to discount the dangers of this hostility.

The Kurds lying to the north of the road were rather a different matter. Living in the most mountainous regions and doing a good business in highway robbery, the mention of their name strikes awe into the ordinary Persian, though the Russians, too, held them in great respect and certainly over-estimated their ferocity. During the Russian tenure of this road, losses of individual men from Kurdish raiders were very frequent. Comparison was made between them and the Pathans of the North-West Frontier of India, and had this been a true comparison the prospects of the mission would indeed have been dismal.

The meeting with the Russian Army in revolution, and especially with the Bolshevik portion of it, seemed to promise insuperable difficulties, as the Bolsheviks had already, in resentment at the British Government's refusal of recognition, adopted a strongly anti-British attitude.

The Jangalis of Gilan, under the redoubtable revolutionary leader Kuchik Khan, might offer an even greater obstacle to the success of the mission. Mirza Kuchik Khan had forcibly taken over the administration of the whole of the Gilan country, through which lay the last 70 miles of our road, had adopted a fiercely anti-foreign programme threatening death and destruction to all white men who came his way, and was now, in conjunction with the Bolsheviks, holding Enzeli, the only port on the Caspian from which we could hope to embark.

Difficulties of this sort usually melt away when firmly confronted, but should they be all successfully overcome, we would be eventually landed in the port of Baku, more strongly Bolshevik and anti-British at this time than any point in the Caucasus.

Next, the question of food supply for fifty-five officers and men would certainly prove difficult in a famine-stricken and war-devastated country in the depth of winter; and finally the question of petrol supply was extraordinarily difficult and was naturally the key of the whole situation, as every pint had to come from Baghdad, and the difficulty thus increased in geometrical progression with every mile of road traversed.

The risk of failure of petrol supply was very considerable, but in the end no such failure occurred. From

A PLEASURE TRIP ON RECONNAISSANCE

Baghdad to Kermanshah, where we met the first Russian detachment, we carried our own petrol, filling up from the last dump 150 miles from Baghdad. From Kermanshah onwards the Russian authorities helped us.

Major Barttelot and Captain Goldsmith left on January 24th with an escort of one light armoured motor-car under Lieutenant Singer, having orders to proceed as far as Hamadan, ensure the petrol supply and await the arrival of my party there.

The risk of so small a party entering Kurdish territory would have been considerable; but the moral effect of the armoured car is enormous, and the advent of winter had driven most of the Kurds to the lower valleys on the Mesopotamian side.

By January 26th my party had grown to fourteen, and at last the moment had arrived when a start might be made. During these days of waiting, I had had to consider whether it would not perhaps be better for me to push on to Hamadan alone, and so get more in touch with local conditions and begin collecting information. But I decided against this plan for two reasons, firstly because it would make communication with London more difficult, and there were many important minor points not yet settled; and secondly because a possibly long halt in Hamadan would attract attention to the mission and give our numerous ill-wishers plenty of leisure to plan out annoyances for our further move.

I had cabled home stating that I had decided to stay in Baghdad till a small party of officers had been collected, and then to hasten on a non-stop journey through to Enzeli, thence straight on boardship and to Baku, where I would arrive, if all went well, in about twelve days, and before any of the various enemy plans to stop us could mature. In theory the idea of the non-stop journey was delightful; as a matter of fact the journey eventually involved more stopping than travelling.

The soldiers' worst enemy, or best friend, the weather, turned against us at the start, and put a stop to anything in the nature of rapid progress.

At last, at 7 a.m. on January 27th, the forty-one Ford cars were lined up outside the walls of Baghdad waiting for the word to start. I had chosen the following officers to accompany me: Captain Dunning, A.D.C., Lieut.-Colonel Duncan, A.Q.M.G., Captain Saunders, G.S.O., Captain Stork, Staff Captain, Captains Hooper, Jackson and Annett, representing Infantry, Artillery and Cavalry; Major Brunskill and Captain John, Medical; Captains Campbell and Aldham, Supply and Mechanical Transport; and as clerks, Sergeants Routledge and Watson.

For fighting purposes we could muster forty-one rifles from among the drivers, and we had one Lewis-gun in charge of Captain Hooper.

With a punctual start and fine weather the distance to Khanikin, 94 miles, was covered without excessive delay. But even under such favourable conditions it took ten and a half hours to cover the distance. As it is imperative in such circumstances to keep a convoy together, all cars must halt at intervals till the repair car at the rear of the column joins up and reports "all correct." The delay, therefore, to be expected when travelling with forty-one cars is roughly forty-one times the average delay when travelling with one car. It may be considered a good day when the average speed approaches 10 miles an hour.

Since my arrival in Baghdad the weather had been uniformly fine, but it seemed too much to hope for a continuance of the blue sky. Sure enough, as we approached the mountains the clouds gathered over the distant hill-tops, and there was every indication of the worst possible weather, an indication completely fulfilled in the next few hours.

A PLEASURE TRIP ON RECONNAISSANCE 17

After spending a very comfortable night in a ruined Turkish building at Khanikin, and receiving much kind hospitality from the British garrison there, we left again on the 28th for Pai-Taq, 61 miles, reaching our destination in a violent gale accompanied by sleet, after a run of about ten hours. We had averaged only 6 miles an hour owing to bad roads, bad weather and bad luck with repairs. The rain started almost as soon as we left Khanikin, and amply fulfilled the gloomy prophecies of yesterday.

The village of Pai-Taq at the foot of the Taq-i-Giri Pass afforded us shelter of a sort for the night. The wretched villages all along this road had been destroyed time after time by Russians and Turks in turn, in the course of the fighting during the two previous years. The remaining miserable inhabitants wander, gaunt with famine, among the ruins, and tearfully regard the advent of yet another host of invaders, of yet another nationality. They will soon learn that the new-comers are not destroyers but restorers.

From Pai-Taq the next stage of the journey was to land us in Harunabad, but starting on January 29th it was not till February 2nd that we actually completed those 41 miles. The road from Pai-Taq ascends for the first 3 miles very steeply up the face of a cliff, and as we got under way at break of day in the worst sort of weather, our prospects did not seem very bright. We soon found that pushing our cars up the incline by hand was good enough exercise, but not helpful from the point of view of progress.

At the top of the cliff it was pleasant to find a rosy-faced Hampshire lad sitting on the edge of the rock, a sentry from one of the last picquets that guarded our road for us. This war has produced many scenes of marvellous contrast, but I think the picture of that young soldier was among the most striking. There on the road from Persia to Babylon, the road trodden by the Medes and Persians, on the rocky barren hillside of the Persian mountains sat a youngster from the kindly Hampshire downs.

When the top of this the steepest portion of the road has been successfully climbed, another 3 miles of bad road remains before the watershed is reached. It remained to be seen whether this second half would be at all passable in the snowstorm, which continued with unabated vigour. At this point we found the camp of the 1/4 Hampshire Regiment, close to the village of Surkhadisa, and a halt was made to fill up our petrol tanks and await a break in the weather before bidding a farewell to the last outpost of the Mesopotamian army, and finally launching out on our own resources. The longed-for break occurred soon after 1.30 p.m., and the journey was resumed in high spirits. But not for long. The sun shone brightly for precisely ten minutes, when down came the snow again in a blinding whirl that made further driving, on a mountain road that was entirely obliterated, a matter of absolute impossibility. So after one or two ineffectual charges into snowdrifts, we had to bow to the inevitable and get back to Surkhadisa, where we tucked ourselves up very comfortably in a ruined caravanserai. Most of the roof was down, but enough remained to give shelter to us all, and the presence of two dead horses did not prevent us from feeling glad of the shelter.

Evils and blessings balance as a rule. As witness those horrible horses. In summer time they would have made the whole atmosphere unbearable. As it was, being frozen, they were only remarkable to the eye. So with the insects of these filthy serais; they were all dormant for the winter and left us in peace.

So again with the Kurds. The same snow that annoyed us had driven them down from the hills, and

A PLEASURE TRIP ON RECONNAISSANCE

had left the few who remained very disinclined to molest us. Under normal summer circumstances the risk of bullets from Kurds, and typhus from insects, would have been considerable. "Autant de gagné sur l'ennemi."

In the serai at Surkhadisa we were fated to stay for several days, each day reconnoitring with a view to getting the cars to the top of the pass; but as snow fell daily and the drifts became deeper and deeper as the top was approached, it seemed that we might be compelled to stay for an indefinite time.

At last, on February 2nd, I decided to make an early start and try to get over the pass before the snow-surface melted.

Starting at 4 a.m. in bright moonlight, the top of the pass was reached by 7.30 a.m. Nothing could exceed the beauty of the narrow snowclad glen which leads to the summit, and as we pushed the cars slowly over the crisp snow, we were confronted every now and then by grey visions of passing Kurds, who flitted harmlessly by. The only test of the hostility of these heavily armed figures is when they open fire.

The British Consul at Kermanshah, which lay some 70 miles ahead of us, had evolved a system of road-guards from among the Kurds themselves, making it difficult for the new-comer to be certain whether any particular individual was there to guard us, or whether he was the Kurd we were to be guarded against. In any case there is not much in it. He could assume either character as the occasion dictated.

However, the mere fact of there being road-guards and consuls ahead of us, and bank managers, and alongside of us telegraph and telephone wires, made us feel that, however wild the land we were in, we were not quite out of touch with civilization. True, the telegraph and telephone wires were hanging in festoons, but the poles and insulators remained, and the line could be restored without much difficulty. These consuls and bank managers are the real heroes whose tale is seldom told. Through all the troubles and vicissitudes of these years of war, they (and their brave wives with them) have kept the flag flying in these remote corners of the earth. Harried by Turks, threatened by local disturbances and sometimes compelled to fly for refuge, leaving all their wordly goods behind them, they reappear when the storm is over and complacently continue their truly imperial tasks.

The rate of progress to the top of the pass was just one mile an hour, and this only achieved by dint of pushing and pulling and occasional digging. However, at 7 a.m. we found ourselves with a nice down slope before us and the worst part of our labours over. At Surkhadisa we had been joined by a light armoured car as escort, but it was quite impossible to get anything but the very light Fords over the difficult road, and we had to leave this escort behind.

Up to this point signs of famine were numerous, and we not infrequently passed the corpse of some poor, weary, hungry fellow who had given up the struggle by the roadside. At Karind, 20 miles from Pai-Taq, we encountered gangs of villagers, men and women, working under the guidance of an American missionary at the usual form of famine relief—road-improvements. This was part of an extensive system of relief inaugurated by the British Consul at Kermanshah.

From Karind another 20 miles brought us to our destination of Harunabad, having covered the distance of 41 miles in twelve hours, or at the rate of a little better that 3 miles an hour.

At Harunabad, a typical Kurd village, we passed a very comfortable night in some of the few houses still left standing, and nothing occurred to disturb our slumbers

A PLEASURE TRIP ON RECONNAISSANCE 21

except a visit from a donkey who insisted on sharing our sleeping apartment.

At 6.30 a.m. on February 3rd we were off again for Kermanshah, and managed to do the 40 miles in seven hours, a good deal better timing than yesterday's.

The road was mostly across the flat-bottomed valleys common to this part of Persia. The most important of these valleys is the Mahi-Dasht, which we were lucky to cross in the early hours of the day. This plain is usually a sea of mud of the consistency of cream, and in wet weather forms an impassable obstacle.

At the outskirts of the town we found two Kuban Cossacks on their shaggy horses, waiting to show us the way to our billets. They were fine-looking fellows, belonging to Colonel Bicherakov's " partisans." Circling the town under their guidance, we came to a well-built Persian house standing opposite to the British Consulate, the Imperial Bank of Persia and the American Mission. This house had been arranged for our accommodation, and provided the bath of which we were very much in need.

It will be necessary now to introduce Colonel Bicherakov, a truly heroic figure, as he and his picturesque Cossacks have much to do with the further narrative. Bicherakov is a man of about forty years of age, slightly built and of commanding presence. He is an Ossietin Cossack, one of those semi-wild tribes that are typical of the North Caucasus. Throughout the war he has done splendid service, and has been wounded on many occasions. His men worship him as a fearless leader. Incidentally, he is C.B., D.S.O.

At the time of our meeting he was commanding a mixed Cossack force of all arms. His men, though not unaffected by the undisciplined ideas of the revolution, had resolved to be faithful to the death to Bicherakov's person, and their unflinching loyalty to him has since enabled him to accomplish great feats. Why the Russians have chosen the name of " partisans "[1] for this force I do not know. With this detachment was Lieut.-Colonel Clutterbuck, of the Indian Army, acting as liason officer, a Russian scholar and a great favourite with the Cossacks. In addition to these troops Kermanshah had a Russian wireless installation worked by men of the New Zealand detachment.

Our welcome from the European community was warm, and the contrast of sitting at an English dinner-table in the Consulate with white linen and glass made us smile as we thought of the friendly donkey and the dirty rooms of the night before. Colonel Kennion, the well-known traveller and "shikari," is the representative here of His Britannic Majesty's Government. Mrs. Kennion, who shares his risks and dangers, is one of those brave Englishwomen, of whom I have already spoken, who do so much in an unobtrusive way for the needs of the Empire.

Delightful as Kermanshah was, it was not possible to spare time for a halt, though the cars would have been glad of a day's rest, so on the following morning, February 4th, at 5.30 a.m. we started for Hamadan (103 miles), hoping to do the trip easily in two days. From the start things did not go well with us. Within the first quarter of a mile we had a broken axle that delayed the column for an hour and a half. At 20 miles we passed Bisitun, with the ancient rock inscriptions of Darius I, thence over a single arch bridge blown up by the Turks, but with just sufficient of the arch remaining to suit the width of our wheels. The ground here was free from snow, the sky was blue and the road so good that a Staff

---

[1] EDITOR'S NOTE.—The word "partisan" is used equally in Bulgarian to express that familiar fauna of the Balkans called by the Turk the "komitadji," by the Greek the "andartis," by ourselves the "irregular."

A PLEASURE TRIP ON RECONNAISSANCE 23

Officer yielded to the fatal temptation to say, "Well, we've got over our troubles now; this is like a pleasure trip." He made that remark at about the fortieth mile, and at the forty-first mile we reached the foot of the small but steep Sahneh Pass where we had to man-handle each car up the slope, taking three hours to cover the distance of one mile. At the fifty-sixth mile the cars were running well, and we reached the town of Kangavar where, close to the ruins of a temple dating back to classical Greek times, a small Russian detachment welcomed us in the overwhelming style of Russian hospitality, with a hot meal for officers and men. It was getting late now, 4 p.m., and we had 22 miles still to do. It was obvious that we should get belated in any case, and might experience increased difficulties and dangers in the dark. But on the other hand we might never reach our destination at all, and the chance, therefore, of giving the hungry drivers at least one full meal was too good to be lost. Moreover, we now had with us a guide, in the person of Lieutenant Georgiev of the Russian Army, who had been detailed by Colonel Bicherakov to accompany us as far as Hamadan; a most useful officer, without whose aid we would probably not have reached Asadabad at all that night.

So, having yielded to temptation, we left again at 5 p.m. Darkness soon came on, and the road was generally just a cross-country track often hardly distinguishable from the surrounding plain. The drivers were almost too sleepy to carry on, and at 8 p.m. I was nearly tempted to halt in the open plain. The night was exceptionally fine, and nothing seemed less probable than a change in the weather. However, by good fortune as events proved, I decided to press on, and we eventually reached Asadabad and got the cars and ourselves into a fairly clean serai, where we fell asleep with the pleasurable anticipation of an early start on the next morning, a stiff climb up the pass, 7,600 feet high, and an easy run into Hamadan only 25 miles ahead. The drivers had been at their work on this day for eighteen hours, and doubtless looked forward as much as any of us to the prospective comfort of decent billets and a day or two's halt. This was the night of February 4th. The cars did not reach Hamadan till February 11th!

I was up at 4 a.m. and stepped outside our little sleeping room to see that things were getting ready for the start. My horror and surprise may be imagined when I found a foot of snow on the ground and the sky filled with fast-falling heavy flakes. My first feeling was one of thankfulness that I had not camped out for the night on the open plain: had we done so, it is hard to see how we should ever have extricated ourselves from our difficulties. The next was naturally one of exasperation at further delay just when time was becoming more and more valuable. "Pleasure trip," indeed! Let me dissociate myself on this one occasion from my Staff's views.

The whole of the day was spent in endeavours to clear the pass, but as fast as we dug through the drifts the snow came down and obliterated our work. On the third day, February 6th, large gangs of villagers were employed but without success, and the snow continued to fall.

On February 7th I determined to ride over the pass with one Staff Officer. After procuring two decent ponies and a local guide, Colonel Duncan and myself set off in the early morning, reaching Zageh on the far side of the pass at about noon, and motoring thence into Hamadan in a Russian car with Lieutenant Zypalov, who had been sent out from Hamadan to meet me.

My object in getting to Hamadan ahead of the party was to procure assistance from that side in getting the cars over (they were eventually got over with drag ropes)

"Colonel Duncan and myself set off in the early morning."—7th February, 1918

A PLEASURE TRIP ON RECONNAISSANCE 25

and also to meet the many important people awaiting me there. Firstly there was General Offley-Shore, recently returned from Tiflis, who was to post me in all the latest information concerning the South Caucasus. Major Sir W. Barttelot and Captain Goldsmith, who had been collecting local information and arranging petrol supply, should also be here. In addition to these, there was valuable knowledge to be acquired from the Consul, Mr. McDowell, and from the Bank Manager, Mr. McMurray. And here I was to meet General Baratov, lately commanding the victorious Russian Army that had fought the Turks on this road. He was now most uncomfortably remaining in command of revolutionary troops who would obey no orders.

The problem of the evacuation of these disorderly troops was most difficult. Under normal circumstances an evacuation is difficult enough, but with troops that defy all authority it was obviously an almost impossible task. The great point was that the individual soldier was most anxious to get home, so he was certain to move, with or without orders, in that direction. With General Baratov was Colonel Rowlandson as liaison officer.

On arrival at Hamadan we found most comfortable quarters at the Bank House. The same roof sheltered Major Barttelot, Captain Goldsmith, General Shore and others, and the charming and indefatigable hostess seemed prepared to welcome any number more.

Throughout all the varying fortunes of the force in North Persia the Bank House at Hamadan stands out as a landmark, a never-failing refuge for the weary, a centre of genial hospitality and a focus of all the local political news.

The first thing to do now was to send on Captain Goldsmith to explore the further road to Enzeli and to see about our petrol. He accordingly left on the following day, and fate ordained that we should not meet again.

As he travelled singly on a road crowded with retiring Russian troops, he attracted no attention, and, being an adept in finding his way through difficult places, he reached Enzeli and thence Baku before local suspicions were aroused. As my party did not reach Baku till seven months later our prospect of meeting was small, and he had by that time joined up with Colonel Pike in the North Caucasus.

On February 11th the cars at last got over the pass. On arriving at Hamadan the entire party of officers and men were most hospitably entertained by the American missionaries, who could not have welcomed their own men more warmly. Comfortable billets were found for all, the cars were overhauled and all was ready for a start, when further falls of snow blocked the Sultan Bulaq Pass which lay just ahead of us, rendering it impossible to start till February 15th. On that day we got away by 6.30 a.m., and now that we were on the well-made Russian road we had every hope of making good progress, a hope that was, this time, not to be disappointed. The snow would have again blocked us, but the evacuating Russians in their anxiety to get themselves home worked as they had never worked before, and the drifts were soon cut through. We crossed the pass without great difficulty in fine weather, and reached Aveh (75 miles) by 2 p.m., an average of about 10 miles an hour. The next day, February 15th, we reached Kasvin, where again we enjoyed the hospitality of the Imperial Bank of Persia, represented here by Mr. Goodwin. Kasvin is a town of 50,000 inhabitants and is one of the many earlier capitals of Persia. It lies at the junction of the Enzeli-Teheran road with the road by which we had come. Here it was useful to be able to consult with Sir Charles Marling, the British Minister in Teheran, before moving on to the Caspian and possibly leaving Persia finally behind us. Acting later in the Caucasus,

A PLEASURE TRIP ON RECONNAISSANCE

a thorough knowledge of the Persian situation would be indispensable, and it was a great advantage to have had the experienced opinions of this Minister.

Kasvin itself did not seem to welcome us at all. In Hamadan there had been a few smiles among the crowd, but as we entered this city we got only scowls; the populace, however, instead of resorting to violence, contented themselves with holding anti-British meetings in the mosques, and passing fierce resolutions. Our party of twelve officers, two clerks and forty-one drivers was certainly not strong. But the forty-one cars gave quite a false impression of strength, and we also had now with us as escort the armoured car under Lieutenant Singer that had preceded us to Hamadan. It is probable that but for the armoured car the resolutions might have ended in action, although this would have involved the breaking of a well-established rule.

At Kasvin we learnt that further progress was impossible. Mirza Kuchik Khan, the leader of the Gilanis whose district we were about to enter, had vowed not to let the British through, and his Committee were working at Enzeli in conjunction with the Bolshevik Committee, who were equally determined not to allow our passage. Still, so many of these granite difficulties had up till now turned out tissue-paper, that it was obviously necessary to see if this last "impossible" could not be managed. Arrangements were accordingly made for an early start on the following morning.

A short description of the "Jangali" or "Gilan" movement is now necessary.

The Elburz Mountains, the highest peak of which, Demavend, near Teheran, ascends to over 18,000 feet above sea-level, form a wall separating the Persian plateau from the Caspian Sea. The watershed lies about 50 miles from the shore, to which the spurs gradually descend through thick and beautiful forest. The country comprised in this area is divided into two provinces, Mazanderan composing the eastern half and Gilan the western. Through the latter country runs the road connecting Persia viâ the Caspian with Europe. Resht, the capital of Gilan, lies on this road about 20 miles from the Enzeli-Kazian port, whose double name requires explanation. The harbour is formed by two long sandspits running from east and west like the jaws of a huge pair of pincers, enclosing a large shallow lake. On the western spit lies the old Persian town of Enzeli, on the eastern spit the new Russian town of Kazian, built by the Russian Road Company in connection with their valuable trade concessions. Only a few hundred yards of water separate the two towns, and while the wharves lie almost entirely on the Kazian side, the merchants' residences, the banks and all the hotels lie on the Enzeli side, where all business is transacted.

The inhabitants of Gilan are spoken of as "Jangalis" for no other reason than that they live in a forest country or jungle. It is a misleading term, as it is apt to convey the idea of something wild and fierce and uncivilized, and the Gilani is none of these things.

The so-called "Jangali" movement was started by a well-known revolutionary of the name of Mirza Kuchik Khan, an honest, well-meaning idealist. His programme includes all the wearisome platitudes that ring the changes on the will-o'-the-wisp ideals of liberty, equality and fraternity. "Persia for the Persians" and "Away with the foreigners" are other obvious items, a further enumeration of which is not necessary in view of the fact that they are all obvious, all fallacious and the world is already tired of them all.

The next scene in the play is also an unvarying one in such dramas. Kuchik Khan appoints a Committee to assist in the control of affairs, and from that date the Committee run Kuchik, who thinks he still leads, while being merely pushed. And do the Committee really lead, or are they also being a little pushed ? The answer to this question is one which affords point where we find the solution to many such problems—German and Turkish agents and propaganda. Kuchik's troops are led by a German officer, von Passchen, and are drilled by Austrian instructors. Turkish machine-guns and ammunition form a large part of the material of his army. So we have first the leader Kuchik Khan, not very intelligent, but a high-minded enthusiast. Pushing the leader we have the Committee, each member of which has private ends to seek. Pushing the Committee we have on one side Germany with promises of pecuniary gain, and on the other Turkey with spiritual appeals to religious fanaticism and a machine-gun or two. What a thing it is to be a leader! Now the attitude of these Gilanis towards the Russians may be explained. The general feeling of the North Persians towards the Russians may be described politely as one of extreme dislike; but with the advent of the revolution, the proclaiming of the fraternity business and the withdrawal of the troops, the dislike is temporarily put on one side. Kuchik Khan is only too glad to see the Russians leaving Persia (as he hopes for ever) by the road that passes through Gilan. This enables him to buy huge stocks of rifles and ammunition at very low prices. So their passage is in every way facilitated, and a combined Committee of Bolsheviks and Jangalis run the port of Enzeli, united in the common desire to thwart the British: the Bolsheviks chiefly because they imagine that the British are out to prolong the war, the Jangali because, having at last thrown off the Russian burden, they fear lest the British take their place and lest their conception of " Persia for the Persians " be once more indefinitely deferred; and both of them because they are the victims (mostly unknowingly) of subtle propaganda.

Mirza Kuchik Khan claims to have 5,000 troops, and he probably has that number of armed men. What numbers he can induce to take the field, and what will be their fighting value, are questions that later events will answer.

CHAPTER III

THE SEA! THE SEA!

AS our convoy passed out of the Resht gate of Kasvin at daybreak on February 16th, the hearts of all were elated at the thought that by to-morrow night the last obstacles would have been surmounted and the party embarked on the Caspian, heading for Baku. There were not really any serious grounds for believing that we should get through. On the contrary, the hindrances loomed larger than ever. But our party contained no pessimists, and we felt confident that whatever difficulties arose would be overcome.

Since leaving Hamadan the whole road had been blocked with Russian troops evacuating in disorder; Kasvin was filled with them, and though mostly friendly in a general sort of way they were obviously going to be a nuisance on the road.

The weather at any rate was in our favour; no snow fell, and we crossed the last high pass near Buinak, 30 miles from Kasvin, without difficulty. Here, as on the Sultan Bulaq Pass, the retiring Russians had cut a first-rate road through the snowdrifts.

From Buinak to Menjil, 40 miles, the road winds down a rather desolate valley, crossing the streams occasionally by well-built bridges, and finally emerging on to the small open plain of Menjil, on which some fine clumps of very old olive-trees help to vary the monotony of the landscape. Our halt for the night was arranged for in the little post-house belonging to the Russian Road Company, where large advertisement boards of the "Grand Hotel" in Teheran with "Cuisine Française" made our "bully stew" taste less luscious than usual.

The only impediment on the road had been the Russian troops, whose transport consisted chiefly of the enormous Persian country carts with four horses harnessed abreast, not an easy vehicle to get by on a narrow mountain road. The troops themselves were cheerful, and showed no signs of making themselves unpleasant to us. Life for the time being was very pleasant for them, and as all men are brothers they wished it to be pleasant for others as well. The principles of freedom and fraternity were applied with great zeal to poultry and other unconsidered trifles that lay not too far from the roadside, and the tedium of the march was relieved by shooting the insulators off the telegraph poles, or testing marksmanship for a small bet on heedless crows. No formation was kept, except occasionally among the mounted troops. Parties pottered along in twos and threes or larger bunches, and now and then a tired soldier would beg for a lift, or try to get one without begging by jumping on to the back of one of the vans, an athletic feat that was generally beyond his powers.

At the serai, where we went with a special permit to draw petrol for to-morrow's journey, we were surrounded by a crowd of soldiers, and enjoyed some rather amusing and instructive conversation. The soldiers wanted to know where we were going. I replied, "To Enzeli." "And then?" "That depends on circumstances, we want to help you who are our allies." The invariable reply to this was "We are not your allies; we have made peace with Germany, and you only want to prolong the war." This was the parrot-like refrain that never varied

The Kasvin-Resht Road—16th February, 1918

and had evidently been carefully taught to the men by some ardent propagandist.

Asked as to their political ideas, the general replies may be reproduced somewhat as follows : " We have had a revolution because we were ill-treated and oppressed. Now we are free, but ignorant and uneducated. We don't know how to rule ourselves. Everything is in disorder. I am a Bolshevik, but I don't know what Bolshevism means, as I cannot read or write ; I just accept what the last speaker says. I want to be left alone and helped home, and as the Committee in Kazian is Bolshevik, I am too. If it were anything else I would be that."

Great curiosity was evinced as to the real reason for our presence in their midst, and the general consensus of opinion was that we were up to no good. The peasant mind is naturally suspicious, that of the Russian peasant especially so, and the guileless Englishman has an unfortunate reputation in Russia of being very cunning ; so our party was regarded with mixed feelings of suspicion and dislike tempered with good-natured tolerance.

Menjil lies at the head of the fifty-mile valley that runs down to the Caspian Sea through Resht, and the narrow gap in the hills, through which the Sefid Rud, or White River—generally red, by the way—flows down to the sea, acts as a funnel for the north wind that blows in a perpetual hurricane throughout the summer and has made Menjil infamous as an intolerable place of residence. Luckily this wind does not blow during the winter months, or we should have had a miserable time. We had scant leisure for exploring the neighbourhood: darkness soon came on, and we were only too glad of an excuse for turning in early and getting a good night's rest before embarking on to-morrow's adventures.

The next day, Sunday, February 17th, we were off at dawn in fine weather for the last and most critical stage of our journey, with the pleasant prospect of crossing the Caspian Sea on the following morning if the fates were good to us. But we were beginning to realize that the fates would have to be extraordinarily good to bring it off.

The beautiful 70 miles of road from Menjil to the sea have been described by every traveller, and I am obliged to add my modest contribution. Leaving the post-house, the road winds downwards with a gentle slope for about $1\frac{1}{2}$ miles to the Menjil Bridge, where the Sefid Rud is crossed and the final descent to the sea begins. The bridge is well built of stone and iron, and lies in a sharp V-shaped gap in the hills where the road turns due north. After crossing the river the road winds along the left bank for the next 40 miles, when the flat country is reached. From here it diverges slightly to the left, reaching Resht at about the fifty-second mile and Enzeli at the seventieth.

On entering the gorge immediately beyond the Menjil bridge, the thoughts of the soldier are inevitably drawn to the terrible natural difficulties confronting any army that might endeavour to force this defile against a determined enemy. The road is cut out of the rock in many places; the cliffs tower above on the left, while on the right there is a sheer drop to the roaring torrent of the Sefid Rud, impassable at all times of the year. The rocky spurs and sharp ravines on the right bank of the river give excellent cover to an enemy for sniping the troops on the road, and any attempt to advance would obviously entail a parallel movement on both sides of the river.

So far, although the traveller feels most distinctly that he has left Persia behind and has entered an entirely new country, the real forest has not begun. The lower hills are still barren but not entirely devoid of trees; large groves of olives line the road and fill all the hollows on the mountain side, while higher up a glimpse can be caught of the upper forests of pine and oak.

The real forest is not entered till the twentieth mile from Menjil, where the Russian toll-gate of Nagober is passed and the road plunges into thick woods with dense undergrowth. Here we feel that we have not only left Persia but Asia behind, when we stop for repairs beside a mossy bank on which primroses and cyclamen are just coming out, and farther down the road we find banks of violets and snowdrops. The trees are not in leaf, with the exception of a few evergreens, and it is hard to identify them in a rapid glance from a motor-car, but chestnut and a tree resembling a beech are the most noticeable, while the undergrowth is chiefly composed of box.

At Imamzadeh Hashim, about 40 miles from Menjil, the hills abruptly cease, and from here on to Enzeli the road runs on the level, at first through alternate forests and rice-fields and later, as Enzeli is approached, through pasture land and sand dunes.

It was hardly to be hoped for that we should be allowed by the fierce Kuchik Khan, after all his threats, to pass through the Menjil defile unopposed, and it was necessary to arrange the convoy so that at the first sign of opposition all possible fire should be brought to bear on the enemy. Our only chance would lie in acting with determination and rapidity. But at the same time we were handicapped by having to leave the firing of the first shot to the Jangalis, as until that shot was fired it might be possible to bluff our way through. And bluffing is far better than fighting when you have very little to fight with.

The armoured car under Lieutenant Singer led the way, Captain Hooper with the Lewis-gun was well up in front, and each driver had his rifle and a hundred rounds ready to his hand. Frequent halts were made to ensure the cars being all kept together.

Through the forest belt we encountered no signs of opposition at all, but as we neared Resht we passed here and there fierce-looking and heavily-armed warriors. With successive bandoliers of cartridges arranged round their bodies so as to form a very showy waistcoat, Mauser pistol on waistbelt and rifle in hand, these soldiers really looked as if they meant business. But Persia is a land where most things are done by "looks," and any attempt to ensure military success by other means need not be tried till that method has failed.

At Resht we halted for half an hour to meet on the roadside the British Consul, Mr. Maclaren, and his Russian confrère, M. Grigorievitch. The former, together with Mr. Oakshot, of the Imperial Bank of Persia, bravely keeps the British flag flying under most adverse circumstances. After Kuchik Khan's recent announcement of his feeling towards the British, it required some nerve to continue to reside in the Jangali capital. As a matter of fact both were shortly afterwards taken prisoners, and suffered very much at the hands of the Gilanis before effecting their escape.

After a short and useful conversation with them the cars again moved off, passing through Resht undaunted by more scowls from more desperadoes, and covering the remaining 20 miles to Enzeli in good time and without incident, puzzling our brains to guess why after such fierce threats we had been allowed to come through unscathed.

It was about an hour before sunset that the proximity of the sea was announced by the sand dunes, a moment later—Θάλασσα! Θάλασσα!—the blue waters of the Caspian became visible in the distance, and we were soon in the outskirts of the Kazian settlement.

Now we had to see how the Bolsheviks and other brands of revolutionaries would receive us. Curiosity was much more evident than hostility, in fact there never was much of the latter except from the Bolshevik officials (numerous enough) and a small proportion of really anti-British

LIEUTENANT SINGER IN THE ARMOURED CAR

THE SEA! THE SEA!

agitators. The attitude would therefore be as dictated by the officials, and it remained to be seen what their attitude would be. There were at this time about 2,000 Russian disbanded troops in the town, and as we drew up in front of the Persian Customs House the whole 2,000 flocked round, eager with curiosity and betraying no sign of hostility.

In Persia the Customs are entirely run by Belgian officials, and we were given a most hearty welcome by M. Hunin, who, with his wife and children, occupies the spacious building here provided for the head of the Customs.

The arrangements which had been made for our reception were as follows. I was to have the honour of living with the Hunins, the cars were to be parked inside the Customs yard, the drivers were to be accommodated in a Customs shed close by, and the officers in a very comfortable building in the Fishery Depot about a mile away.

More unsuitable arrangements could not be imagined. Hitherto at every halt we had all lived together with our cars in our midst, officers and men sharing the same quarters and the same bully-beef stew prepared by our indefatigable and cheery cook, Private Pike of the A.S.C. Under such circumstances, whatever happened we could give a good account of ourselves, but scattered all over Kazian as we now were we could hardly do our best in the event of a row.

But at this late hour to set out, followed by a gaping crowd of Bolsheviks, to make other arrangements was not to be thought of, and I had to accept matters as they were and take certain measures to bring things together in the event of a crisis. The only thing that I had absolutely to decline was the extremely kind personal invitation for myself, and I threw in my lot with the other officers in the Fishery Depot. It was sad to think that any mind could conceive arrangements based solely on comfort, the last thing we desired. All we wanted was safety and strength.

I could not, however, be so churlish as to refuse the warm invitation for myself and a Staff Officer to dine with the Hunins, which was therefore duly accepted.

The cars were soon stowed away inside the courtyard, but as many of the crowd as could squeeze in were inside as well.

How to get them out ?

The conversational method appeared to be the easiest, so Captain Saunders and myself commenced haranguing the men, who were deeply interested in our remarks and flocked around to listen. The topics were simple. We talked of the latest war news, we agreed that liberty was a fine thing and admitted that all men were comrades ; in the British Army, at any rate, officers and men had always regarded each other as comrades.

On their side questions were asked as to uniform ; was the Staff badge worn on his cap by Captain Saunders (a crown surmounted by a lion) meant to be the badge of the Persian lion ? As to the war, when would it end ? For Russia it had already done so. Thus pleasantly conversing we gradually approached the door, passed through the archway and into the open space, the crowd following us as if I was the Pied Piper of Hamelin. Then, during a continuance of the discussion, the doors were quietly closed and a sentry posted.

It was now possible to move down to the wharves and see what ships would suit us, but we were not able to do more than make a note of their names and a rough estimate of capacity, as we were followed at every step by a gigantic crowd that listened to every word and rather hampered our movements. The first thing to be done, therefore, was to shake off the crowd, which we eventually succeeded in doing, getting our men into their shed and installing ourselves in the Fisheries house. Here we occupied ourselves with toilet arrangements, during which a crowd, hostile this time, assembled in the open space before the house and began to look rather ugly. Before, however, we could take steps to deal with these people some one in authority evidently gave the word "not yet," and the mob gradually dispersed.

After devising secret methods of ascertaining shipping facilities, and setting on foot inquiries regarding the local situation, we prepared to set forth for our most ill-timed dinner-party. At this moment an unkempt individual appeared with an important-looking note from the " Revolutionary District Soviet. The Military Revolutionary Committee of the East Persian [sic] Circle of the Caucasus Front." The note that followed this grandiose and unabbreviated title was curtly worded as follows: " The Committee desire your attendance at an extraordinary meeting of the Committee to explain the arrival of the motor-cars and the mission." No time was mentioned, and it was obvious that if I had dinner first I should have time to think. So we decided just to carry on with the dinner and see what would happen.

The dinner was certainly excellent, and we were doing thorough justice to it when the sound of heavy boots was heard in the hall outside and the Persian servant hurried in in great agitation to announce that the Revolutionary Committee had arrived in the house, demanding to see the British General. I reassured my hostess, who was horror-stricken at the invasion, and left the roon at once to meet the visitors, of whom I expected at least half a dozen. As I entered the sitting-room I was rather surprised to find only two representatives, Comrade Cheliapin, formerly a clerk in a shipping office and now President of the Enzeli Bolshevik Committee, and a swarthy sailor in uniform.

I at once shook hands warmly and begged them to be seated, when the following conversation took place:

"May I ask what I can do for you?"

"We sent you a note that you were to attend a Committee meeting to explain your arrival here and to answer other questions. Did you not get the note?"

"I got the note, but as it contained no mention of time I was waiting for a more precise invitation."

"We desire you to come with us now and make the necessary explanations to the Committee who are waiting for you."

"The Committee must be very tired, as I am, after the day's work, and I suggest that if you could assemble at 11 a.m. to-morrow we could talk over all matters pleasantly and at length. Meantime I may tell you briefly that we are animated only by feelings of friendship for Russia, and have no ideas of setting up any counter-revolutionary movement."

After this I expressed my surprise and pain at their general attitude. I had expected a warm greeting from them, and felt sure that to-morrow I could at least count on their fullest assistance in all matters. I was only too anxious to explain, as I knew that their ideas and mine would probably coincide on all points. I thanked them very warmly for taking the trouble to come and see me, and after smoking a cigarette and exchanging further complimentary remarks (not quite an exchange, as the compliments were mostly on my side) we shook hands once more and parted with the usual Russian expressions of politeness.

I was anxious to defer any meeting with the Committee till we had learnt something of local conditions, and until I had heard the result of the inquiries now on foot as to shipping facilities. It was very necessary for me to learn the situation before entering into any discussion. With full knowledge of conditions on their side, and complete ignorance on mine, any controversy would be a very one-sided affair.

I was now able to return to the dining-room and relieve the anxiety of Madame Hunin, who had expected to see me dragged off to instant execution. Dinner was soon finished, and after an excellent cigar we made our apologies and withdrew. The night was young and there was a good deal to be thought of before turning in to rest.

First of all the shipping reports came in. Two ships were available and willing; but no ships were privately owned, all were "nationalized" and entirely in the control of the Bolshevik Government. Any idea therefore of getting on board in the dark and making a run for it was out of the question. Next as to accommodation on board. The ordinary steamer would take from 100 to 500 men, but none could take more than ten cars. Therefore if we endeavoured to slip away in one steamer we should have to leave thirty-one cars behind, a fact which alone sufficed to negative any scheme of stealthy departure.

Other items of intelligence were also not very encouraging, and it appeared likely that we should be faced with the problem of being unable to go forward and equally unable to go back.

Our house was watched from every corner by sentries concealed, to stop or give notice of any suspicious movements on our part. These sentries were posted each night during our stay in Enzeli.

To-morrow we would see what the day would bring forth, and I had reasonable hopes that the Committee would fall in with our ideas. I still feel certain that they would have done so if left to themselves, but with Kuchik Khan's emissaries at their elbows, and German agents in their midst, it is not surprising that they were led into a hostile attitude.

Rain had begun last night, and we woke on February 18th to find a dull, drizzly morning, with the landscape entirely enveloped in mist. We were soon astir and about our various tasks. Our movements in the town still attracted some attention, and apart from the curious crowd there was of course always a reporter from the Committee dogging our footsteps. It was therefore difficult to accomplish much by direct inquiry, and we had to rely chiefly on secret agents, of whom we had one or two who were sincerely acting on our behalf, but whose reports were frequently incorrect or exaggerated.

At 11 a.m. Captain Saunders and myself duly presented ourselves at the small building where the Committee held its meetings. Happy soldiers in full enjoyment of the delights of freedom lounged round the entrance. The delights of freedom were chiefly indicated by the bestowal of silly smiles instead of salutes, the neglect of ablutions, unbuttoned uniforms and dirty belts and rifles. Passing up the wooden steps we entered a crowded ante-chamber, where more soldiers and sailors smoked and talked and indolently regarded the new-comers. In a short time the door of the inner room opened and Comrade Cheliapin advanced with outstretched hand and an official frown that fitted the seriousness of the occasion. Hands were solemnly shaken in token of equality, and our leader ushered us into the adjoining room, where we found ourselves in the presence of the redoubtable Committee.

The twelve individuals composing the Committee were seated at a long table that almost filled the room, and each had before him in the most correct manner paper, pens and ink, to show that he could write if called upon to do so. There was no general rising on our entry into the room, but each rose or half rose as we exchanged the usual hand-grips, and on the whole we received a welcome that showed a general desire to be polite while remaining severely formal. The members were all young men, mostly soldiers and sailors in uniform, and those who wore tunics buttoning up to the neck left the collars undone, as a further sign of their recently won freedom. Throughout the entire period of my relations with revolutionaries I noticed this distinguishing sign of the unbuttoned collar: To look the part of a revolutionary, grow your hair long, refrain from brushing it and leave your collar undone, or if in mufti wear an open turned-down collar cut as low as a lady's dinner frock, and the disguise is complete.

The flouting of the greybeard is also a revolutionary sign. The absence of the men of experience from among revolutionary officials leads to many false moves that wiser heads would have avoided; but youth will have its fling, and in all ages and in all civilizations there is always a permanent undercurrent of revolution on the part of the young men who know everything, against the older men who are considered out-of-date and incapable of understanding their brilliant schemes of reform. But it is good to be young, and the effervescence of youth is possibly of some small value in the general scheme of life.

I was not able to say all this to the Enzeli Committee, though I should have liked to have done so. Time pressed and I was anxious to get through with the business.

It was known in the town that Kuchik Khan's Persian Committee were urging the Russian Committee to arrest us, while the Bolsheviks were anxious to throw the onus on the Persians. There was no reason why either side should hesitate, but there is a good deal of prestige about the British flag, and neither party so far cared to put our strength to the test. There was moreover the armoured car, which looked as if it would account for a good many of the attackers if an attempt was made to take it. Still, there was the prospect of our own arrest, as Captain Saunders and myself were entirely in their hands, and to make us realize the serious nature of our predicament an armed guard surrounded our chairs. This guard soon grew tired, and when they concluded that their presence was not producing any great impression on us, they sat down on benches round the room and made themselves comfortable.

We were accommodated with seats at the table, and the discussion opened with a short speech by Cheliapin, in which he informed the Committee that the English General had been invited to attend this meeting to explain the reason of his sudden descent into their midst, and to answer questions generally as to the future intentions of his party.

In reply I stated briefly that I was astonished at their attitude, that we had come solely to help them and were pained at the very poor welcome we had received.

It was necessary for me to be very careful in my replies to the volley of questions that now ensued, each member determined to justify his existence by taking a part in the cross-examination. My desire was naturally to adhere strictly to the truth, not always an easy task when one is in possession of State secrets, and very difficult in this case where the entire object of the mission had been kept a very close secret, and where it would be unwise to avow all the details of our plans before a hostile assembly such as that before which we were undergoing cross-examination.

This difficulty was at once removed by the kind President, who informed me that he knew all about our plans for going to Tiflis and helping the Georgians and Armenians to continue the fight. He was too anxious to show me how hopeless our case was when he knew so much, but he could have used his knowledge as a much better weapon had he waited till he had succeeded in getting false replies from me and then produced his bombshell.

It appears that the Bolsheviks had full information

from the Tiflis side of the objects of the mission, and of the date of our probable arrival at Enzeli, and they had peremptory orders (at German instigation) to stop us at all costs.

The result of the meeting may be summed up as follows: The Committee stated that Russia was no longer our Ally. Russia had made peace with the Germans, Turks and Austrians, and among all nations mistrusted only Great Britain, as a symbol of Imperialism, and the Tiflis people whom we proposed to help, as being anti-Bolshevik.

At Enzeli they possessed the telegraph and telephone line, the wireless apparatus and the petrol supply. All shipping was in their hands, and a gunboat lay ready to open fire on any ship endeavouring to leave the port without their permission. They forbade any endeavour on our part to reach Baku. Baku was under the Bolshevik Government, and had already been informed of our arrival by wireless, and had replied that the party was to be stopped at all costs. For Russia the war was over, and they objected to a mission whose avowed intention was to prolong the war.

On my side I protested that our only object was to help Russia, without taking notice of political parties, that I should in spite of their threats carry on with arrangements to proceed to Baku, that we had sufficient machine-guns to enable us to overcome any resistance, and that we did not recognize the right of the Bolshevik Government to impede our movements.

I expected that the announcement of this determination would lead to our arrest, but while some members were doubtless in favour of this, there was lack of unanimity, of which I took advantage, and rising with the usual expressions of leave-taking Captain Saunders and myself walked out of the room without interference.

The rest of the day was spent in feeling our way as

regards shipping facilities and calculating chances. A visit to the wharf left us rather hopeless. All steamers were strongly guarded, and out in the stream lay the vicious-looking gunboat with guns prepared for action.

With the Bolsheviks and Jangalis around us, Bolsheviks ahead of us and Kuchik Khan waiting for us on the road behind, it was not easy to see one's way through, either forward or backward. One thing only was certain, that the longer we delayed the smaller would be our chances of escape. Yet I felt it necessary to hold on for at least forty-eight hours in the hopes of something turning up. What I really looked for was some sign of assistance from our friends on the other shore, some indication that if we got as far as Baku we might count on at least a few helpers. There were people over there who were undoubtedly looking forward to our arrival—the Armenians especially—and surely they would be sending emissaries to suggest some plan and help us through.

But the hours passed by and there were no signs of any such helpers, and it was obviously useless to hope for anything from this source. My later experience has taught me that these people are glad enough to ask for help, but having asked they sit with folded hands, and when help arrives they welcome you warmly and say, " Now we give you a free hand, just carry on and we will sit and watch how well you do it ! " This is exactly what happened when we eventually reached Baku about six months later.

I sat up most of the night weighing the intelligence that had been collected during the day, and balancing the pros and cons of each possible solution.

We might face the situation, seize a steamer and risk the gunboat. I knew a method that seldom fails of stopping the fire of the latter. I considered that there was almost a sufficient prospect of success in this scheme to justify its attempt, but it was negatived by the fact that as the steamer could only take at the most ten cars, thirty-one would have to be left behind to fall into the hands of the Bolsheviks, and my party would receive a warm reception from the Bolsheviks of Baku, informed by wireless of our impending arrival. Finally, at the very best, we should be landed in the Caucasus, leaving the road by which we hoped the remainder of the party would arrive in the hands of a very irritated enemy, who would see to it that no further parties got through. Under such circumstances our position in Baku or Tiflis would be ridiculous.

Colonel Pike was at Tiflis as Military Agent and was anxiously awaiting our arrival, but it was impossible to expect that he could do anything to help us, his own position being fairly desperate until we could get through to him. Captain Goldsmith would also now be with him, but was out of touch with us, owing to the impossibility of communication.

The next plan to consider was the possibility of our remaining in Enzeli, establishing friendly relations with the local Government and wheedling them into a better attitude. The risks of this plan were too great. The combined hostility of the Persians and the Bolsheviks would certainly burst into flame, and one or other would at last pluck up the courage to put our strength to the test, and find that the strength was all weakness. Moreover, the rumour that we had large stores of gold with us made such an effort all the more tempting.

Comrade Cheliapin himself proposed another plan, that we should officially recognize in writing the Bolshevik Government (our non-recognition being the chief cause of their hostility) and proceed to Baku under Bolshevik auspices, leaving our further movements to be directed by the Bolsheviks. This meant, in fact, becoming

Bolsheviks. He offered to wire to Baku in these terms, but did not anticipate agreement.

I had no particular objection to becoming a Bolshevik, but to take up the Bolshevik programme of non-resistance to the invader would be rather far away from my orders. Cheliapin also suggested that the Tiflis business was a played-out game, and if we threw in our lot with the Bolsheviks we would be much more useful in the Moscow direction. And he said all this without a smile!

The upshot of my midnight deliberations was a decision to get out of Enzeli while there was time, run the gauntlet of Kuchik Khan on the Resht road and get back to Persia, call up my second party and watch for a favourable opportunity to renew the attempt.

There is a telephone line all along the road from Enzeli, with Persian operators, and I could hardly hope to get through to Menjil without my movement being notified, but we should just have to take our chance of that.

In accordance with this decision I sent a message to the Revolutionary Committee early on the morning of the 19th, asking them to assemble at 11 a.m. and to allow me to address certain remarks to them.

At the appointed hour I arrived at the Committee room with Captain Saunders, and we were ushered in with the same ceremony as before. The only difference on this occasion was that the smiles were now frowns, and the intimidating guard was largely increased in numbers and looked most impressive.

I opened the discussion by stating that I wished to know finally whether the Committee had changed their minds and were willing to give us all the assistance in their power, or whether they adhered to their former ill-advised decision to thwart us. The answer was a quite unanimous one in favour of the latter proposition.

I then asked to be allowed to speak to Cheliapin alone, which request being granted I withdrew with him into a

THE SEA! THE SEA!

separate apartment, where we were as much alone as revolutionaries are ever allowed to be. "Trust no one" is the sound motto of all revolutions.

I informed him that I regretted I was quite unable to accept the Bolshevik proposition, that I was undesirous of bloodshed, which would be the natural result of any effort on his part to thwart our forward movement, that I was quite convinced by his eloquence, and consequently decided to withdraw my party. I congratulated him warmly on the very admirable manner in which his government of the town was conducted, and made him feel that I regarded him as a peer among men. I then begged for and got a signed order for all the petrol I required and, after requesting the Committee to keep my intended departure a secret, I withdrew from the assembly.

In paying such compliments as I did to Comrade Cheliapin, I was not altogether romancing. I could sympathize with the difficulty of his position, the endeavour to carry on the business of government with no experience and little education, and I wish to record here the fact that I consider he did extremely well in maintaining a semblance of law and order amid the chaos of a revolution. Anyway, I shall always be grateful to him for the petrol.

In spite of my request for secrecy the news of our intended departure was beginning to leak out, as of course I knew it would, and it would be a very good thing to get through Resht before Kuchik Khan had time to digest and act upon the telephone message he was probably now receiving. I accordingly gave orders for a very early start on the morrow, and after an excellent meal at which bully beef was quite put in the shade by fresh fish and caviare, we turned in for the night.

CHAPTER IV

WE FALL BACK TO HAMADAN

ALL people are apt to change their minds, revolutionaries especially. The night of February 19th was therefore a very anxious one, as, although Cheliapin had agreed to our departure and supplied the petrol, there would be many who would think it a pity to let the Englishmen get away with all those bags of gold they had, and the amount of gold had doubtless been greatly exaggerated. Hence I decided on a very early start.

Long before dawn on February 20th the cars were quietly got out and loaded up, and we were soon on the move; when daylight came we were already some miles on the road to Menjil and ready for the second time to run the gauntlet through the Jangali country. The day was dull and rainy, and the cheerless weather corresponded to our mood, which without being despondent was certainly as cheerless as the sky. It was well to hope for a renewal of opportunity and a prospect of later success, but nothing could compensate for the fact that we had entirely failed to carry out the object with which we had set forth, and were turning back in our tracks.

To-day a conflict with the Jangalis appeared certain; it was not to be conceived that they would let us return through their country carrying that precious load of gold and silver, and we were prepared to encounter

WE FALL BACK TO HAMADAN

opposition as we passed through Resht. But again no attempt was made, the scowls were fiercer and an occasional warrior significantly tapped the butt of his Mauser pistol, but we were not fired on.

We had got accustomed to the playful Russian habit of firing at anything along the road, and keeping up a cheerful fusillade most of the night, as this had been the usual state of affairs ever since our arrival at Hamadan; but it made it very hard for us to guess whether the sounds of firing we now heard ahead of us meant just the usual insulator and crow shooting, or whether business was really going to begin.

A great deal depended on the cars, which had now run some 700 miles from Baghdad over poor roads and without proper overhauling; however, they behaved splendidly and there were no serious breakdowns. A three hours' halt for repairs, such as we often had to endure later, would have brought about a most uncomfortable situation in the forest country.

Menjil was reached at 5.30 p.m., and we rested again in the post-house with the tempting advertisements.

At 6 a.m. on February 21st we started for Kasvin, but it was going to be a day of misfortune, and we only reached the town on the following day. The cars were getting tired, and breakdowns were frequent. A halt of two hours was necessary before we were out of sight of the village: this considerably shortened our day, but we trusted with luck to make up time and did very well till midday, when a second halt of three and a half hours removed all hope of reaching Kasvin that day.

The weather was fine and there appeared to be no need to get over the pass to-day. The drivers were tired, and we could very well spend the night in the village of Bikandi on this side, and have quite a short run into Kasvin to-morrow. I was very much tempted to do this, but choice fortunately decided against it. We pushed on and crossed the pass at sunset, and two miles farther on found an excellent serai that held us all for the night.

The same startling change took place in the weather at night as we had experienced at Asadabad. We woke to find the whole country buried in snow, and a first-class blizzard in full progress. Had we remained last night on the far side of the pass we might have been held up for a week. As it was, the distance to Kasvin was only 20 miles, and the road, when you could find it in the snow, was not bad. Driving was difficult with freezing hands and the glass screen obscured with clinging snow-flakes, but we got in by noon after an unadventurous journey, and were glad to be able to tuck ourselves into warm billets.

The people of Kasvin had not looked as if they liked us when we passed through on our way down; it was not likely therefore that they would be any more amiable now. It was certain that we would not have a very pleasant time in the town, and it would be too lively for our permanent resting place. For this reason I selected Hamadan, where we could occupy a good defensive position outside the town and on the higher ground, and whence communication with Baghdad would be facilitated through the Russian wireless station.

Before proceeding to wind our way through the narrow and muddy roads of the town, I halted the convoy behind a vineyard near to the principal gate to enable them to close up and make a smart entry. At this moment we were greeted with a sudden outburst of rapid firing and the sound of bullets whizzing quite as near as an aimed Persian bullet would be likely to be. However, they proved to be not hostile but friendly bullets; a large wagon filled with Russian soldiers came slowly round the corner through the snow, and the occupants were indulging with rather more than usual vigour in their favourite pastime of firing a *feu de joie*.

WE FALL BACK TO HAMADAN

We proceeded on our way through the town to the British Consulate, where Mr. Goodwin had again made all arrangements for the comfortable housing of officers and men.

Our arrival had caused quite a stir in the town. Reports went round to the effect that Kuchik Khan had stopped us at Resht and allowed us to go back as an act of clemency, after relieving us of our cash and valuable stores. We were naturally regarded as a defeated party, and the determination to wipe us out was more vigorously made then ever.

It must be remembered that at this time the whole of North Persia was full of arms and ammunition, and any mob that turned out would be a mob armed with Russian, Turkish and English rifles; so if they could only screw up their pluck sufficiently to substitute action for talk we might anticipate a rather warm time. Meetings were held in the mosques, and inflammatory placards posted on the walls of the houses.

The next day, February 23rd, was spent in Kasvin thoroughly overhauling the cars. It was most desirable to get on, but the cars were not up to it. During this day the proceedings of yesterday were repeated in a more marked way, and all the mob now required was a leader, which they luckily failed to find—plenty of talkers but a dearth of leaders.

I was now able to send home by the Indo-European telegraph line which passes through Kasvin a report of the occurrences up to date. This had not been possible at Enzeli, where there was only the Russian wireless station, which was naturally not placed at our disposal.

I cabled to the effect that the mission had failed to get beyond Enzeli and were only enabled to withdraw from there by sheer good fortune; that it would be useless to make any further attempt to reach Enzeli until we either fought or came to an agreement with Kuchik Khan.

At Kasvin I received an official intimation from this leader that his troops had been ordered to attack the column if any attempt were made to repeat the experiment of passing through his country. We also became aware of a plot, the failure of which accounted for our not being molested on our previous journey. It appears that the Jangalis had determined to ambush the convoy on the road, but had feared lest the Russian troops marching in an endless procession down the road might throw in their lot with us and act as reinforcements. They had therefore addressed the Russian leaders on this point and begged from them a promise of non-interference. There is reason to believe that there was considerable delay in the Russian reply, which, however, in the end proved to be a refusal to give the required guarantee. Although according to their own point of view they were no longer our Allies, any other decision would have been disgraceful, and we must be grateful that even the revolutionary soldiers proved themselves to be "white men" in this matter and refused to be parties to such treachery. The Enzeli Committee were in favour of letting the Jangalis have their own way, but the troops on the road were against it.

I had also the interesting news that a strong detachment of Red Guards from Baku had arrived at Enzeli the moment after our departure. This probably explains the effusive manner in which Cheliapin begged me to stay one more day as their guests, to enable a reply to be received to a certain message he had sent asking if we could possibly be allowed to proceed.

The Red Guards were to do the work the Enzeli Committee were afraid to undertake—the capture of the British mission.

During February 23rd no outbreak occurred. The

WE FALL BACK TO HAMADAN

night was kept lively with perpetual firing, but it was only the usual expression of Russian joy, although it sounded as if a fierce battle were in progress.

At 8 a.m. on the 24th our procession once more passed through the Kasvin streets with the formidable armoured car acting as rear-guard, and we were soon bowling along the really good road and enjoying a spell of fine weather. We reached Aveh at 4 p.m., and shared the small and dirty post-house with some Cossacks. On the following day we crossed the Sultan Bulaq Pass in deep snow, but as before, with a good road cut through the drifts, and reached Hamadan in the evening.

Here we got the men into good billets on the premises of the American Mission, while for the officers we were able to secure two good bungalows in the vicinity. Colonel Duncan, Captain Dunning and myself were accommodated in the Bank House, which is alongside the mission compound. We were thus very suitably situated as regards defence—cars, men and officers in close proximity and ready to turn out at a moment's notice.

The ancient town of Hamadan, or Ecbatana, the treasure city of the Achæmenian kings, lies on the northern slopes of the Elvend range, the highest peak of which runs to 11,900 feet. The lower part of the town is 6,500 feet above the sea, and the foreign settlement which I had chosen for our position lies at about 7,000 feet, which means something like an Arctic climate in winter. A better position could not be imagined; the site is healthy and entirely overlooks the town, and water is plentiful from the streams that flow down from the mountain side, and which we were able to use without fear of pollution.

The city itself is quite uninteresting, the houses being of the usual type in Persia and Northern India, the better kind well built of brick surrounded with mud walls, the poorer of sun-dried bricks. A few ancient domes with the remains of coloured tiles brighten the general dulness of the city; these are either mosques or tombs, among the latter being those of Esther and Mordecai. On the east lies the big mound supposed to be the site of the ancient palace, of which no trace now remains. In fact, it would be hard to find any city with half the history of Hamadan possessing fewer relics of its bygone glories. It was taken and plundered by Alexander the Great and was the scene of some of his wildest orgies. Successive conquerors appear to have most effectually removed any trace of the wonderful buildings described, probably with much exaggeration, in ancient records. The solitary remnant of past glories is the stone lion which lies in the fields a few hundred yards from the north-eastern edge of the town, a piece of sculpture that possibly stood at one of the former entrances. This lion is now supposed to possess all sorts of magic qualities, and is much appealed to by those to whom male offspring has been denied or who suffer from some incurable disease.

I should like to quote here a verse from a poem on Hamadan by Clinton Scollard, which I copied from a book on travel in Persia in the possession of the American mission.

> Nought of all the radiant past,
> Nought of all the varied, vast
> Life that thrilled and throbbed remains
> With its pleasures and its pains,
> Save a couchant lion, lone
> Mute memorial in stone
> Of three Empires overthrown,
> Median, Persian, Parthian,
> Round the walls of Hamadan.

A mountain stream flows through the centre of the town and helps to brighten the dull surroundings and simul-

WE FALL BACK TO HAMADAN

taneously to provide water and a drainage channel for the inhabitants.

Hamadan is a place of considerable commercial importance, being noted among other things for leather manufactures and carpet weaving. The population is about 50,000, including a considerable proportion of Jews and Armenians. The people of the district are partly of Turkish origin, at least one half belonging to the Turkish Karaguzlu tribe, and Turki is more spoken in the villages than Persian.

The town is surrounded by cultivation, and is very beautiful in the spring when the young wheat is coming up and the fruit-trees are in blossom. From our quarters we looked out over the plain which lies unbroken to the north for 50 miles as far as the Sultan Bulaq Pass.

The site we had chosen was ideal from a military point of view. The Turks had equally selected it when here, and the house which was now my Head Quarters had a year ago been theirs. It is due to the Turks to say that very little damage had been done by them to the Bank House.

The original plan having for the time being quite broken down, we needed to take our bearings and see what could still be done to thwart the Turk in these regions.

The first obvious thing was that by remaining where we were, if we could hold out, we could interfere with the numerous Turkish and German agents who were at work in this part of Persia, while awaiting a change in the situation which might enable us to make another dash for the Caucasus. Meantime the Persian internal situation was very complicated and required watching. In any case, as snow now continued to fall almost daily, all passes were completely blocked and no move could be attempted; we were quite cut off from Baghdad and nothing could possibly reach us. A Russian party with ammunition loaded on pack transport had lost six men and thirty animals frozen to death on the Asadabad Pass, which we had crossed a fortnight ago, and it was clear that we were in for a long spell of bad weather.

I was able through the Russian wireless to communicate with Baghdad and thence with London, and received instructions to remain where I was, to watch the Persian situation and to move forward if any possible chance occurred.

The next thing to do was to consider if there were no other routes by which we could enter the Caucasus. The only other possible route was from Kasvin through Tabriz and Julfa, where we could get on to the railway to Tiflis. The distance from Kasvin to Tabriz is over 300 miles, the road is impassable for motors in winter and lies through the Shahsavan tribe with the Jangalis on our right flank. Balancing pros and cons, it did not seem in any way possible to attempt any movement by this road with any prospect of success.

Troops were now urgently needed, as Persia was on the verge of very serious internal trouble, but as long as the Arctic winter remained it was not possible properly to equip and march men up the road by which we had come. So we had just to stay where we were and to carry through with bluff.

In the eyes of the Persians we always looked stronger than we were. The mere sight of the armoured car inspired awe, and the forty-one cars were probably each supposed to contain some fearful weapon. The forty-one drivers, too, looked most imposing, the Persians not being aware of the fact that their military training hardly extended beyond the technical knowledge of their motor vehicles. But these drivers deserve all the praise I can give them. With their two Sergeants, Harris and Watson, they performed marvels, and never grumbled under the most trying circumstances.

"A MOUNTAIN STREAM PROVIDES WATER AND A DRAINAGE CHANNEL."

WE FALL BACK TO HAMADAN

The situation and the measures taken to meet it were as follows :

The Persian Government were quite naturally sitting on the fence, and leaning rather towards the side of the Germans, whose propaganda and rose-coloured war news enchanted the Teheran people. Teheran was still neutral in practice as well as in theory. While the Turks and Russians had been freely using the Kasvin-Kermanshah road as a battle-ground, the sanctuary of Teheran remained undisturbed. Alongside of the British Legation the flags of the Turkish and German Legations floated proudly on the breeze, and the Turks had a free hand for propaganda and intrigue. The Germans, however, in spite of the laws of neutrality, did not seem to regard the Persian capital as a healthy place of residence, and though the flag flew over the building the Legation was actually closed.

The Kuchik Khan movement was also in the ascendant. Our retirement was undoubtedly attributed to his action, and his prestige was duly enhanced. His reform programme recommended itself to all the serious democrats as well as the usual turbulent element that wants any change that brings disorder and prospects of loot. He had sympathizers in the Cabinet itself, Kasvin was full of his agents, as well as Hamadan and all other large towns. He was acclaimed as the saviour of Persia, who was going to turn the foreigners out and bring back the golden age. Added to all this was the fact that the spirit of Bolshevism was in the air, and the microbe of revolution was spreading through all the nations of the world : it was not likely that Persia would escape. One would have thought that the object-lesson provided by the Russian troops would have acted as a deterrent, but it apparently had the contrary effect.

It was clear therefore that Kuchik Khan had only to display his banner, march on Kasvin and thence on

Teheran and establish a revolutionary Government in Persia. With all the leading officials, as well as the greater part of the populace on his side, success was certain if only he struck now. The time was ripe, but the weather was bad, and by the time he eventually decided to move we were able to checkmate him. Behind him he had the very strong propelling power of German and Turkish agents and the Mahomedan Committee of Union and Progress, and against him he had nothing, but he failed to snatch the opportune moment and Persia was saved. The interesting details of this movement will appear in a later chapter.

My situation was affected by the movement to the extent that, if it were successful, we were obviously among the obnoxious foreigners who were to be got rid of, and the large number of sympathizers in the town of Hamadan ought to feel it their duty to show their sympathy by getting rid of us on the spot. But any plan for our direct removal was shelved as usual for the more exciting but less efficacious method of plot and intrigue, against which we were more proof than we were against bullets.

The first step to ensure our own safety and to render services that should be very valuable to the Allied cause was to start a good intelligence system. This was at once inaugurated under Captain Saunders and achieved most valuable results. Nothing could have been better than the work done by the officers in this department, and no greater compliment could be paid them than that contained in the following extract from an intercepted letter written by one of the many plotters, "the English hear even our whispers." Through our agents we were at all times thoroughly in touch with the general situation in Persia, the local situation in Hamadan and the strength and position of the nearest Turkish detachments. We were also able eventually entirely to check all movements of spies on the stretch between Kasvin and Kermanshah,

WE FALL BACK TO HAMADAN

and several quite good fish fell into the nets that we spread for them. As regards local intelligence we were able to know the exact degree of complicity with enemy agents of every single man of importance in the neighbourhood, and knowledge of this sort is very literally strength.

Endeavours had also to be made to get in touch with Colonel Pike and Captain Goldsmith at Tiflis, and special messengers were dispatched for this purpose, but all our efforts to establish communication with Tiflis failed.

From among the Persians themselves we recruited a very few but very good agents. These men worked for money, but money alone would not have produced the results; they threw their lot in most whole-heartedly with us, and one of them at least was as brave a man as I have ever met in my life, risking his life for the sheer pleasure of risking it, and no danger or threats ever prevented him from following up a clue. The Russians were still occupying Hamadan; the whole town was full of them, and sleep was much disturbed by their unrestricted indulgence in night-firing. Their Head Quarters were in the small summer resort of Sheverin, about 3 miles away, and the prospect of their quitting the neighbourhood seemed very remote.

General Baratov was in command, with General Lastochkin as Chief of the Staff, and our sympathies were very deeply with these officers in their difficult task of endeavouring to control troops who had broken away from discipline, and any prospect of the restoration of discipline had disappeared since officers had been forbidden to wear any badges of rank. Bicherakov was still at Kermanshah, but a small detachment of his men were here, and represented the only unit that had any respect for law and order.

Among other matters that required attention was the question of supplies. Our own needs were considerable, and we had also to be prepared for any number of troops that might be sent up later to these parts. In the midst of the terrible famine that was now at its height I did not wish to draw supplies from the country that would still further reduce the stock available for the starving people. But we soon had accurate intelligence on the supply question and found that there was sufficient grain and fodder for all, though no abundance, and it was only being held up to secure higher prices. Unfortunately, however, the result of our small purchases was to send prices still higher, and each fractional rise meant the death of many individuals. Only a properly regulated wheat control system could meet the case, and we were not at present strong enough to enforce our views on this subject, but we were able later to undertake the necessary measures when Brigadier-General Byron came up to Hamadan as my second-in-command. General Byron remained for a long time in Hamadan and was able to deal with the famine and wheat control in a businesslike way which did much to enhance our popularity.

As it was impossible to forecast how long we were likely to be in Hamadan or in North Persia generally, it was necessary without further ado to tackle the language and get to know the officials and the people. Those of us who had a smattering of Persian soon learnt to improve our pronunciation, and those who knew none began taking lessons.

The visits to the various officials and land owners were interesting and instructive. The principal officials in a Persian town are the Governor, the Deputy Governor, the Kar-guzar, who deals with foreign matters, and the Head of Police. In Hamadan we had also a special official appointed in connection with the liquidation of the Russian debts. The official who held this appointment at the time of our residence in Hamadan was Haji Saad-es-Sultaneh, a most enlightened Persian who had

WE FALL BACK TO HAMADAN

travelled much, and to whose society I am indebted for many a pleasant and instructive hour.

In Persia all people of any consequence are known by titles, and their names are never known to their ordinary acquaintances. This makes it hard to trace people, as titles change frequently, and the title bears no reference to the nature of employment. Thus a gentleman of noble birth who bears the title of "Leader of the Army" has no connection with any military occupation. "The Governor of the Kingdom" is a pronounced democrat, "Headman of All" is a humble person of no importance, and one of the most dunderheaded illiterates I ever met was entitled "The Ocean of Knowledge."

Within a few days of our arrival in Hamadan we had begun to make acquaintances among the people. The inevitable football was produced and the men were able to get a little relaxation and exercise. The Persians joined freely in the game which, owing to the presence of the American Mission here, was not entirely new to them, the graceful extra-long-tailed frock-coat they wear looking quite an unusual garment on a football ground. It certainly is more attractive than the football jersey, and any one who has seen the tails of a Persian frock-coat flopping in the breeze, as its owner flies down the ground, will realize that there is no comparison between the two. The boys who had been under the influence of the mission school were usually more correctly but less quaintly garbed.

It seemed as if the drivers might have much leisure for football as the cars would not have much chance of running for some time. Not only were the passes quite blocked, but the petrol question had become very acute. We now relied entirely on the Russians for our supply. General Baratov was most anxious to help, and took steps to ensure an ample supply, but with the roads blocked and with subordinates not amenable to discipline the petrol seldom arrived. A certain amount was always to be purchased in the town, and we laid in a stock of this at most exorbitant rates. This petrol found its way into the bazaars through the Russian drivers, who added to their slender incomes by disposing of a proportion of their consignments in this way.

Our first efforts at establishing friendly relations with the people were not entirely successful. The prospects of our success in this direction naturally called forth increased anti-British efforts on the part of the local officials. The Governor and all the chief people of the town spared no means to set the people against us; while the politicians of every shade, Extreme Democrats, Moderate Democrats and Social Democrats, held the usual meetings denouncing us and decreeing our immediate extermination.

Although we had been in Hamadan only a few days the people were informed that the rise in the price of bread was the result of our purchases of wheat (which were so far nil), that we were the advance-guard of an army, and if we were allowed to live, the army would arrive and eat up all the country and commit all sorts of atrocities. On the other hand, if we were slaughtered, the army would never dare to come. I thought it worth while to take a leaf out of their own book and try the effect of a printed proclamation. I therefore had notices posted in the town to the following effect: "The British are here as quite a temporary measure, and have no intention at all of remaining in this part of Persia, where our presence is only necessary in order to counteract that of the Turks. In all lands our first care is that of the people, and it is well known that wherever the British flag flies it stands for freedom, peace and prosperity. We have made no purchases of wheat and we are anxious to help to alleviate the famine. The present high prices are not due to our purchases, as we have so far made

WE FALL BACK TO HAMADAN

none, but to a deliberate plot of the democrats who intimidate grain dealers and bakers and force up the price artificially in order to drive the people into a frenzy."

This proclamation produced a considerable effect in the town, and helped to discredit the agitators. Nor was the good effect much reduced by their counter-proclamation which consisted chiefly of abuse, but contained the following amusing sentence. "The British General says he comes to bring peace and prosperity. Did we ask for it? Let him keep his peace and prosperity till we demand it. Persia represents a civilization that was in its prime long before the British were ever heard of, and consequently we are not likely to learn much from them."

I do not think that the sentimental appeal to patriotic pride in their ancient civilization interested the people half as much as my statement that our policy would be to help to alleviate the famine conditions. The fact is that the presence in their midst of a new type of soldier, who behaved himself with dignity and paid good prices for the articles he purchased, was beginning to sway popular opinion in our favour, and the more this feeling on the part of the people became apparent, the more vigorously did the democrats plot and scheme to turn the tide against us.

In a few days the change of feeling in our favour was quite marked, and the intelligence department was beginning to make our presence felt in other beneficial ways. A complete system of agents and messengers was organized to cover the whole area from Hamadan to the Caucasus, and we were soon able to mark down and later to deal effectively with the most violent of our opponents.

Meanwhile there was the question of our further parties now assembling in Baghdad. The mission had been officially designated "Dunsterforce," and a Dunsterforce camp was formed at Baghdad, and afterwards at Ruz, to accommodate the various parties till orders could be issued as to their disposal. The unofficial designation was "The Hush-Hush Army."

I was anxious to get up another batch of officers, but we were not yet quite sure of our ground, and motor transport for them could not at the time be spared from Baghdad. I thoroughly realized the unfortunate situation of these officers and men arriving from some active theatre of the war, full of hope for the chance of great achievements, being obliged to kick their heels in camp in Mesopotamia; but for the moment things must remain as they were, and the only thing for them to do was to undertake the study of Persian or Russian—a dull enough task for men who were primarily fighting men and who had never expected to be asked to qualify as linguists.

The following is an extract from an appreciation of the situation which I dispatched at this time:

". . . The real combination we are up against is not only the Bolsheviks but the Pan-Islamic scheme uniting the Tartars of Baku with the Jangalis of Enzeli—a very strong anti-British combination backed with German money and German officers. . . . As regards Tiflis, we are out to help people who cannot agree among themselves and seem to want not British interference but just British money, and that is all. Had it been possible for my mission to have been in Tiflis by the autumn of 1917, I would have devoted the whole of my energies to the drawing together of the two Christian peoples, the Georgians and the Armenians, while trying to bring the Mahomedan Tartars into line with them. On this basis alone could complete success be achieved.

"But what has happened during those six months? So far from sinking their religious differences, both sides have accentuated them, and the attitude of the Christian communities has driven the Tartars into a leaning towards the Turks. As regards the immediate future, let Persia and the Jangalis be first settled, and the road is clear at least as far as the South Caspian. . . ."

To deal with the Jangalis effectively troops would be required. As long as we had no troops on the ground Kuchik Khan refused to enter into any negotiations. Once troops were visible he would either fight or more probably admit the sense of a mutual agreement.

CHAPTER V

AN ALLIANCE OF PHANTOMS

BY the middle of March we were firmly established on a fairly solid foundation in Hamadan. The strength of our position was much improved by the Persian habit of exaggeration, which leaned very much in our favour. We were fortunate in being able to see most of the telegrams that passed between various officials, and which generally ran something on these lines:

"From X. to Z.
Why have you not reported the numbers of British troops in your neighbourhood? You do not do your work properly and you will have to be removed."

"From Z. to X.
I do my best to get information, but it is hard to find out what troops there are. They do not allow us to come near their place of residence."

"From X. to Z.
You must ascertain personally and give me accurate information. I must know what numbers they have. You must obey orders."

This peremptory message worries and annoys Z., who in his exasperation lets himself go as follows:

AN ALLIANCE OF PHANTOMS

"In compliance with your orders I send figures that are reliable. They have here about 500 men and twelve armoured cars, each of the latter has four large guns. I have seen all this with my own eyes. They also have about 150 motor-cars."

Then Z. probably smiles to himself as he thinks of the delight of X. at receiving such authentic information.

We were beginning to get about the country a good deal now, and small parties with three or four Ford vans might be seen in various towns, each party resulting in a similar telegram to the above. When X. came to add up the totals received from his various informants our party of twelve officers, two clerks, forty-one drivers and one armoured car must have assumed the dimensions of an army corps. I purposely omit names and official titles from these telegrams for obvious reasons.

The Turks were certain to have better information, but probably also much exaggerated, and I do not think they ever realized that the 240 miles of road from Kermanshah to Kasvin was being held by twelve officers and two clerks plus the armoured car. They were so close—in Shenneh, for example, only 100 miles from Hamadan—that a raid on our party would have been easy and probably successful. We were, moreover, surrounded by individual Turks; in fact there were so many that we could not possibly undertake to arrest them all as we could spare neither guards nor rations. One or two of the more active among them had to be arrested, but the remainder were left in peace. They were in most cases our sincere well-wishers, chiefly men who had recently deserted from the Turkish detachments to the North-West, or from the army that had fought with the Russians on this road in 1916–17. Some of the latter had settled down in the villages as peaceful inhabitants and had married and begun to raise families.

The Russian evacuation was proceeding now with some rapidity and we would soon have nothing but the men of Bicherakov's detachment left. This would place us in a far more favourable position. I had at this time a great deal to do with General Baratov and his Staff, and it was necessary to discuss many things with reference to the evacuation.

There were two points to be settled, one the question of finance, the other the question of handing over of material.

I have mentioned General Baratov before as being the original Commander of the Russian Army that had in the earlier stages of the war done so much to help the Allied cause by operating against the Turks on this road through North-West Persia and by linking up with our right flank on the Turko-Persian border.

General Baratov is himself a Caucasian, with his home in Tiflis, and naturally had his heart very much in any scheme that would tend to the restoration of law and order in that region. But during a revolution those who previously possessed most influence become the least influential of all, as they represent the very class against which the people have risen. The more valuable therefore his services had been and might still be to Russia and her Allies in this war, the more the Bolsheviks demanded his blood; and the Enzeli Committee asked me to convey a polite message to him that if he would only come down to Enzeli, they were very anxious to try him by court martial (verdict and sentence a foregone conclusion). Under these circumstances I could expect little help from him except in the matter of advice.

Had it been possible to utilize his services in the Caucasus there is no doubt that his personality would have been a great asset. He is an extraordinarily able speaker and always exceedingly popular. In North Persia the Russians had done little to endear themselves

General Baratov

AN ALLIANCE OF PHANTOMS

to the people, but the feelings of friendship and affection with which General Baratov was regarded by the people who had least cause to like him, are evidences of a very fine character. He was at this time more particularly odious to the revolutionaries as having been one of the principal supporters of the Russo-British Volunteer Corps, which they regarded as being a counter-revolutionary movement. The history of this corps is briefly as follows:

When it became evident in the autumn of 1917 that the Russian troops were going to evacuate their portion of the line in North Persia, leaving a gap of 400 miles on the right flank of the Mesopotamian army, it was thought that a force of volunteers might be raised from among the retiring troops, who would continue to serve under British control and on British pay, and this would obviate the necessity of sending up troops who could ill be spared from Baghdad. These volunteers were raised under the direct command of a very distinguished Russian officer, Colonel Baron Medem, but they were a failure from the very start, and when I saw them in February it was obvious that they would never be of any use.

The idea had been that, with Russia in a state of anarchy, a large number of men would be glad to remain in a well-paid service until a change in affairs might render a return to their homes a more pleasant prospect than it was at present. This scheme was undoubtedly attractive, and a fairly large force might have been raised under British officers. But it was decided that the force should have Russian officers, which was not acceptable to the men. The eventual failure was due to the Bolsheviks, who declared the movement counter-revolutionary and threatened with death any who supported it. And it was no real loss to us.

Judging from the few specimens I saw I am convinced

that the force at its best would have been quite worthless. Even under British officers proper military discipline could never have been restored, and the men composing the force would have been only the spiritless loafers who wanted to draw good pay and rations and avoid the turmoil of their own country, while equally refraining from risking their lives or undertaking any arduous tasks for the "cunning" Englishmen in Persia. We should therefore be grateful to the Bolsheviks who nipped in the bud a scheme that was destined under any circumstances to be a complete failure.

A good deal of my time was also taken up in discussing with General Baratov the possibilities of British assistance in the matter of the costs of the Russian evacuation. It was clear that it was to the interests of all that the Russian troops should be got out of Persia without delay, and as the Russians had no money it would be advisable to afford whatever financial assistance might be necessary. This had been agreed to, and the payments were carefully controlled by a local board, of which Mr. McMurray, of the Imperial Bank, was President.

But there remained the question of the Russian debts, and on this subject the British Government was adamant.

The position was certainly unpleasant for General Baratov personally, but it could hardly be expected that we could allow arguments of a sentimental nature to have any force.

The British Government had offered, under certain guarantees, a fixed sum payable at certain periods, which was calculated to meet the difference between a sum to be received by General Baratov at intervals from the Tiflis Government and the actual cost of the evacuation. The Tiflis Government failed to produce their share, and the Russian Commander had to make up the deficit by the issue of payment requisition orders in lieu of cash. These paper obligations now amounted to a considerable sum, and General Baratov begged that the British Government would undertake their redemption in order not only to clear his personal honour, but to uphold the prestige of the European in Asia, a matter which he maintained affected British credit as much as Russian.

His heart-rending appeals were met by constant and unqualified refusals, and it was my painful duty to convey the news of these reiterated refusals on each occasion.

The arguments adduced by the gallant General would have melted the heart of a stone; but as they could not be cabled home in full the heart of the British Government remained quite unmelted.

"See, Lev Lvovitch," he would say to me in introducing a picturesque allegory, "there on the floor before you lies a dead body. Whose body is it? It is that of Russia. Have you no tears of pity for it? Can you forget that that friend, who now lies in the awful stillness of death before you, saved you and saved all the Allies in the first year of the war? Because we have fallen from grace, are you to take no account of our earlier heroism? You stand before me, Russia's friend. Before you lies, uncared for and unburied, the dead body of your friend. Do you mean to tell me that you will not even pay the funeral expenses? The redemption of the requisitions which I demand from your Government, is only to save your deceased friend from a pauper's grave!"

The contrary contention was, however, firmly upheld, and the requisitions were in the end only partially redeemed by other means.

Another matter that absorbed much time was the question of paying the Russians for material taken over from them. All supplies we were glad to have and took over without hesitation. Wheeled transport, telegraph equipment and certain military stores would also be of great value. But there were certain items which could hardly be seriously entertained. Among such repudiated items I give the following specimens:

1. Payment for the military telegraph line from Hamadan to Enzeli. *Answer*: Totally destroyed and of no value.
2. Purchase of military roads constructed by the Russian Army. *Answer*: The question of roads constructed in Persia must be referred to the Persian Government. Whatever sum of money I paid for these roads would not make me their owner.
3. Purchase of bridging material. *Answer*: Permanent bridges having been constructed, this is not required.
4. The Russians had meant to repair the Asadabad road and had collected a lot of metal by the roadside; will the British purchase this? *Answer*: No.

Then when it was decided to take over certain things the question arose: "Who was the owner?" There was General Baratov representing the Tiflis Government, but there were also various other bodies such as the Zemski Soyuz, a charitable Red Cross institution, and these bodies did not hand over their rights to him. So we generally found that the things we bought from one man belonged to another, and when the latter's claim came up it was generally a very nebulous one.

With regard to some telegraph material I arranged to purchase, I found it already belonged by previous agreement to the Persian Telegraphs, and while we and the Persian Telegraphs were considering the matter, the stuff was removed by a third party who had a very doubtful claim, but wisely decided that possession was

AN ALLIANCE OF PHANTOMS

nine points of the law and walked off with it. This individual afterwards showed me the document on which his claim was based, and which was simply a chit signed by a Russian Second-Lieutenant to say that "the bearer can have the wire if he wants it."

Between these Russian negotiations and the endeavour to establish reasonable relations with the Persian community, it may be understood that our time was fully taken up. Measures for defence were also necessary in view of the rumours, based undoubtedly on real intentions, of an attack on the mission. Sometimes it was to be the townspeople themselves urged on by the political agitators, at other times it was to be wandering bands of desperadoes, raiding tribes, and professional highwaymen. It may have been just the fact that we were always prepared both night and day that prevented any of these bloodthirsty schemes from materializing. As long as the Russians were near us, it was possible that they might help us in case of difficulty, but it was equally possible that revolutionary soldiers might be tempted to join in with the other programme, that included, like all good programmes, the looting of the bank.

The weather remained very bad, and this factor was more for us than against us, causing a reluctance on the part of would-be attackers to undertake operations in the snow, which fell frequently and rendered movement difficult on foot and impossible in wheeled conveyances.

After a heavy fall on March 16th the weather cleared for a spell, enabling the last of the Russians to get on the move, leaving only Bicherakov's detachment at Sheverin, 3 miles out of the town.

My thoughts being still fixed on the Caucasus, many schemes were put up before me for consideration, but not one of them showed any reasonable chance of success.

I was interviewed frequently by individual Russian officers, who, inspired with the desire to do something for their country in her desperate plight, propounded schemes that belonged more to the realm of fairyland than to that of practical possibilities.

One such scheme commenced with a suggestion of the payment by the British Government of fourteen million pounds in a lump sum and ended with the restoration of order in the Caucasus and a triumphant entry into Moscow. Other smaller minds suggested the capture of a gunboat on the Caspian by aeroplane, forgetting that when the aeroplane had captured the gunboat the latter would have no port to put into and would have to spend its time till its oil fuel gave out, wandering round and round the Caspian.

Our supply question was also a matter of some difficulty. I wanted not only to supply our own needs, but also to begin laying in stocks for the troops that must eventually move up this road. But we were hampered by the famine conditions, by the resistance of the local officials and by an order issuing from the Government at Teheran that the British were to be prevented from getting supplies of any sort. The food we got was good enough, but not the sort of ration to keep a British soldier fit. Meat was not hard to obtain, bread in the form of Persian "Sangak," somewhat like the Indian chupattie, could be procured at a high price, fresh vegetables were not to be had, and their place had to be taken by dried figs and apricots. The men ate their rations cheerfully enough without caring much for them, the British soldier being a very staunch conservative in the matter of his food. But the Persian bread was too much for their digestions, and they began to suffer from stomach trouble which would in the end have become serious had we not managed at last to set up a small bakery and turn out some quite decent bread. This bakery we were enabled to construct out of some of the useful gear we had taken over from the Russians.

We began now to add to the strength of our force by taking into our service several Russian officers, of guaranteed integrity and proved ability, who had fled from the clutches of the Bolsheviks of Baku. These helped us greatly to keep touch with the Baku situation, and two of them were at once dispatched on a secret mission. All of those who entered our service at this time were men who had already distinguished themselves in the war and who would stick at nothing to prove their merit; they nobly maintained their reputation.

The last of the Russian regular army having withdrawn, Bicherakov's men were now getting restless, and he informed me that he had the intention of following the rest of the army and leaving Persia as soon as his transport could be arranged. If he carried out this move, all chance of retaining our hold on North Persia would be gone. I could continue to hold out in Hamadan, but I should be able to exert no influence farther north, and there would be nothing to prevent Kasvin falling into the hands of the Jangalis, who would certainly be getting on the move now that the weather showed signs of improvement.

It was therefore necessary to tempt him to throw in his lot entirely with us, and to draw up an agreement that would be advantageous to both of us. After many discussions on the various points we finally settled on the following terms :

1. That he would not withdraw his troops from Persia till I could replace them with our own troops.
2. That I would assist him financially, as he had great difficulty in paying his men, but that he was in no sense a mercenary, would accept no money

for any service performed but only for expenses actually incurred for military operations.

3. That neither would undertake operations without consulting the other, and that any financial assistance from the British Government would cease if he undertook operations not in accordance with the general plans of the Allies.
4. That the first operation to be undertaken would be an attack on Kuchik Khan's army and the clearing of the road from Kasvin to the Caspian.
5. That if he would fall in with my plans in Persia, we would try to evolve a mutual plan for later operations in the Caucasus, where my assistance to him would be as valuable as his to me.

This excellent agreement had no sooner been drawn up than an opportunity occurred of testing its value. On March 23rd we received reliable information that the Jangalis were preparing to march on Kasvin and that Kasvin was preparing to welcome them. They were now holding all the strong points on the Resht road and had entrenched themselves in a position to cover the Menjil bridge and close the road to all traffic.

On March 24th we pushed off a small detachment of Cossacks to Kasvin, and the remainder moving by route march reached that town in the nick of time. Kuchik Khan's scheme was for the moment thwarted and Kasvin saved. The situation there had become so critical that the bank had had orders to close, and all officials to withdraw. The bank at Resht had been looted; the bank manager, Mr. Oakshot, and the British Consul, Mr. Maclaren, had both been arrested and were now prisoners in the hands of the Jangalis. Captain Noel, endeavouring to reach me with dispatches from

Tiflis, also fell into their hands. The two former were allowed a certain amount of freedom and escaped to Enzeli after some months' captivity; the latter, however, was treated with great rigour from the first and was kept a prisoner for five months until released under the terms of peace made after the defeat of the Jangalis. He had made several attempts to escape, being thwarted in each case by sheer bad luck, and each unsuccessful attempt resulted in increased severity in his treatment which, without going into details, was far from being in accordance with the rules of civilized warfare, though Kuchik always maintained that in such matters he was on a par with European nations.

It would now be possible for Bicherakov to move forward on the Menjil road and he was anxious to do so. As I had as yet no troops to put up behind him this would have left me in a very bad position, and I was able to make him defer his departure by the promise of aeroplanes and armoured cars to support his move if he would only wait another week. In this way I was able to keep him hanging on for ten weeks, by which time the needed troops had arrived and the scheme was brought to a successful issue. Those ten weeks were not a very happy time for either of us, and we got dangerously near to what are politely called "mutual recriminations."

A suggestion that Persian levies and irregulars should be raised was at once taken up and added considerably to the heavy tasks which fell on the small number of officers available. It was decided therefore to get up a second batch of officers and N.C.O.'s.

My present duties were now defined as being to take energetic and immediate measures to frustrate enemy penetration through North-West Persia. We had already had considerable success on these lines, and a rather valuable Austrian army officer fell into our hands on March 21st. He was captured through the agency of the Cossacks, together with a Turkish sergeant who was acting as his guide and interpreter. The officer was disguised as a Persian lady, but his height and gait aroused suspicion, while the Turkish sergeant was more easily disguised as a Persian peasant, and could have passed muster if alone. The only special request the Austrian had to make was that he might be given some European bread to eat, and he was astonished and disgusted to hear that we had been eating "Sangak" ourselves for two months and had nothing else to offer him: a week later we could have given him the treat he asked for, when our famous bakery had got under way.

In the surrounding villages some drilling was going on at this time under Turkish instructors. This was all part of the scheme to exterminate our party, and we took steps to interfere with these parades; not that they seemed likely to result in anything very serious for a considerable time at least, but the actual drilling of well-armed men is certainly getting nearer to action than the passing of resolutions to which the plotters had hitherto confined themselves.

Famine relief had already commenced and was beginning to work well; a description of the work undertaken will be given in a later chapter. The evidences of famine were terrible, and in a walk through the town one was confronted with the most awful sights. Nobody could endure such scenes if he were not endowed with the wonderful apathy of the Oriental: "It is the will of God!" So the people die and no one makes any effort to help, and a dead body in the road lies unnoticed until an effort to secure some sort of burial becomes unavoidable. I passed in a main thoroughfare the body of a boy of about nine years of age who had evidently died during the day; he lay with his face buried in the mud, and the people passed by on either side as if he were merely any ordinary obstruction in the roadway.

AN ALLIANCE OF PHANTOMS

Spring was now beginning to show signs of its advent, but on April 1st down came the snow again and for a time winter regained the supremacy. It was not possible to dispense with fires till May.

On this day we really thought that the expected climax had actually arrived. Breathless messengers from the town brought the news that the people were taking up arms, and the Governor himself was issuing rifles and ammunition to the mob with orders to destroy the English. This was very much like the real thing, and we prepared for our destruction. But investigation proved that the alarm was false and the occurrence was of quite another nature. As I was by this time a firm friend of the Governor I could not believe that he would behave quite so treacherously. It is a good maxim to trust no one in war time, and I never trusted my Persian friends to the extent of relaxing all precautions, but I always found that the measure of trust I considered judicious was never betrayed.

In fact all that had happened was that a Persian Cossack had been arrested and imprisoned by the Governor. Bicherakov's Cossacks got the idea that it was one of their comrades who had been confined, galloped into the town and prepared to storm the prison. This was too much even for the very yielding Governor, who quite rightly met the situation by arming his men and proceeding to defy the Cossacks. A conflict was only avoided by the arrival of General Baratov, who called a truce, examined into the facts of the case and persuaded the Cossacks to return to their quarters.

On April 3rd General Byron arrived with the second party, a very welcome addition of twenty officers and as many N.C.O.'s to our little force. The party were well selected and included Captain Donohoe, the well-known war correspondent, who was doubly welcome on account of his knowledge of Russian, and Captain Eve, equally a Russian scholar, of the Royal Engineers, a service so far unrepresented in our small detachment. Another useful addition was Lieutenant Akbar, a Persian gentleman with business connections in England, whose services proved of the greatest value.

Looking back on our first passage through these mountain defiles, I never cease to marvel at the fact that while travelling on the road from Baghdad to Enzeli and thence back to Hamadan, only one single shot was fired at the party. The Russians did not fare so well, and always ran into trouble. A motor lorry containing six Russians was ambushed near Hamadan at the end of March and all the occupants killed. Another car was attacked beyond the Sultan Bulaq Pass and three officials killed, and a third attack on a motor lorry at the foot of the pass was successfully beaten off.

I do not think that this necessarily showed excessive hostility to the Russians as compared with ourselves, but more perhaps the utter neglect of precautions which was characteristic of the former's happy-go-lucky methods. The same tragedies continued to be enacted on the Enzeli road till the last of the Russians had gone. Lorries were continually being held up and burnt and the occupants killed, whereas with the exception of the casualties involved in actual fighting, we never lost a car or a man on the road throughout the whole period of our occupation.

A small detachment of the 1/4 Hants Territorial Infantry, consisting of thirty rifles, joined our force at Hamadan at the end of March, and on the same day the first aeroplane arrived from Baghdad. The former though not a large body of troops was quite a formidable addition, as things go in Persia, and was promptly reported to Teheran as being a whole battalion; the latter produced a moral effect that was of more value than many troops. It was an unmistakable sign of strength and suggested the proximity of the Baghdad army.

Neither the Russians nor the Turks had been able to use aeroplanes in these parts, and the effect of our aeroplane was much enhanced by its novelty.

The news of the arrival of numerous aeroplanes and the battalion of infantry had a good effect in the distant capital, where enemy propaganda had lately been running with great vigour and had resulted in various disturbances and the holding of the usual anti-British meetings. The position of the British Legation was very precarious.

The Persian Government now made a rather clever move. Seeing that by our alliance with Bicherakov we had secured Kasvin and had thwarted the movement of Kuchik Khan, and that such an alliance was likely to be most beneficial to our cause, an attempt was made to separate us from the Russians. A peremptory message was sent to Bicherakov ordering him to remove his troops at once from Persia, in accordance with the previous agreement between the Russian and Persian authorities, under which the former had promised to evacuate Persia by a date already far past. Dire threats were made as to what would happen if there were any further delay in compliance with this order. But it did not result in any hastening of the withdrawal, Bicherakov explaining that he was getting along as quickly as he could, and was only delayed by the presence of Kuchik Khan's troops on the road.

The mission now began to assume quite an international character, being joined by three French officers. These officers were on their way under Colonel Chardigny to join the French mission in the Caucasus, but attached themselves to me till they could get a chance of reaching their destination. Two of them later returned to France, leaving with us Lieutenant Poidebard, an excellent fellow, who remained with us from this time onwards until the fall of Baku.

Several cases occurred of officers being shot at, but without casualties, the firers preferring to keep a good distance away, and they were not at all good at long shots. The only case of shooting at close quarters was where a Persian drew his revolver on an officer, but the latter was fairly handy with his weapon and got in his shot first. With the exception of these few instances there were no attempts at violence, and the town began to look on us as permanent, and not at all unwelcome, residents.

CHAPTER VI

WE GET TO KNOW OUR HOSTS

THINGS were much more plain sailing from the latter end of March, when the Russian troops had completed their evacuation and Bicherakov and ourselves had a clear ground to work on.

The agreement we had entered into was very sound as long as it lasted, but there was always the risk that the impatience of the Cossacks to get back to their homes in the North Caucasus might lead to their breaking away from us. They were already chafing at the delay, and I knew it would be many weeks yet before their further move towards the Caspian would suit our plans. It seemed very doubtful whether we should be able to hold them till our troops were up.

In any case, in the absence of our troops, although the Persians estimated my body of twelve officers, two clerks and forty-one chauffeurs with one armoured car and thirty soldiers as representing several thousand troops, it was obviously not possible to conduct operations with this phantom army, and active operations would soon be necessary. It was clearly a case of the Cossacks or nothing.

In describing the various phases through which the work of the mission passed at this time, it is difficult to adhere to an exact sequence. We were simultaneously engaged in so many parallel tasks that it is only possible to make the situation clear by devoting separate chapters to each phase. These chapters therefore do not describe events following one another, but events actually taking place concurrently.

Thus in the last chapter I endeavoured to set forth the situation as between the Russians and ourselves. In this chapter we must hark back to the time of our first arrival in Hamadan in order to explain our relations with the Persians.

As soon as it became apparent that our stay in Hamadan might be prolonged, I set out to make the acquaintance of all the officials, the landowners, the politicians and the merchants. The numerous visits and return visits constituted a somewhat arduous task, but the experience was on the whole enjoyable. Certainly the Persians have no monopoly of the virtues, neither have they of the vices. They make very poor soldiers in these degenerate days, but the most pugnacious people are not necessarily the most amiable, and I see no reason why the Persian should be despised because he has adopted a line of philosophy which regards fighting as an anachronism and prefers the tongue to the sword. The Chinaman divides his nation into two classes, the braves and the non-braves, and the Persian follows much the same line of thought. Certain classes, such as highway robbers, make a profession of being brave and have to live up to it (though they don't!); others openly profess not to be brave and are consequently not expected to encounter, but rather to flee from, danger. "I drew the feet of security under the skirt of contentment" is a Persian phrase that expresses the feeling quite neatly.

In my earlier calls I was very kindly conducted by the British Consul, Mr. MacDowell, who interpreted and advised me on points of etiquette. Our first visit was of course to the Governor, Nizam-es-Sultan, an ultra extreme democrat as far as political nomenclature went,

COSSACKS HOMEWARD BOUND

but otherwise an aristocrat in ideas and tendencies. He was renowned as being so " ultra extreme " that his views were practically anarchical, and altogether he promised to be a very difficult person to tackle. It was for March 3rd that our visit had been fixed, and at 4.30 p.m. on that date we arrived at the Governor's residence, where we were received by a general salute from the police guard and escorted to the room of audience by a uniformed retainer.

Captain Saunders, and Captain Dunning, my A.D.C., accompanied me, the former, who had served in Seistan, possessing some knowledge of Persian and being quite in his element in visits of this kind.

We received a polite and frigid shake of the hand from the Governor who, after introducing his friend Haji Saad-es-Sultaneh, the special delegate for Russian affairs, begged us to be seated and ordered tea to be served.

Nizam-es-Sultan was a nice-looking Persian gentleman of about thirty-five years of age with the polished manners of Teheran society; his companion was a good-looking man about ten years older, who had travelled much in Europe, spoke French fluently and had adopted European manners and, with the exception of headdress, European costume.

Some time was absorbed in the usual inane remarks of polite society. The Governor remarked that there had been a lot of snow, to which one could but assent, and that there would very likely be more, to which probability I equally agreed.

On my part I spoke of deaths from famine and deplored the uncertainty of life, commenting also on the execrable nature of the road between here and Asadabad. This brought us immediately out of inanities into realities. The Governor at once woke up and fired off a volley of questions at me.

" Was the road really very bad ? "

"Where had we come from ?"
"Why had we come ?"
"How many men were there in the party ?"

With the exception of the last, these questions were easy to answer, but this demand for information was rather disconcerting though easily warded off with a good square lie ; but in this instance I was able to answer that there were "quite a lot, and a lot more coming and then lots more."

In order to prevent a pursuance of this embarrassing theme and fearing to be asked for a precise definition of the meaning of the word "lot," I now switched off the conversation on to Kuchik Khan, a topic which immediately caused the inquiries as to our numbers to be put aside. "Excellent fellow this Mirza Kuchik Khan," I said, "I rather like him, although so far he and I have not quite agreed about things ; but that is only because we have not yet been able to meet and talk. If we could meet I am sure he would find we had nothing to disagree about. I suppose your Excellency is in sympathy with him ?"

This brought forth the pained and indignant denial I had expected, but a denial that did not convince me. The intentionally abrupt introduction of the subject had taken him rather off his guard, and there was a hesitation in his manner that indicated a mind not altogether innocent. The fact of the matter is he was not of those who had actually thrown in their lot with the Jangali movement, but was among the wiser ones who were waiting to see which way the wind blew.

The other official joined in the conversation and tried to get various admissions out of me, but I trust he drew a blank, and as this was only an official call I made a point of withdrawing early, which put an end to any further cross-examination.

WE GET TO KNOW OUR HOSTS

I am sure that the British residents of Hamadan will smile when I say that I took a great liking to Nizam-es-Sultan, their point of view and mine not being likely to be the same. Their first objection to him would be that, though a Governor, he did not govern. But the question arises are Persian Governors meant to govern? In no case among my many acquaintances with Governors was there any indication of a serious effort to govern in our meaning of the word. They represent government, and their real function begins and ends with that. To take actual examples, at a time like the present the question of famine relief should be the first step of a Governor. Was there one in Persia who even mildly interested himself in it? At all times the question of sanitation is a vital one. Is there a Persian Governor in the whole kingdom who cares twopence for it? No! My friend was all he should be according to Persian lights, a nice gentleman and a charming representative of Teheran, but he did not govern!

Other visits followed, to the Kar-guzar, and to the chief landowner, Amir Afgham, the former a pleasant fellow, hating his enforced residence in a dull provincial town and never ceasing to regret his inability to get a decent game of Poker. This regret was shared by the Governor, and both prayed fervently for a transfer to Teheran, where they could taste again the delights of society in that gay capital and play Poker to their hearts' content.

But the other, Amir Afgham, was a very fine type of the Persian country gentleman, a little man about sixty years of age, hale and hearty, with a boisterous laugh that could be heard half a mile away; enormously wealthy and, as is usual with very wealthy people, always very hard up. He was quite naturally a great hater of democrats and politicians generally and of the Governor especially. At the time of our visit he had the Deputy

Governor staying with him, and the latter was present while we conversed. It was another insight into Persian affairs to hear the old man revile the Governor in the most biting terms, while the Governor's right-hand man sat there and applauded.

The real cause of the Amir's indignation was that the Governor had, in the routine performance of his duties, demanded from him the payment of very considerable arrears of taxes. The taxes were undoubtedly legitimate and very much in arrears; but to demand them seemed so very uncourteous! Such forgivable lapses of memory ought not to be drawn attention to, and the old gentleman resisted the tax collectors by force of arms, the incident ending, as such incidents fortunately do in Persia, without bloodshed. And the taxes remained unpaid.

To see the Deputy Governor heartily sympathizing with the wicked old man in this flouting of authority enabled me to realize the difficulty of a Persian Governor's really governing. Perhaps, after all, the Persian system of letting things take their own course is as good as any other.

The Persian point of view was set forth in the reply to my printed proclamation, of which I have already spoken—" Our methods may be deplorable, but they are our own; they suit us, and we don't want yours, which don't suit us."

My visit to the Amir certainly threw a new light on the question of a Governor's position. You may abuse him for not governing, but it must be a hard task to administer public affairs when the biggest man in the neighbourhood defies your authority and resists by armed force your attempts to enforce it, while your assistant sides so strongly with the cause of all the trouble that he severs all connection with you and goes to live with the enemy.

WE GET TO KNOW OUR HOSTS

Incidentally it was gratifying to realize how such Gilbertian situations strengthened our otherwise weak position in Hamadan.

The old Amir did not put me to any very severe cross-examination; he seemed rather glad than otherwise at the prospect of British troops coming to this part of Persia. He felt that any rule would be preferable to the rule of democrats, who paid little respect to his position and had the effrontery to suggest the payment of his arrears of taxes.

A few days after these visits the return calls began. The Governor, the Kar-guzar and Haji Saad-es-Sultaneh arrived in due state with official escorts, and the conversation this time was not quite so frigidly formal; the ice was beginning to thaw. The Amir called with a most imposing retinue, including a handsome pony led by a retainer carrying only his pipe and tobacco and a brazier of lighted charcoal, the latter looking rather an uncomfortable load for a fidgety pony; but perhaps sad experience had taught the tobacco pony not to fidget. During this time the other officers were getting into touch with minor officials in the town, and famine relief work had already begun brought us into contact with all classes, so that by the end of the month we formed an integral and indispensable part of local society.

But the cross-examination of myself and my Staff continued with unabated vigour and was becoming insupportable. I knew the sort of telegrams the Governor and others were receiving from the Minister of the Interior ordering them at all costs to discover the exact strength of the British detachment, so I could hardly blame them for making some sort of a show to carry out their orders. My studies in Persian were progressing famously, and a renewal of my early acquaintance with the "Gulistan" of Sa'adi proved of great value to me in the fencing matches that ensued.

It is a marvellous thing that while all Persians are brought up on the wisdom of Sa'adi and other deep and attractive thinkers (and there is not a problem in life that has not its solution in the writings of these poets), they read them and quote them and are never guided by them. They look feebly for enlightenment to the West, when all that we have worth knowing, except modern science, we have got from the East.

In the eighth chapter of the "Gulistan" I found what I was looking for, a quotation that I could learn by heart and which would shield me from the shower of embarrassing questions that the Governor made a point of putting me at each interview.

I finally protested on these lines: "My visits to you and yours to me are a source of undiluted pleasure to me, but I do not think that we conduct our conversations on proper or fair lines. I talk to you of the weather, the crops, the pleasures of life, the uncertainty of existence and the ultimate destiny of mankind. Your conversation on the other hand consists of a series of oft-repeated and most uninteresting questions, such as : How many troops have you got ? How many rifles have they ? How many rounds per rifle ? How many more are coming ? When will they arrive ? Where are they now ? Conversation on such lines is extremely wearisome to me, and must be equally so to you. I could quite easily answer all your questions by telling you lies, because obviously my Government does not expect me to lay bare official secrets, but I have a great objection to telling lies, and in that respect I may represent a type quite new to you; but I repeat that falsehood is most repugnant to me. I might, according to the well-known Persian saying, wrap up my principles in the napkin of oblivion, but I prefer not to do this. In answer therefore to all questions you have so far put to me and intend to put to me in the future, I give you the following quotation from Sa'adi :

WE GET TO KNOW OUR HOSTS

> Not every secret that one has in one's heart
> Should one reveal to the best of friends—
> God knows, he may be an enemy to-morrow!
> And not every possible injury
> Should one do to an enemy—
> God knows, he may be a friend to-morrow!

This settled finally the irritating cross-examinations, and I was never really bothered by them again. Now and then in response to a peremptory order from Teheran, a fitful effort was made to revive the old process, but it was not even necessary to produce the quotation; it sufficed to say "Eighth Chapter," and with a smile my interlocutors turned to brighter themes.

It is not to be imagined that my unassisted Persian would run to these flights of eloquence. The conversation was sustained partly by the combined efforts in Persian of Captain Saunders and myself, partly by means of the Consul or Mr. McMurray acting as interpreter, and partly by making use of French in addressing the Haji.

Our friendship with the local notables was now firmly established, and bore ripe and luscious fruits for both sides. The monetary basis, which is the ordinary, useful, but sordid method of gaining one's ends, was entirely absent from our relations, and though when any kindly act was done, the other politicians invariably scented a bribe, I can truthfully say that whatever was done to help us at this time was done without any recourse to money payments.

I can give an example, however, from our dealings with an official, not mentioned by name, which occurred in another town at another time.

This official was a great personal friend of mine, and showed the reality of his feelings in a very marked way. The question of obtaining supplies at the time of which I am speaking, was becoming one of daily increasing difficulty.

On a certain morning I was made aware of the fact that a cipher telegram from a person in high authority had been delivered to the official in question. And it was also made known to me that the contents of the telegram were as follows : " You are to see that the British get no more supplies of any sort. All their contractors are at once to be imprisoned." This looked as if we might expect rather more active opposition in the matter of obtaining supplies, but there was nothing to do but " wait and see." We had not long to wait before we saw.

The first report I got was from the Supply Officer, who informed me that supplies promised for delivery that morning had not turned up. This was soon followed by a wail from families bereft of their breadwinners to the effect that the heads of the families who were our contractors had been thrown into a dungeon.

An urgent message was sent to the official asking for an explanation, and begging for a release of the men. This drew forth a reply couched in polite but severe language stating that the men had been arrested on certain charges and could not be released.

Now was the time for choosing between two diametrically opposite lines of action. Should we parade the twelve officers, two clerks and forty-one drivers and endeavour to rescue our contractors at the point of the bayonet, or should we put our friendship to the test and see if our friends would act up to their professions ? The latter course commended itself to me, and I set forth with a Staff Officer to interview the obstructive official. I was afraid he would say he was ill and unable to see me, which is the usual Persian method when trouble is brewing ; I took it as a good sign, therefore, when we were admitted without hesitation to his residence and courteously received by him in his most severely official manner. After the usual exchange of compliments we commenced business by my asking for an explanation of the tyrannical treatment of my contractors. In reply I received the following statement:

"With regard to the imprisonment of the men you refer to, I regret to state that I am acting under orders which in my official capacity I am bound to obey. You may not believe it, but I will tell you in confidence that I have just received explicit orders to the effect that every measure is to be taken to prevent you from getting supplies, and your contractors are to be forthwith imprisoned as a first step to giving effect to this decree. Your presence is not desired in Persia, and it is intended to make your position here impossible. Why do you disturb the peace of a neutral country like Persia by bringing troops here?

"As regards the imprisonment of the contractors," I replied, "surely it is not possible in your country to put men in prison without bringing a legal charge against them, and surely there is no law in this land prohibiting the sale of grain to any would-be purchaser!"

To this the official retorted, "You do not know our laws and you are not therefore competent to discuss them; they do not resemble yours. I am ordered to arrest these men and I have done so."

I then explained, not for the first time, that as to the remark regarding our presence here in a neutral country, we were most unwillingly forced into that position. If Persia would keep her neutrality there would be no need for our presence here, which was solely necessitated by the activity of the Germans and Turks in this neutral country. The Persian Government seemed to acquiesce in Turkish occupation and German intrigue, and to claim the laws of neutrality only as regards one of the belligerents. There was no great need for entering on such a discussion at this time but Orientals do not like to be hurried, and it is polite to talk a little round your point before you come to it. So after interchanging a few more opinions on these general subjects, I deemed it time to work back to the original point, which I did in these words: "I am grateful to you for your detailed explanation of the circumstances leading to the present trouble, and as a soldier I would be the last person to suggest disobedience of orders. I see that the course you have adopted was the only one open to you and I admire the promptness of your obedience. You have now fulfilled your duty, and can report your having done so, with a clear conscience, to your superiors. That quite finally settles the official side of this interview may be regarded as closed.

"Now may I address you as a friend? In that capacity I feel I can rely upon you to do whatever you can for me personally. So far our friendship has consisted of words, not deeds. Were those words sincere? If so, translate them into deeds. As a friend therefore I beg you to release all the contractors at once. And, as a friend, I equally trust that the question of the supplies may not be made too difficult."

The happy ending to this annoying episode was the release of the offending contractors and a withdrawal of all obstruction in the matter of supplies. At a later meeting I congratulated my friend on his ready solution of the difficulty, and he suggested that if the great nations now at war had been only half as sensible as he and I were, there would not have been any war. Which is a fact.

I have given a general idea of what I may call the pleasant meetings. But there were other categories which were most unpleasant, those with the leading merchants, and those with the leading politicians.

WE GET TO KNOW OUR HOSTS

The merchants were cheerful and effusive, but had none of the charm of the refined Persian gentleman, and they had no views on any subject outside their little business. The sentimental business man is a type not yet developed, more's the pity. I was generally able to bring an uninteresting meeting with such gentry to an abrupt close by referring to the horrors of the famine, and suggesting a handsome contribution from them for the purpose of famine relief.

The politicians were mostly men of humble origin, some genuine idealists, some who were only "in it for what they could get out of it." For a long time they fought against coming to my tea-parties, but in the end they were brought along in twos and threes until at last the uncompromising leader himself, Ferid-ud-Dowleh, was persuaded to put in an appearance, and we spent a most cheerful afternoon together. The extraordinary difficulties involved in inducing these people to enter into any sort of relations, even purely social, with their avowed enemy, was chiefly overcome by Mr. Moir, who acted as political adviser to me, and with a great command of the language and intimate knowledge of Persian customs was able to work wonders. Mr. Moir had been working in Persia for years as representative of a large business firm and also in the capacity of Vice-Consul, and had now thrown in his lot with my mission, where his services continued to be of great value throughout the operations. I was also very greatly helped by one of my Persian friends.

These meetings were only useful as helping to form an estimate of character, and as tending to abate in a very small degree the virulence of the agitators. I had no hope or desire of converting the conspirators, but I brought them to a frame of mind which rendered them less anxious to conspire.

The intelligence office under Captain Saunders was

now achieving such success that there was practically no information I required that I did not get. In all such work money plays a great part, but money alone will not achieve the best results; there has to be a good deal of inspiration both on the part of the Staff and of the people they employ, and a very complete system of counter-check to avoid the acceptance of false or misleading information.

All this time there was a Turkish Consul just a hundred miles away, with a military escort strong enough to wipe my party off the map; but the fighting spirit had quite left the Turks since the fall of Baghdad, and with his exaggerated notion of my strength he was more afraid of me than I was of him.

This official was naturally in touch with the Turkish Legation in Teheran and spent a great deal of time and money in telegraphing to them. These telegrams had to pass through Hamadan, and without any treachery on the part of the telegraph officials we secured them all. Some were in plain language and were useful to us, others were in a cipher of which we did not yet possess the key. The result of our manipulation of these telegrams was a plaintive appeal sent by special secret messenger from the Turkish Consul to the head of the telegraph office at Hamadan, to this effect: " What has happened to your office ? It does not seem to be working properly. I have received by messenger from one of my agents the information that of nine telegrams lately sent to Teheran two have altogether failed to reach, and the seven that reached are altogether undecipherable. The fact of the two being missing is traceable from my numbers. Will you please be more careful in future." One might have expected the Consul to have guessed the answer to this very easy riddle: he probably solved the problem later.

With such a complete and reliable system it was easy to secure documentary evidence of the state of mind

WE GET TO KNOW OUR HOSTS

and aims of the local Democratic Committee, headed by Ferid-ud-Dowleh. Their correspondence was most enlightening and enabled me to appreciate the local political situation with accuracy. Letters passed almost daily between the leaders and Kuchik Khan in one direction and between them and the Turkish Legation on the other, and most of these letters passed through my hands.

To the former they wrote somewhat in this strain: "The British are here, but in very small numbers. At a sign from you we can rise and destroy them, but you should send some of your soldiers to help; we have not many fighting men here, and the British are well armed. All the people of the town and most of the leaders are heartily in your favour, and we only await your signal. We are short of funds." To the latter they wrote: "The British force here is a small one. We hear that German troops are being passed through Baku by the Russians. When they come, if you could send some here, we could easily destroy the small British garrison and all the other English here. Or send some Turkish troops. We do all we can to help the aims of the Germans and yourselves and are ready at a moment's notice to lay down our lives for the cause. We could accomplish more if we had more money." These letters show that the politicians realized our weakness better than the officials did. Their common final note is a searchlight on Persian politics.

With a good deal of such information at my disposal I was thoroughly prepared for my guests at the afternoon tea-parties. One party took place within a few hours of the writing and dispatch of two such letters as the above, and I was privileged to read these letters just before my guests arrived. After a considerable discussion of such topics as the weather and the famine I changed the subject to a direct inquiry concerning Kuchik and the Turks. The fact that my guests lied to me is of course not remarkable; had they been the most upright people in the world they could not have been expected to give truthful answers to my questions, and to have done so would have been to betray their own cause. But with letters in my hand containing their very latest expressions of opinion, their falsehoods were distinctly entertaining. It would have been still more amusing had I confronted them with their actual letters with all their signatures attached. There were occasions later when it paid to do this; to do so at the present moment would be to acquaint them with the fact that their letters were falling into our hands, which would at once dry up this fount of information.

"I hear a great deal," I went on, "in the shape of rumours in the town of your hostility to my mission here. I pay no attention to such rumours, but of course we have to face facts. You naturally resent our presence here; we regret that it is unavoidable. You obviously sympathize with Kuchik Khan; why shouldn't you? You are democrats, and he is said to be the chief of democrats. But you might remember also that I am a democrat, in the sense that I represent the only truly democratic country in the world, and in a way I sympathize with Kuchik. The only mistake he makes is in making an enemy of me and closing the road to the Caspian: that will in the end get him into trouble."

Loud murmurings of dissent greeted this speech. "What baseless rumours! what fanciful ideas! How could we possibly sympathize with Kuchik Khan, who is an upstart and endeavouring to lead a revolution, whereas we represent law and order."

"But you must very strongly resent our intrusion here, although we have most excellent reasons for it, and I understand from placards and manifestoes that you intend to murder us all in our beds. The Jangalis might help you to do that." More protestations of inno-

WE GET TO KNOW OUR HOSTS

cence ensued, and I switched off on to the question of their most right and justifiable love for the Germans and the Turks. " The great advantage of having the German or Turks, or both, here in preference to ourselves is that by this means you ensure stability of government. We have no intention of staying here, and our eventual withdrawal after we have won the war would throw you back again into the chaos which is the normal state of Persia. Now with the Germans and Turks there would be no risk of that. Once here they are here till the crack of doom, and a stable form of government is assured in perpetuity. German rule would be a nice bracing tonic for Persians who, as you yourselves complain, are too lethargic. There won't be any lethargy left when you've had a dose of Kultur. And as to the Turks, well! you know more about them and their methods of government than I can tell you. Still, all these advantages are only to be gained *if* the Germans win the war, and they won't. Therefore I think that on the whole your leaning to them and antagonism to us is not going to do you any good." This produced quite a volley of negatives. " What an unheard of thing to suggest that we have any sort of leanings towards those horrible Germans whom we loathe and the Turks whom we despise. We have the greatest admiration for the British, but we are a neutral country, and you must leave Persia at once. We intend no open hostility to you and will even offer you protection in case of trouble, but the people of the town are fierce and will not be controlled by us."

This will suffice to give an idea of the entertaining conversations with which we whiled away the pleasant hours. They were both amusing and useful to me—I doubt if they were useful to the democrats, but they must have been extraordinarily amusing. To think how easily the British General had swallowed all that stuff about their hating Kuchik and loathing the Germans and Turks! Ha! ha!

CHAPTER VII

FAMINE

IT is hard to convey to any one who has never been in a famine even the faintest idea of the horrors that dearth of food entails. In the struggle for existence the human side of nature gets thrust out of sight and only the animal, like a ravening wolf, remains.

Many may be acquainted with famine conditions in a country like India where, however great the suffering may be, the Government undertakes full responsibility, and private charity properly organized assists in the endeavour to alleviate the sufferings of the poor. Even then the misery is appalling. But imagine what the conditions must be in a country like Persia, where the State makes no effort and where private charity would be regarded as lunacy.

Signs of the famine had greeted us at the very outset of our journey in January when we encountered the dead and dying on the road, and passed through half-ruined villages with their starving inhabitants. But as time went on conditions went from bad to worse, and it was obvious that the distress must increase until the reaping of the next harvest some six months hence.

The famine was due to many causes. Firstly, owing to war conditions and bad weather, the harvest of 1917 had been a bad one. Secondly, the demands of the troops, Turkish and Russian, had been considerable and had much reduced the quantity of grain on the market. Thirdly, the extraordinary rise in price had opened such vistas of wealth to the landowners and grain dealers that they had made a ring with a view to keeping these prices up and forcing them still higher; and although there was always wheat enough for the food of the people, the holders of wheat refused to put their stocks on the market, waiting for still better prices, regardless of the fact that every fractional rise in price meant a large increase in the death-rate among the very poor. The wheat was there, but not the money to pay for it.

The apathy of the townspeople of Hamadan was extraordinary. Among the population of 50,000 over 30 per cent. were on the verge of starvation and for a very large percentage death was inevitable. But Hamadan contains a very large number of wealthy people, and the well-to-do community could easily have saved their poorer brethren from starvation had they but parted with a very small percentage of the enormous profits they had already made out of wheat transactions. But not only would they take no steps themselves, but when I took the steps for them I had the greatest difficulty in getting prominent men even to assist in the organization of the gangs, distribution of tickets, etc.

When we arrived in Hamadan there were already two centres of famine relief at work, one at the Imperial Bank of Persia and the other at the American Mission; but the numbers they were able to deal with fell far short of the 15,000 people who were in acute distress. These relief centres were run on purely charitable lines, no work being exacted and no money paid, but good food issued on tickets.

The relief I proposed to undertake would be on the

lines of cash payment for a day's labour, without demanding any special standard of work.

The most suitable form of famine relief work appeared to be the construction of new roads and the improvement of those already existing in the neighbourhood. I therefore begged that a sum might be allotted for this purpose, and my request was sanctioned without delay.

Having received permission to incur the necessary expenditure, all that remained was to get the men to work. None of us had any experience of famine relief work, and the problem before us appeared fairly simple; but it was not. The problem was this: " In this town are, say, 10,000 men and boys on the verge of starvation. Of these we can employ 5,000; but these 5,000 must be chosen only from the very poorest. How can we be certain of getting the poorest ? How can we best notify conditions as to work, time, place, etc ? How can we ensure the men we want turning up and no others ? With so few officers superintending and such large gangs at work, how can we be certain that the men we pay out at pay-time are the men who actually did the work ? "

These are not the only questions we had to ask ourselves; there were a great many more, but these were perhaps the main problems, a solution of which was indispensable to satisfactory commencement of the work.

In discussing this on paper I may be giving the false idea that we had carefully considered all these questions beforehand. We did nothing of the sort, and only realized the necessity for various lines of action as we learnt day by day by sad experience.

There were too many other things to be attended to, and it was not possible to devote oneself entirely to the problems of famine relief. We were even ignorant of the numbers to be dealt with, as to which it was not feasible to obtain any reliable estimate; we could only find out by trial.

Our earlier efforts were great failures, but we soon got things in order, and in the end achieved remarkable success.

For the first day's work no one seemed quite certain if the people would turn out at all, and we were certainly quite unprepared for the enormous crowd of applicants we had to deal with. It was announced in the town on the previous evening that the British desired to have some work done on the roads and would pay workers three krans a day, that the work was intended to help the starving people, that only the very poorest would be accepted, and that intending workers were to assemble at a spot near the eastern exits of the town at 8 a.m.

At the appointed hour on the next day I sent Captain John, with two other officers to assist him, to start the day's proceedings. The instructions I gave him were these: "As soon as you get your men assembled make them sit down in rows. Pick out all the robust ones and send them back to the town till you have reduced the numbers down to the level we can afford to pay. Divide up into gangs of fifty, choose a likely man as head of each gang and get to work."

There was not for a moment any doubt as to the number of people applying for work. The entire town rose as one man and rushed to the rendezvous, the unfortunate officers were overwhelmed and lucky to get out alive, although the disappointed crowd showed no malice. There was nothing to do but to give up any further effort for that day and try again to-morrow, having in the meantime thought things out a little more and issued further explanatory proclamations in the town.

Tickets were also printed, to be given out on the

ground to each man before commencing work and to be presented by him as a coupon for payment at the end of the day.

The next day, with a strong escort of drivers, Captain John again proceeded to his task, but again returned reporting a failure.

I was not pleased with this repeated lack of success, and explained to the officer in charge that it was simply owing to his lack of ordinary intelligence. Colonel Duncan quite agreed with my reproaches and added, "The mistake you make is in not making the men sit down. Once they are sitting it is quite easy to keep order."

The next day again I received a despairing message from Captain John to say that he was powerless to do anything with the mob. I replied that I would send Colonel Duncan out to show him how to do it.

So Colonel Duncan forthwith proceeded and, after making some such remark as "Now you watch me," addressed the crowd in Persian, as follows: "Sit down, sit down, sit down! Nothing till you sit down. Sit down!" Whereupon the crowd of several thousands sat down. Then the interpreter announced, "The gentleman will now give tickets to those who are entitled to work. No one must move, all must remain seated."

Perfect order reigned, and a triumphant smile enlivened the features of the Staff Officer. "Now all you have to do is for each of you to go round with a bundle of tickets and issue them to the most hungry-looking"; with which remark he stepped forward with one ticket in his hand to demonstrate the process. In one moment the whole six thousand were on top of him, and he returned sadder but wiser, admitting another failure, after having been severely trampled on.

Our next scheme was to issue tickets the evening

before through the Consul and any of the prominent citizens of the town who would undertake to be responsible for the various quarters in which they resided. From this time on things worked more or less satisfactorily. But in manipulating any charitable scheme the whole world seems to be against you; genuine helpers there were none, and the recipients of the charity were as bad as any in their dishonesty. The great difficulty was to ensure that only the poorest got the tickets; but the poorest are the weakest, and the weakest go to the wall, and it was hard to prevent fairly robust men coming to the works while the really starving were pushed out in the scramble for tickets.

Then there was a traffic in tickets which we were powerless to stop. Assuming that one of the men deputed to issue tickets acted conscientiously in his distribution, he could never be sure that the same applicant had not been up three times and received three tickets. Or, if he were not conscientious, there was nothing to prevent him from giving five tickets straightaway to any favoured individual.

These tickets gave the right to work for one day and receive a payment of three krans; the normal value of a kran is a little less than fivepence. The lucky holder of five tickets could go round the town, sell the five tickets for one kran each, enabling the purchasers to earn two krans by putting in a day's work on the roads, while he pocketed five krans without having to do any work at all. Nothing could put a stop to this kind of fraud except the co-operation of the well-to-do Persians, but so far there was no sign of any desire on their part to help us. I had already begged the Governor, the other officials and all the big men of the town to show some interest in the scheme, but they showed none. The only sign of interest displayed by notables came from the politicians, and took the form of the most active opposition.

They realized that I was fulfilling the promise of my proclamation, in which I had stated that the British always interested themselves in the welfare of the people; they saw that we were gaining in popularity, and they infinitely preferred the death of their neighbours to such an undesirable contingency. It was the same unuttered thought of all revolutionaries: "Life must be sacrificed in this good cause; so let any life but mine be freely offered up."

The next step of our opponents was that when I had provided the starving people with money to buy bread, they closed the bakers' shops by intimidation and insisted on the people dying "in a good cause." This difficulty we also overcame.

Then there was further trouble on the ground. With so few officers to supervise, how could we be sure that the ticket-holders did any work at all? It was hard to prevent a man from getting his ticket, sneaking off into the town and either selling it or turning up himself at pay-time after having done no work. And work was only exacted in proportion to strength. Some were only capable of pretending to work as we came along to inspect, feebly patting the ground with a small implement, and ceasing this effort as soon as we had passed. Of these a certain number lay dead on the ground by the time the day's pay came to be issued. It seems horrible that men should have to work under such conditions, but Government funds are not available for issue in the form of simple charity, though we got as close to that as we conscientiously could.

As time went on the deaths entirely ceased and within only a few days each man was capable of doing some appreciable work without over-exerting himself, and no Persian is prone to over-exertion.

Our system of having gangers to each fifty was the only workable one; but the gangers were not to be

FAMINE

trusted, and they probably got their mite out of each member of the gang. The most we could do to thwart this was to make all payments ourselves direct to the workers, a British officer actually putting each man's money into his hands; but this would not prevent the ganger from applying afterwards what the Chinese appropriately call "Squeeze." This task of direct payment by an officer was very toilsome, but we never swerved from it.

We employed no women, and it was now suggested that while we were giving each man the bare amount to support his own life, there was nothing over for his family, who starved as before. This difficulty was overcome in a very simple way, by increasing the value of each ticket to an extent that would enable the worker to buy enough bread for his wife and children as well as himself.

Like all these simple solutions, this was doomed to instant failure and had to be at once withdrawn. What we intended to happen did not happen, and instead the result was wholly unfortunate. The agricultural labourers who were just making both ends meet in the surrounding villages, hearing of the good wages I was paying, flooded the town, elbowed the starving townsmen out of the way and secured a large proportion of the tickets. My intended boon to the poor had a quite contrary result and had to be withdrawn. Any one of experience would have foreseen all this, but we had no experience and had to learn as we went along.

By the time the second party—the first addition to our force—arrived, we had got things going fairly well, but were still hampered by paucity of officers for supervision. I entrusted the future working of the scheme entirely to General Byron, who was very soon able to introduce many much-needed improvements. Arrangements were made for a portion of the wage to be paid in cash, and the remainder issued in the shape of food from soup kitchens established in the town. The reduction in cash payments, while supplying food in kind to the workers, helped very much to eliminate the stronger members who had hitherto been our chief difficulty. They wanted the cash only, and the necessity of drawing part payment in the shape of food from the soup kitchens successfully choked them off.

The work on which the officers and N.C.O.'s were engaged was undoubtedly a noble one, but it was the exact reverse of any task which these essentially fighting men had expected. Chosen especially for their martial qualities, and panting to achieve " The bubble reputation at the cannon's mouth," it was indeed a dispiriting step on the path to glory to find themselves dumped down in a Persian village, issuing soup to the poor. All I could do was to cheer them by putting before them the prospect of more lively events later.

Cases of cannibalism were not uncommon, and the punishment of such offenders as were detected was worse than the crime. It is easy for a mullah with a full stomach to condemn to death miserable beings who are insane from the pangs of hunger. Two culprits, a mother and daughter, who had cooked and eaten one of the family (a boy six years of age) were stoned to death in front of the telegraph office by order of the religious authorities. In this case the offenders were women, who are of small account; and they had eaten a male child. There may have been cases equally bad where the culprits were male and the victims female, but I know of none such being brought to light. It was always the women who were brought up.

We are taught from early youth that only properly organized charity is of any avail, and that fortuitous charity does more harm than good. It is impossible always to act up to principles, and the extreme pleasure of being able to relieve the immediate sufferings of some wretched individual is apt to lead into indiscretion. Such a case occurred to me and gave me a lesson which I shall remember for the rest of my life.

I was walking through the bazaars with my friend Haji Saad-es-Sultaneh when we came opposite a bread-shop, where the long strips of "Sangak," or Persian chupatty, were hanging temptingly on pegs, looking more like dirty cloths than bread. In front of the shop was an emaciated child of about nine, looking longingly at the bread with its eyes half out of its head. I looked round and saw there was no sign of any other beggars in the street, fearing that, if there were, any gift to the child might cause a scramble. The temptation was too strong to resist and I hastily paid for a large chupatty (they are about five times the size of the biggest Indian specimens), and presented it to the wretched infant. In one instant the whole bazaar was in a state of pandemonium, hosts of starving people, hitherto invisible, appeared to drop from the sky, and before I could realize what was happening the unfortunate holder of the prize was literally buried beneath a mass of fighting and screaming humanity, each with murder in his heart trying to obtain possession of a morsel of the food. "Beastly!" you may say. But why malign the beasts?

The restoration of order was a difficult task. Without aid the owner of the bread would undoubtedly have been killed; as it was the bread was torn to scraps, rubbed into the mud of the road and the fragments swallowed whole by the lucky holders, in the intervals of fighting, scratching, biting and strangling each other. There was not one that was not covered with blood.

The work was continued till the harvest was at hand, when the holders of grain stocks began to release them, proving thereby the correctness of my previous statement that there was plenty of wheat in the country which I could have drawn on if I had been able to apply military force to bring it on to the market.

In the early days of famine relief it could not be expected that the workers would show much return for the expenditure; in fact, for one month we did little more than keep them alive. After that, rapid progress was made and much useful road-work undertaken. The first task was the construction of a road entirely encircling the huge straggling town. The advantages of such a road were very great both from the point of view of tactics and also of general convenience of convoys, of which there would be many when the hoped-for troops began to move up. Without such a road a driver who approaches a Persian town from one side with a view of reaching some place on the other, is very severely handicapped; to find his way, for instance, without being able to speak the language, through the tortuous streets of Hamadan, would be well-nigh impossible. Added to this is the fact that in many streets only the smallest cars could get through, and big lorries would get stuck. By means of the circular road, lorries could pass rapidly and without hindrance from any one point to another, and in case of trouble in the town the armoured cars could get round to any point in a very short time, avoiding the risk and difficulty of forcing their way through the narrow streets. The next road undertaken led from the upper ground where we were billeted to the aeroplane ground on the low plain east of the town. The remainder of the work consisted in a general improvement of existing roads.

Up till March 28th all the various tasks described up to this point were undertaken by the small original party, and our days were more than busy. On the 28th and 29th the thirty rifles of the Hants and the aeroplane had arrived, and from this date our position might be regarded as secure. The time when the hostile demo-

A Courtyard in the Bazaar, Hamadan

crats might have hoped to have attacked us with some prospect of success was gone for ever, and the feelings not only of the townspeople but also of the surrounding districts had changed from an attitude of suspicion and hostility to one of honest liking for the new-comers. Our agents returning from far-off villages in Kurdistan and elsewhere brought back tidings of our reflected glory in the form of bazaar reports in those neighbourhoods, that we had done wonderful things with the famine in Hamadan, and intended shortly to extend our charitable operations over the whole province, a hope which it was quite impossible for us to convert into a fact. We had been able to do much for Hamadan where we felt it incumbent on us to do what we could, but the whole of North Persia was famine-stricken, and the horrors of other towns and villages equalled or exceeded those of Hamadan. The fame of our relief works spread down even as far as Gilan, and Kuchik Khan, in his pose as an enlightened ruler, felt called on to undertake relief work on somewhat similar lines but on a smaller scale.

At the beginning of April, as it was now certain that either myself or my second-in-command would be in Hamadan for a long time, I shifted my quarters from the hospitable dwelling of the McMurrays and set up my own establishment in a small house lent me by the Bank.

About this time the constant firing at night which was carried out with a view of terrifying us ceased almost entirely. It had never been very dangerous, the shots being always unaimed, except one or two which struck my bungalow but did not even break a pane of glass.

On April 24th arrived a squadron of the 14th Hussars, under Captain Pope.

Supplies were now easier to obtain and Captain Campbell, the Supply Officer, was able to report that our stocks had reached a figure that made the prospect of any further crisis very remote. Even if supplies were not always easily obtainable we knew where the wheat hoards were, and only required troops to insist on their surrender at a fair price. Thus, except for the bacon and jam part of the ration, we could guarantee to feed a large number of troops without difficulty.

As soon as the snow began to melt on the lower hills I sent a small party under Captain Hooper to examine and report on the road over the Asadabad Pass. The party consisted of three officers and two drivers, and while carrying out their task of reconnaissance they became engaged in a very minor military operation. Half-way up the pass it was found that the cars could proceed no farther, and a halt was ordered, to enable the party to examine the road on foot. At this point a descending caravan of pack donkeys was encountered, and the owners complained that they had just been looted by thieves who had taken refuge in a village near by. As it would be necessary to get labour for road improvements from these villages close to the road, Captain Hooper decided to inquire about the prospects of obtaining coolie gangs here, and with this view moved with his little party, leaving one man in charge of the cars, towards the village, expecting at the same time to run into the robber band.

If the robbers had kept quiet nothing would have happened, but on seeing the approach of the very small party their guilty consciences led them to decide on flight. They emerged from a house on the outskirts of the village and fled towards the hills, pursued by all the villagers and the plundered merchants, who overtook them, gave them a sound hammering and recovered the stolen property.

The amusing thing about all this is, that what the villagers and merchants accomplished with merely the moral support of one or two men with rifles, they could have equally accomplished without, another example of the effect of lack of leadership.

It was not Captain Hooper's duty to interfere in a case of this sort, the policing of Persia forming no part of our responsibilities, but the movement in the direction of the robber band coincided with the legitimate movement towards the village for other purposes. The guilty consciences of the bandits settled the rest of the matter.

On April 21st the real advent of spring was heralded by the appearance of the first blossoms on the fruit-trees, and we were glad to feel that we had said good-bye to the snow. Two days later an Armenian doctor arrived from Baku, bringing suggestions from the Armenian National Council there with regard to possibilities of our helping to put things straight in that part of the world.

The Bolshevik Government was still in power under the leadership of an Armenian named Shaumian, but there was a growing feeling on the part of the people against them, and their influence was distinctly on the wane. Very serious disturbances had broken out in March in connection with the disarming on arrival at Baku of troops from Persia, street-fighting had ensued and a large number of very valuable buildings in the Tartar quarter had been destroyed by Armenian troops. The result of this was naturally to accentuate the animosity already existing between the Tartars and the Armenians, and to make the plight of the latter very unenviable in the event of the Turks eventually taking Baku. The British Consul, Mr. MacDonnell, was still in the town, and he was able to furnish very useful statements concerning the situation.

The schemes propounded by the doctor were all based upon British military support in the shape of actual troops, and he stated that he was not authorized to accept our aid merely in the form of leaders and organizers. I had to make it very clear to him that I had no troops and could make no promises as to the dispatch of troops from Baghdad. So we could agree upon no plan suitable to both parties, and nothing came of our conversation.

On this day a Turkish naval officer surrendered to us. He was tired of wandering about Persia and wanted decent food and a rest-cure. It is not likely that he had been actively engaged in any of the enemy schemes in this part of the world, but it was just as well to have him out of the way.

On May 1st we had news of the entry of the Turks into Tabriz, a move that we had long been expecting and that might threaten our position at Kasvin, if they had the energy to push down the Mianeh-Zinjan road towards that town; and there was nothing to stop their doing this. The move was obvious, but indecision on the part of the Turkish Commander fortunately delayed it until September.

Having firmly established ourselves in Hamadan we might now hope to secure a similar position in Kasvin, and I accordingly dispatched a small party of officers and N.C.O.'s under Major Hay, to get a footing there, spy out the land, start famine relief and reconnoitre for billets and supplies. I purposely made the thin end of the wedge as thin as possible, but to make some small display of force in this direction I also dispatched the squadron of the 14th Hussars, who went into camp at Sultanabad, about 5 miles on our side of Kasvin.

The third party had now arrived, and provided sufficient personnel to enable us to undertake further enterprises. With a view to thwarting Turkish efforts to win over the Kurds and other tribes lying between them and us, and to raising levies and irregulars among these tribes for our own purposes, I dispatched Major Starnes with a party to Bijar, 100 miles north-west of

FAMINE

Hamadan, and Major Wagstaff with a similar party and and an armoured car to Zinjan, a little more than 100 miles west of Kasvin on the road to Tabriz. These two parties, consisting only of officers and N.C.O.'s without troops were dangerously weak, but it was all we could do at the time, and with the Turks already in Tabriz and also threatening an advance towards Hamadan from the direction of Sauj-Bulaq, south of Lake Urumiah, I hoped that this very weak screen would for a time at least baffle their enterprises in our direction, while the possession of Zinjan would stop the artery by which Turkish agents were communicating with Kuchik Khan and supplying him with arms and ammunition.

Having set on foot arrangements for the raising of local levies I decided to visit Kasvin and see how our small party were faring there, and what could be hoped for in the way of recruits for levies in that neighbourhood. I was also anxious to get to Teheran for a few days to try and get a grip of the internal situation, and obtain the Minister's advice on the subject of the levies and other kindred matters.

I accordingly left Hamadan on May 12th, accompanied by Captain Saunders and Captain Topham, who had now taken over the duties of A.D.C.

CHAPTER VIII

A PAUSE AT HAMADAN

BEFORE leaving Hamadan for Kasvin I wrote a letter, in which I endeavoured to make as clear as I could how things stood at the time of writing. The following extracts from the letter in question will probably be of general interest, and help the reader to form a correct mental picture of the general outlook.

"HAMADAN,
"*May* 5, 1918.

". . . There are so many situations here, that it is difficult to give a full appreciation of each. There is the local situation, the all-Persia situation, the Jangali situation, the Persian-Russian situation, the Turkish-advance-on-Tabriz situation, the question of liquidating Russian debts, the Baku situation, the South Caucasus situation, the North Caucasus situation, the Bolshevik situation and the Russian situation as a whole. And each of these subdivides into smaller and acuter situations —for there is no real Caucasian or even North or South Caucasian point of view, there is no unity of thought or action, nothing but mutual jealousy and mistrust. Thus the Georgians of Tiflis regard the problem from a Georgian point of view and play only for their own hand; the Armenians and the Tartars in the south, and the Terek and Kuban Cossacks and the Daghestanis in the

A PAUSE AT HAMADAN

north, do the same. And not even these small races can agree among themselves as to any line of policy, because they have two distinct lines of thought, that of the greybeards who cling to the traditions of their forefathers, and that of the young bloods who think everything contemptible that is not brand new. This applies with especial force to the Cossacks, who have hitherto been entirely ruled by a council of elders.

"Bolshevism is far from being firmly rooted in the Caucasus, but its malevolent tendencies have permeated the blood of all the races in this part of the world: the present ultra-democratic movement in Persia is really the same spirit as Bolshevism. The name is new, but the spirit is the old spirit of revolution, the spirit of men gone mad. 'What is yours is mine and what is mine is my own; all men are equal and brothers; discipline and control are contrary to the spirit of freedom, and all men are free.' And out of this always emerges the insane doctrine: 'The more blood we can shed the freer we shall be; and it doesn't matter whose blood it is as long as it isn't ours.' The mobs are bloodthirsty and cowardly and are at the mercy of any disciplined force, however small.

"Here, to begin with, the situation is enormously improved. As regards troops, I have at present one squadron of cavalry and two armoured cars at Kasvin and fifty rifles and two light armoured motor-cars here. The detachment of fifty rifles 1/4 Hants Regt. have no nights in bed, being all used up to furnish ordinary guards and to guard the numerous prisoners I collect. I have at present one Russian officer suspect, one German civilian spy, one Turkish naval officer, two Turkish soldiers and four Indian deserters. I have to use N.C.O.'s as privates and officers as N.C.O.'s.

"Being practically without troops my weapons have been propaganda, winning over leaders by personal methods, and also famine relief work. All of these have been successful and have resulted in turning the inhabitants of this district from an attitude of hostility to one of marked friendliness. Unfortunately the forces of good are always more or less passive and the forces of evil are extremely active, so that while in this town of 50,000 inhabitants I have 49,950 well-wishers, there is a nucleus of fifty sincere haters who have the power to cause a great deal of trouble. By an excellent system of intelligence worked by Saunders I know the details of all their plots, and we are so far able to counter them.

"Occasional shots are fired at officers, and they have sometimes sniped my house at night with the object of terrifying me. I have no troops to spare for a guard. I have been informed that I shall be shot in the town some day, but there has been no attempt to put this threat into execution. I have made friends with the leading democrats, but get little results from that, as, so far from my friendship with them leading to friendly relations with the democrats in general, it merely has the effect of putting the other democrats against them.

"One of my friends, a high Government official, called on me the other day and showed me a threatening letter he had received—written in red ink to suggest blood, and with a picture of a Mauser pistol at the top of it. The letter said that it was obvious that he had sold himself for money to the English and if he continued to visit me he would be shot.

"On the other hand the fame of the famine relief work has spread far beyond the limits of the district and is much spoken of in the bazaars of Sinneh and Bijar, which all helps the cause, and I have been able to improve existing roads and to construct some 9 or 10 miles of useful communications. So on the whole

A PAUSE AT HAMADAN

the situation is as good as it can be under the circumstances.

"The Persian situation fluctuates, but is never much in our favour. The people are attractive; they are good workmen but lazy, and they have only one real political idea, fair terms for farmers and a guarantee of order. They have no other political ideas, but in their hatred of the present tyrannical system of landlordism they unconsciously become true democrats as opposed to the political democrat who does not know what the word means. Politically 'Democracy' is only a banner to wave, and the programme, so far from being democratic, is merely a stupid combination of an anti-European movement with an attempt to bring about disorder in which every poor man would hope to possess himself of the rich man's hoard.

"The Jangali situation is quiescent and is perhaps reaching a point of stagnation owing to the fortunate interposition of Bicherakov's partisans . . . at Kasvin and Menjil. It was an extraordinary piece of luck that his troops were late in evacuating, and I was able to get him to deal with the Jangali problem just in the nick of time. He reached Kasvin on March 28th about the date on which Kuchik was to have taken over the town unopposed. Had Kuchik succeeded in that, Teheran would have raised the Jangali banner on the following day and North Persia would have gone. In the East a small success spreads like a flame, and Jangali sympathizers in Teheran include a portion of the Cabinet. Success would bring all the waverers in and Persia would have started another revolution. It has to be remembered with gratitude that although so far he has had no actual fighting, Bicherakov alone solved this very precarious situation.

"I would like to meet Kuchik Khan personally and talk things over, but his German advisers would go to any length to prevent this. Meantime I hope to bring about a meeting between Stokes and a representative of Kuchik's, and we may perhaps come to a settlement. If one has no troops one has to try the tongue. Kuchik Khan himself is a man of humble origin, poses as a religious enthusiast and is not of much intelligence. He is, I rather think, a true patriot, which is rare in this land, but like many true patriots, goes the wrong way to achieve his objects and does not realize that he is being made a tool of. He has a nucleus of about twenty foreign officers, German, Turk and Russian, who he thinks are his servants but who really are the mainspring of his movement and are trying to push him over the precipice in order to achieve their own ends. Meanwhile he is at least clever enough to pause on the brink, and if I could only whisper a word in his ear I think he would be saved the fatal leap.

"Bicherakov makes rather large financial demands, and the War Office asks if he is worth it. He certainly is. I do not consider his demands exorbitant, when you realize the task he is accomplishing and the fact that he alone can do it. We have no alternative.

"At present rates it costs but very little under one pound a day to feed a horse, bread and meat are one shilling and tenpence a pound, sugar three shillings and sixpence and tea four shillings and sixpence, so that a million krans, which looks a big figure, does not go very far. Whatever we pay him does not get into his pocket, but is honestly spent for military purposes, though with his system of accounts there may be a leakage among the subordinate grades.

"Mixed up with his situation is the question of the liquidation of Russian debts. So far our Government has refused this peremptorily, but I have advocated it and still do so. . . .

". . . The Baku situation is obscure. It is separate

A PAUSE AT HAMADAN

from the Caucasus question generally. At present the Armenian colony there and the Bolsheviks are holding out against the Caucasus-Islam Army—The Georgians of Tiflis, who heartily dislike the Armenians, offer no help. How can we help them in any way that would hold out a chance of success ? It appears to me quite impossible. Troops alone could restore order—and we have no troops. A few officers, a few armoured cars and liberal finance would not turn the tide ; in fact such an effort would probably add fuel to the flames.

"The South Caucasus situation has long been hopeless. They must go on killing each other until they are tired of it : we may then get a chance of pulling things together again. But for the moment the racial and religious animosities are so fierce, the spirit of Bolshevism is so rampant and the usual mistrust of the supposedly self-seeking Britisher is so strong, that an opportunity for us to help seems far away. When they appeal to us for help they mean money, money, money. We are to them the goose that lays the golden egg. We should be temporarily popular with those who secured the egg, but we should get no real gratitude even from them, and we should earn the more intense hatred of the others. The North Caucasus is the same, but not to so acute a degree. There is less racial and religious hatred, but there is a hearty dislike of the South Caucasus and the poison of Bolshevism is also in their blood. The Bolshevik himself is not of much account ; but it must be remembered that those who fight against the Bolsheviks are themselves unconsciously impregnated with this vile spirit of Bolshevism —the poison innoculated unnoticed into their veins by the German propagandist. The Tiflis Government is anti-Bolshevik, but the members are probably as much inspired by Bolshevik ideals as the Bolsheviks themselves.

"The famine here has been awful. The highest

price I know of quoted for wheat has been 230 tomans, or about £70, for one kharwar=800 lb., the normal price being 12 tomans or, say, 70 shillings. We are buying forward crops at 40 tomans and hope to get some for less. Cases of cannibalism have occurred in the town. Many die daily, and men have sometimes died while actually on relief work. Now that the snow has melted and spring has begun the people go out and graze in the fields like cattle.

"Meantime, though wheat and barley are short, they do exist. I could collect by force enough to feed the troops and stop the famine, but I have no force to employ. I know where the wheat is, but have difficulty in getting it. Firstly, the owner holds on in the hope of higher prices; secondly, the villagers resent it being taken from a village while they starve; thirdly, brigands attack grain convoys on the road; fourthly, the extreme democrats threaten to kill any one who supplies the British; and fifthly, the Governor shows me an order he has received from the Government at Teheran to the effect that he is to see that I get no supplies. . . . In spite of this, supplies come in very well, and I could supply a Brigade in actual bread and meat between here and Menjil. There is a shortage also at Resht, but rice is obtainable there, and is much cheaper than wheat. The country is naturally rich in grain, fruit and sheep, and there will be no supply difficulty as soon as the new crop is in. At this elevation (6,500 to 7,000 feet) crops are late, but as soon as the lower harvests are reaped the prices will fall here and grain now hoarded will be released.

"Lastly there is the matter of levies. Colonel Kennion (Political) guarantees the road from Qasr-i-Shirin to Asadabad, so I have given up the idea of raising levies from the local Kurds in that section. I am raising one group at Hamadan, and later intend one at Kasvin, each group to consist of one squadron of cavalry and two companies of infantry, total strength 600, with 6 British officers to each group. These levies will not take the place of regular troops, nor will they form road-guards. They will be used to deal with gangs of robbers, to round up German or Turk emissaries, of whom there are many actively employed in propaganda, and to garrison posts at dangerous places on the roads.

"The Persian is not dangerous as a fighting man, but he will be more dangerous in this revolution than in the previous one, because the country is full of arms and ammunition sold by the Russian soldiers or taken from them, and also provided through German agencies.

"The Turkish advance on Tabriz is not being very vigorously pressed, and we may be able with the aid of the Jilus and other tribes south of Lake Urumiah to thwart them entirely. I am sending in a day or two a party of twelve officers and eight N.C.O.'s towards Tabriz to organize this resistance. The recent very successful operations from Mesopotamia against the Sinjabis and the defeat of the Turks at Kifri and towards Kirkuk has enormously improved the situation in Kurdistan and in Persia generally, and will possibly also affect the Turkish advance south of Lake Urumiah.

"The only opposition to the entry of our troops into Persia is political. The people are glad to see soldiers of a new type who . . . bring with them law and order. But even the political difficulty may eventually be overcome. I am not aware of our Government's attitude towards the democratic movement in Persia, but I assume that we make the Persians feel that, being a democratic country ourselves, we cannot oppose a democratic movement in another country, and we are not out to support against them the other party of the big landowners. Nor do we desire the hostility of the latter, who have a more direct influence over the large numbers of people on their land than the democrats are ever likely to have.

It is obviously difficult to support the moderate democrat without alienating the landowner, or at any rate without driving him into too hostile an attitude. It is perilously near to trying to run with the hare and hunt with the hounds.

"I have collected about twenty Russian officers, very specially selected and all capable men, mostly aviators from the school at Baku, with a view to seizing any opportunity that may occur of our intervening in the Caucasus. Meantime they are useful in various ways and enable us to keep in touch with Baku and to get reliable information.

"We have made several efforts to reach Pike at Tiflis, but have not succeeded in getting direct news of him for a long time. He and the remainder of ours, including Goldsmith as well as the French party under Colonel Chardigny, are probably either refugees or prisoners. . . .

"The winter has been long and the cold very severe, but the snow has now melted, except on the hilltops, and spring has begun. Officers and men have kept well, and in spite of a very arduous time there have been only a few trifling cases of sickness among the first party. . . ."

Much of this letter is a recapitulation of events already described, but it will be useful as a means of taking stock of events up to date.

My Staff was now strengthened by the addition of Lieut.-Colonel Stokes, who joined me as General Staff Officer, First Grade, for Intelligence duties. I considered it important to work up our information from the Teheran side and accordingly posted him to the capital, where he could work with the Military Attaché at the Legation, constituting a liaison between my force and the diplomatic representative.

Work in connection with the raising and training of the Persian levies and irregulars had begun by the end

A PAUSE AT HAMADAN

of April, and I will explain in as few words as possible why it was thought advisable to raise them and how they were raised.

The difference between the levies and irregulars may be explained briefly as follows. The levies were to be regularly formed units enlisted from the surrounding districts, and employed at a fixed salary, under British officers, in guarding dangerous points and defiles on the road, reconnoitring the country for enemy spies and agents, and furnishing escorts for any parties of mine moving at any great distance from Head Quarters. I knew that it would be useless to employ them against the Turks, and from the outset I had no intention of putting their valour to this test. They would be good enough to encounter robber bands, but were not likely to face the fire of any sort of regular troops.

The irregulars, on the other hand, were meant to fight. They were to be raised from among the Kurds and other tribes lying along any probable line of Turkish advance. They were not to be formed into regular bodies, nor submitted to the regular training of a soldier as the levies were.

Levies would be regularly formed and trained, would be liable to service anywhere, but could not be relied on to fight against the Turks. Irregulars were merely bands of tribesmen under British leadership, not liable to service anywhere but on their own ground, and organized only with a view of fighting the Turks and harassing their communications.

Before we could do anything on the lines of " irregulars " it would be necessary to get thoroughly in touch with the tribes, and this was accomplished by the dispatch of Major Starnes' party to Bijar, and Major Wagstaff's to Zinjan. But with the levies we could and did make an immediate start.

In neither case did we contemplate arming these forces.

There was no necessity to issue arms in a country where nearly every man possessed a good rifle and a quantity of ammunition.

The disadvantages of not arming them were, firstly the heterogeneous nature of the arms employed, secondly the difficulties of ammunition supply during a fight, and thirdly the reluctance of each man as owner of his rifle and ammunition to risk losing the former and expending the latter. But the great advantage which outweighed all these considerations was that we were saved the trouble and difficulty of supplying the arms, and we removed the chief incentive to desertion. With no sort of civil control over the tribes, to issue rifles to men would have been to put a premium on desertions, and the men would have left for their homes, never to reappear, the day they received their rifles from us.

As regards the other disadvantages mentioned above, rules were framed without great difficulty removing the reluctance to risk loss of arms or expenditure of ammunition by a system of rewards and compensation. Uniform was made up and issued on the spot, and in a few days Major Engledue and Captain Henderson, in charge of the first Hamadan group, were able to turn out some very stalwart-looking soldiers, who proved very useful in this land where "looks" go for so much.

As regards the isolated picquets placed at points of danger on the road later on, these would probably have put up only a very feeble resistance to any sort of attack by well-armed robber bands, but here again we relied on "looks," and they won the day. The intending marauders became aware of these uniformed detachments at certain points; they didn't like the "look" of their rifles or their British leaders, so they adopted the line of least resistance and left the road alone.

The levies were to be raised in three groups, two at Hamadan and one at Kasvin. Each group consisted of two companies of dismounted men each two hundred strong and one of mounted men of the same strength, making a total of 600 men. The companies were commanded by Persian officers, and the British personnel acted only as instructors in cantonments and leaders in the field. The first group at Hamadan was raised by Major Engledue from the local people without reference to any particular tribal connections. The second group was raised by Major Macarthy and consisted of a solid block of men taken entirely from the tenantry of a big landowner, and regarded as his special corps, to the upkeep and maintenance of which he was willing to subscribe. These two groups very soon furnished us with sufficient men for our immediate purposes, and were most useful to us. The Kasvin group was naturally more difficult to start as we had not yet made ourselves properly known in that part of the country, and men were shy about coming in to enlist under total strangers. But they came along in twos and threes and we soon had enough men there to help us in carrying out minor police duties.

Although not much of an addition to our fighting strength, these levies were very useful, and more than justified their existence. Among other advantages was the fact that our dealings with them brought us very intimately into touch with a large circle of the people, and this was a very valuable political gain.

Mistakes were bound to occur in our early efforts, and among these were the fact that we accidentally enlisted a complete gang of robbers, who came to us not for our benefit or for that of their fellow-countrymen, but for their own. Their idea was to obtain pay, uniform and authority from us, and then use the latter to extort money from the Persians; in fact the only contemplated change in their careers was that, from being unlicensed robbers, they were now to become licensed. Their method of procedure would be merely an enlightened re-reading of orders. The orders you give are: "All people on this road are to be stopped"—they read this, "People can only go down this road if they pay for the privilege"; you order, "All armed men are to be disarmed"—they issue the improved version, "Nobody is allowed to carry arms without paying a handsome fee to us." In addition to this, another favourite method is to undertake the duties of escort to some well-to-do person, and then at a convenient opportunity to change their rôle from guardian to highwayman, and relieve their charge of his superfluous wealth.

I do not say that any of our men were guilty of these things; the Persians made such accusations against them, but they would have accused them just as vehemently whether they had done the deeds or not. In any case, if they had such intentions, their career was cut very short, as on their proclivities being discovered they were soon weeded out as undesirables.

The usual opposition to all our enterprises was set on foot by the local Democratic Committee. The town was informed by printed manifestoes that to serve the English was to incur everlasting disgrace, and that the assassin's knife would punish any who yielded to such base temptation. But recruiting went on very well in spite of all this, and the murderous threats were never put into execution.

The irregulars did not develop till later on, but I may mention them briefly here. The Turks had two divisions round Lake Urumiah and were holding the country as far south of the lake as Sakiz, 100 miles in our direction. Major Starnes was dispatched with a small party to Bijar, 100 miles north-west of Hamadan, to guard our flank against any sudden move of the Turks from Sakiz. The 150 miles of country between Bijar and Sakiz was peopled by tribes with a genuine reputation for valour and warlike instincts.

A PAUSE AT HAMADAN

These tribes both the Turks and ourselves endeavoured to use against each other by offering rewards for services rendered as levies or irregulars. The equal endeavour resulted more or less in stalemate, which was not an altogether unsatisfactory position from our point of view. Had we made no effort in this direction the Turks would soon have been in Bijar (as they already were in Sinneh, 100 miles south-west of that place), and our position on the Hamadan road would have been very seriously threatened. As it was, we were never worried here at all, owing to the good work effected by Major Starnes' party among the Bijar people.

Exactly similar work was done by Major Wagstaff's party on the Kasvin-Tabriz road, among the Shah-savens. His party was pushed out in the same way towards the Turks, and acted as a very efficient shield for our movements on the Hamadan-Kasvin road, until at last the Turks advanced in force in September and drove us back as far as Zinjan.

Among the most influential men in this neighbourhood was the Amir Afshar, a very remarkable old gentleman, whom I met by appointment in Hamadan when he was staying there as the guest of the Amir Afgham. He is over eighty years of age and a confirmed drug-taker, but for a few hours in the morning his mind is as clear as crystal; my visit to him was therefore paid at the unearthly hour of 5.30 a.m. His estates are in the neighbourhood of Zinjan, and he could easily put up over 1,000 men from among his tenants; but he wanted rather a large price for his services. Firstly he complained that the Russians had punished his tribe, on a groundless accusation of pro-Turk proclivities, by taking away from them a thousand rifles. I must get these back from General Baratov. Secondly, whether I got these rifles back for him or not, he wanted a thousand rifles from me to enable him to take on the serious programme I wished him to adopt. Thirdly (and very wisely), he would do nothing actively against the troops unless he saw our troops at hand to save him from Turkish vengeance, which would be bound to fall on him if unsupported by us and defeated by the Turks. This was a form of support it was difficult for me to guarantee.

In the end I was led to expect very little active support from him in the face of my failure to agree to his third clause. I sent him 250 rifles (captured Turkish rifles sent up to me for this purpose from Baghdad) to see if that would induce the right frame of mind. He acknowledged them with a very flowery letter of thanks and asked for more. To this I replied that he should have as many more as soon as he balanced the account by letting us have 250 armed men of his tribe for active operations. I explained further that when he had received 500 rifles from me I should expect to see 500 of his men in the field. But the 250 rifles failed to bring about the result I aimed at, and he got no more from us. The truth of the matter is that these tribes were willing enough to back the winning horse, but could not make up their minds as to which was likely to be the winner.

The news from France at this time was of the very worst description from our point of view; the victorious German thrust towards Amiens which had begun in March was well advertised by German wireless as far as Hamadan, where it was picked up by the Russian wireless and disseminated among the people. The fact that the German advance was now checked and that there were signs of a turn of the tide was naturally omitted in bulletins from German sources, and news from our sources was regarded with considerable suspicion. On the whole it looked to the Persians as if Ger-

A PAUSE AT HAMADAN

many was going to win the war, and if she did it meant a triumphant Turkey who would ruthlessly exterminate any tribes who had opposed her in the days of her trouble. Moreover, if we won and the Turks lost, we would eventually go away and the Turks would remain very close at hand, so that even in that case they could make it very uncomfortable for any who had shown hostility to them.

It was partly in connection with the subject of our attitude towards these tribes as embodied in our general policy in Persia that I decided to visit His Britannic Majesty's Minister at Teheran at this time.

We left Hamadan on May 12th, arriving at Kasvin on the next day and staying the night there. At Kasvin we were glad to find that Major Hay had been able to get excellent quarters for his party in a large house belonging to one of the best-known representatives of the Persian aristocracy, the Sipah-Salar. This house stood in its own extensive grounds on the western outskirts of the town, and was so situated that the occupants were able to have first turn at the water supply which enters the town from this side. The building had up to this time been used by the Russians as a hospital, and was admirably adapted to our purposes.

Famine relief on a small scale had been started in the town, the people were becoming accustomed to the sight of English faces and English uniforms, and the scowls which had formerly greeted us were already exchanged for smiles or looks of indifference.

On May 14th we left for Teheran, distant about ninety miles from Kasvin, and arrived in the British Legation in the afternoon. The road from Kasvin to Teheran runs due east along the foot of the southern slopes of the Elburz Mountains. The surface is good, but the Russian road company had attempted very little in the way of engineering, choosing a straight line up and down each rise and fall of the natural lie of the land, and avoiding any expense in the way of cutting or embankment.

The country is treeless and for the most part uncultivated, while the southern slopes of the Elburz Mountains that flank the road on the left-hand side are as barren as the usual hills in Persia, and give no indication of the wonderful forest land that lies on their northern slopes.

At our entry into Teheran we were challenged and halted by a guard of Persian gendarmes, and were only permitted to proceed after solemnly entering in a book our names and our father's names, and giving an assurance that we were not conveying arms into the town.

Teheran has a very Europeanized appearance, and is quite unlike any of the other towns with which we had so far made acquaintance. The roads were broad and in many places lined with handsome trees, while frequent signboards in French and Russian notified the presence of numerous hotels and emporiums of every kind. But the general aspect of the town is not very pleasing, and its lack of beauty renders that of the Legation grounds more intense by contrast.

It is hard to describe the beauties of this wonderful oasis. To those who have visited Kashmir it recalls the memory of the old Moghul gardens on the Dal Lake, and gives an idea of what those gardens must have looked like in the days of their youth. But its beauty is enhanced by the abruptness of the transition from unbeautiful things, as the traveller turns from a dusty street, after ninety miles of treeless road, into a fairy-like grove of magnificent plane-trees. And when night falls and the nightingales start to sing, it is hard to realize that one is really living in these horrible days of war and bloodshed.

The Austrian and German prisoners moving freely

in the streets, and the sight of the German and Turkish flags flying over their respective Legations, added to the air of unreality.

We stayed three days at Teheran, during which time I had the honour of making the acquaintance of the American, French and Russian Ministers, and of many of the important Persians, including the Sipah-Salar and the two sons of the Firman-Firma, who are likely to play a prominent part in the future of Persia.

I spent the early mornings riding with Major Barttelot; the later hours of the mornings and the whole of the afternoons were devoted to interviews from which I derived much value.

On May 17th we left Teheran, stayed the night in Kasvin and reached Hamadan on the evening of the 18th, finding the journey a very different affair from what it had been in the winter.

Although the country is treeless, and the unirrigated tracts are very barren-looking, the whole ground is carpeted in this one month with very beautiful flowers. On the higher passes we enjoyed the sight of large red tulips and several kinds of iris, while lower down the hillsides were bright with the varied hues of many unknown flowers. These thrive for a very short time on the water provided by the melting snow, and as there is no rainfall in summer they are soon burnt up, and the landscape resumes its aspect of dreary monotony.

The most beautiful flowers were those on the top of the Sultan-Bulaq Pass, exactly in the spot where we found seven corpses of unfortunate victims of the famine. Such corpses strewed the road between Kasvin and Hamadan at intervals throughout its length.

The general discomfort of a long drive in small cars over rather rough roads was very much increased by the necessity of taking back with us to Kasvin several prisoners who had recently been rounded up by our agents and by Bicherakov's Cossacks. It was becoming very difficult for enemy agents to get through the nets that were spread for them in every direction. With our small forces we could not scour the entire country, and with regard to movements off roads we could only rely on information from our agents, but we were able to render movement on the main roads quite impossible. The road company had established tollgates about every thirty miles along the road, and these we held with small parties of officers and levies, and were thus able to keep a minute check on all traffic.

The present batch of prisoners included one German civilian and one Hungarian officer with his wife and child. This officer had been taken prisoner by the Russians early in the war, had been released in Turkestan when the revolution broke out and, seeing no chance of getting home to Hungary, had married a Caucasian lady, and was now the father of a promising infant. Having heard of the prospect of well-paid service under Kuchik Khan, he was on his way with his family to join that leader when he was arrested. The lady and child presented such difficulties that one almost wished he had been successful in slipping through our fingers. I was fated to have them for companions throughout the interminable day, as I was the only possessor of a touring car, and it was hardly fair to submit a lady, even though a prisoner, to the discomfort of a Ford van.

I unfortunately gave away the fact that I spoke Russian, and I shall never regret anything so much in all my life. We were all very bright and cheerful in the early hours of the day, Madame explaining that she had never been in a motor-car before and was enjoying the trip very much. But after some hours the charm of novelty wore off, and its place was taken by quite another sensation. The lady explained that the unaccustomed motion was making her feel sick, and thereafter frequent halts had to be made to enable her to deal with this dilemma. I was extremely sorry for the poor woman, who was very plucky about it, and bobbed up quite "merry and bright" after each episode, announcing her firm intention of becoming accustomed to the motion, but her pluck was not rewarded with any improvement in this respect. I was as delighted as she was when we eventually reached Hamadan and I was able to hand her over to the kind ministrations of Mrs. Funk, a lady of the American mission.

My short visit to Teheran, and a useful interview I had had with Bicherakov at Kasvin, had decided me to give up Hamadan entirely as Head Quarters and to move forward to Kasvin. Many schemes were now coming to a head. Matters must soon be settled one way or another with the Jangalis, and it would be easier to deal with these affairs if I were on the spot at Kasvin than to do so by messengers and telegrams from Hamadan. Moreover, I had also, on my way through Kasvin, got in touch with certain Russian agents who were willing to be of service in connection with any enterprise in the Baku direction. These latter belonged to the Social-Revolutionary party, and it was due to their influence that the Bolshevik power in Baku was eventually overthrown.

We had also to think of our prisoners in the hands of the Jangalis—Captain Noel, Mr. Oakshot (of the Bank), and Mr. Maclaren (the Consul)—and see if any plan for their rescue or release could be devised. So far we had been able to do nothing for them, and it was difficult to see how we could effect their release except by Kuchik Khan.

Having decided therefore to shift Head Quarters to Kasvin, I sent General Byron up there with three Staff Officers, to enable him to make himself acquainted with the neighbourhood before taking over the command of Hamadan and the lines of communication which I would hand over to him on departure. General Byron was also able to go into the question of supplies, billets etc., and to select a suitable residence for Head Quarters.

On May 25th Colonel Keyworth arrived, bringing with him the fourth party composed of 50 officers and 150 N.C.O.'s, a splendid addition to our numbers, enabling us to put full pressure on to many schemes that had been languishing for want of personnel. This party, as well as the previous one, had walked all the way and seemed very fit after their long march. They brought with them the specially selected Russian officers who had been sent out from home. These officers were mostly from regiments of the Russian Guard, and many of them in the Guards cavalry. The experience of footing it through Persia was one they had never expected to enjoy, but they were a cheerful community and there was no disposition to grumble.

CHAPTER IX

A STEP IN ADVANCE

WE left Hamadan for Kasvin on June 1, 1918, almost exactly four months after our departure from Baghdad.

During those four months work of considerable value had been accomplished and we were entitled to regard our achievements in Persia with some satisfaction. But this feeling of satisfaction in no way removed the sting of our original failure, and all felt elated with the certainty that the advance of Head Quarters to Kasvin was but the prelude to an entry into the promised land of the Caucasus. When the moment for that entry would come none could tell. If troops had been available the moment would have been to-day, but in the absence of troops it was necessary to endure the delay of securing a footing in Baku and to endeavour to neutralize it by means of intrigue. Every day's delay in our movement brought the Turks nearer to the oil city, and the probabilities were that our second failure would be brought about by their capture of the town before we could get our enterprise further under way.

Meantime it can easily be understood that it was very difficult to run the Persian venture at full pressure and at the same time to manipulate affairs in such a way that when the word came to cross the Caspian, we should be able to take with us the necessary complement of selected officers and N.C.O.'s. This in the end proved impossible. To have worked on such lines would have contributed greatly towards our success in the Caucasus, but would have endangered the success of our many schemes in Persia. The proper fulfilment of these schemes demanded our best and had to have them. When, therefore, the time eventually came to risk the Baku venture the greater proportion of officers and men were already employed in Persia in tasks from which they could not be relieved without risking entire dislocation. A considerable staff was necessary for the administration of Persian towns, a large number of officers were required for the levies and irregulars; intelligence and supplies absorbed a great many, and the balance that would be available for service in Baku would be but small.

It is necessary to explain how an undertaking, originally based on the idea of getting to Tiflis and reorganizing local troops there against the Turks, had now been diverted into the fresh channel of the Baku adventure.

When the Tiflis plan proved to be quite out of our reach and it was certain that the enemy would soon be in full possession of the South Caucasus, the question arose as to what must now be undertaken to hinder him in the enjoyment of his conquest. It was obviously impossible to allow him a free hand.

The capture of Baku by the enemy would give him ample stocks of oil for the running of the Caucasian railway lines and the Black Sea shipping (the oil is pumped in pipes from Baku to Batoum), and it would mean the control by him of the Caspian Sea, with all the valuable supplies obtainable from the various ports on its shores, and an open door to Asia and Afghanistan. Any enemy scheme of penetration into Asia through Turkestan would be greatly facilitated by the large numbers of released Austrian prisoners set at liberty in that country by the

A STEP IN ADVANCE

revolutionaries, and now wandering about ready to undertake any task that would procure them their daily bread. It was probable that there were as many as 30,000 of these released Austrians, and it was from their ranks that the Bolshevik army lately operating in the neighbourhood of Merv and Askabad had been chiefly recruited.

On the other hand the possession of Baku by us would mean the converse of these propositions: denial of the stocks of oil to the enemy, and the closing of the door to Central Asia. The retention of the oil in our hands would eventually stop all movement of the South Caucasian railways which are normally dependent on this source of fuel.

To sum up then, our new plan was to get control of the Caspian and, as this could only be achieved by securing Baku, to save this town from the clutches of the enemy. Its importance was enormous and any risk was justified in our endeavour to secure it.

It can easily be understood how hard it was to concentrate on the Baku problem without endangering the Persian situation. We had with great pains built up a fairly solid position in North Persia, and this position was founded on the abilities of the various officers selected for each appointment. To remove them from their Persian responsibilities at a moment's notice and throw them into the Baku scheme would be equivalent to pulling out the foundation stones of the building.

With Head Quarters at Kasvin, we should be in a position to make the best solution possible of the difficult problem before us, and to seize the first fleeting opportunity of a move to the Caspian. We arrived on June 1st and installed ourselves in a comfortable house belonging to the American missionaries, in the neighbourhood of the Sipah-Salar's house, and at once set to work, as at Hamadan, to make the acquaintance of the local notables, while General Byron returned to Hamadan to take over command there. An aerodrome had to be built to receive the four aeroplanes allotted to the force, and landing grounds were made here, at Zinjan and at Mianeh: the one at Hamadan had been constructed a month ago.

We found Kasvin a very different town from Hamadan. In population it is about the same, with probably 50,000 inhabitants. The attitude of the people and the politicians was the same as in Hamadan, the former anxious to be friendly, the latter stirring up hatred and ill-feeling against us.

The town lies at an elevation of 4,000 feet above sea-level, about 10 miles from the southern slopes of the Elburz Mountains: it is not in any way remarkable for natural beauty or striking architecture, but the houses in general have a rather more ambitious appearance than those of Hamadan. In fact the outstanding difference between the two towns is that Hamadan is distinctly a provincial town, while Kasvin tries hard to look like a city. It endeavours to achieve this result by means of numerous inns with the grand names of all the best-known hotels in Europe, and by European shops with actual plate-glass windows, looking very ugly and out of place in an Oriental town. These shops display a variety of goods, from ladies' white satin high-heeled shoes to gents' summer suitings at sale prices, reminding us of much that is least attractive in our own country.

Where Russians are, there will be many haircutters, and Kasvin is full of excellent barbers' shops chiefly kept by Armenians and Greeks. As long as the Russians remain these shops may make a living, but the English soldier pays less attention to his coiffure, and when the Russians depart a good many barbers will have to put up their shutters and choose some other means of livelihood.

The commercial population of the town is very cosmopolitan. There is a large Russian colony, and the retiring troops have left behind them a horde of women and children, who are apparently anxious to follow their lords and masters but don't quite know how to do so. Bicherakov's troops are also here, and a goodly number of Russian ne'er-do-weels, many of whom are in touch with the Enzeli Bolsheviks and looking for an opportunity of thwarting our plans.

With such a population it is much harder to deal with the question of enemy agents than it was in Hamadan. There any one with a white or semi-white face could be arrested on sight, and was certain to be an individual who ought not to be at large. Here if you wished to carry out such procedure, you would have to arrest half the town.

Bicherakov kept order in a rough-and-ready sort of way, and his trusty lieutenant Sovlaiev was quite prepared to take the risk of arresting many harmless people in the hopes that there might be a guilty one somewhere in the bunch. As I had to take over and deal with these prisoners, I soon found the large numbers of indiscriminate arrests rather embarrassing. I complained on one occasion that I had rather a lot of these suspects on my hands, and as there appeared to be nothing at all against the majority of them I proposed to release them. To this Sovlaiev retorted, "There very likely is nothing against most of them, but one can never tell. I don't like the looks of any of them. I suggest you need not punish or confine any of them; just run them all down to Baghdad in a motor-lorry and let them walk home. That will help to keep their heads cool."

Sovlaiev was a magnificent type of Ossietin from the same district in the North Caucasus as Bicherakov. He stood about 5 feet 9 inches in height and was splendidly proportioned, with a muscular development that boded ill for any who fell into his clutches, and as he carried out most of his arrests in person his prisoners could generally testify to the strength of his grip. His methods were probably those best suited to a very difficult situation, where it was impossible to get very exact evidence against any particular person. On one occasion he flew into the Hôtel de France to arrest the proprietor, but the latter saw him coming and fled by a back door. Baulked of his prey Sovlaiev gave a sound hammering to all of the establishment who were within reach and, determined not to come back empty-handed, marched off in triumph with the innocent *chef de cuisine* !

We found prices in Kasvin about the same as in Hamadan, but supplies were not difficult to obtain. Food was quite good but never up to the standard of a private soldier's ration, and our rate of messing, for the simplest diet was 30 krans, or just under £1 a day. Officers receive an allowance of £1 a day for food and lodging; but the cost of living was never within that sum, and later was much above it.

Wheat remained at abnormal famine prices, though the new crop would soon be harvested, and there were still large stocks of the old crop unsold. There is no doubt that the famine was to some extent artificial. Although there had been much loss owing to a bad season in 1917 and the Russian troops had made large demands, still as this part of Persia is so fertile that in normal seasons most of the valleys are capable of producing seven times the requirements of the people, it seems certain that any possibility of famine in this country would be removed if one were able to introduce a system of wheat control.

In Kasvin we were much more in touch with the Russians, and I was able to have frequent conferences with Bicherakov as to plans for the immediate future, which involved the settlement of the Jangali affair, and for the more distant future, which concerned the possibility of our getting a footing in the Caucasus. Discussions on the latter point were rendered difficult owing to the fact that I had no power or authority to guarantee anything, and Bicherakov often petulantly exclaimed, "How can I fix up any arrangement with you, when you have no troops, and cannot even assure me that you are going to get any." Moreover I had, since the failure of our original plans, received no authority to undertake anything in the Baku direction. But as the control of the Caspian was still our aim, I felt sure that the authorities would eventually be convinced that control of that sea would rest with whoever held Baku, and that any endeavour to control the Caspian must therefore involve the holding of that town. The Russian officers who had come out with the last party from home proved invaluable as interpreters, and filled many important posts. One was attached to the squadron of the 14th Hussars, several were employed on dull but useful duties at the tollgates, some assisted in supplies, and Captain Bray, a Russian officer of English descent, was appointed A.D.C. and proved very helpful in my frequent interviews with messengers from Baku.

There were many Russian lady nurses also, who had been left behind by the retiring troops, and it was necessary to do something for them. Many of them had passed high degrees in medical science, and the greater number were sent down to Baghdad for duty in military hospitals.

Our visiting experiences among the Persians here were more amusing than those at Hamadan, but we never got on quite such friendly terms. Sovlaiev's activities brought many people to me in despair. The first to claim my protection was the head of the telephone service, who came flying round the day after our arrival in a state of breathless excitement and poured his tale of woe into my ears. "I come to implore you to protect an innocent man from the Russians. They have declared their intention of arresting me, and that desperate man Sovlaiev is at this very moment scouring the town for me. I cannot think of what I am accused, but whatever it is I am perfectly innocent, as you must be aware. Do I look like a guilty person?"

I must own that he did look extremely guilty, but I could only reply, " I am quite new to this town and know nothing of any of the inhabitants. The Russians have been here for years and must know all about everybody. I cannot therefore undertake to pit my experience against theirs, and I cannot possibly interfere with any arrests they decide to make. As you are quite certain of your innocence I should not resist the arrest. You had better allow Sovlaiev to take what steps he thinks right and rely upon the proofs of your innocence to put matters square."

The Rais-i-telefon smiled a sad smile at this advice and intimated that he was not inclined to take the risk of relying on Sovlaiev's discrimination. As I could offer him neither assistance nor palatable advice, he begged permission to withdraw and was soon galloping off in his little two-horse carriage.

Five minutes later up turned Sovlaiev hot on the trail of his enemy, and very much annoyed with me for not having arrested the culprit. I explained that I had no information as to any charge against him, and I could not be expected to fall in with his idea of arresting people just because I didn't like their looks. On this he flew off to continue the chase, the intended victim continuing to elude him up to nightfall. At daybreak on the following morning he was round again at my quarters with the news that the Rais-i-telefon had taken refuge with the Governor, and he intended to attack the Governor's palace in order to effect his arrest. I dissuaded him from this quite unnecessary act of violence, and we agreed that I should take over the task of further pursuit; I did not, however, immediately press the matter, as it did not appear to belong to the category of events that were going to win the war. I merely asked Captain (now Major) Saunders to find out what it was all about, and awaited his report.

My first official visit was necessarily to the Governor, Midhat-es-Sultaneh, a charming personality of Falstaffian build and humour—a genial philosopher who laughed his way through life and met each change of fortune with an equanimity worthy of the Vicar of Bray. His motto was, " Come what may I will retain my position as Governor of this town," and he told me with pride that he was the only Governor in Persia who had managed to cling to office for more than three years. He had to swing the pendulum this way to please the Persian Government, and that way to please the Russians, and now we had come he was quite ready to swing it any way we liked. As long as we were pleased, he was going to be pleased. In politics he posed as a democrat, but he told me this with a very sly chuckle. He was certainly not the type of man to demand " government by the people for the people," but, as he said, "in these days of politics, for which we have to thank you European gentlemen, one has to be something or another, and the democratic label is the popular one at present." The result of our investigations as to his past leanings and tendencies showed him to be quite innocent of any plots or intrigues. He was pro-nothing and anti-nothing and had only one aim in life, which was to steer his boat clear of all the rocks and whirlpools by which he was surrounded.

After calling on the Governor, we visited the Karguzar, Ihtidar-ul-Mulk, a pleasant young man, who welcomed us with every courteous attention. In conversation he protested a little too much, and went so much out of his way to denounce the Germans and Turks and to sneer at Kuchik that we felt convinced he would prove to be one of our worst enemies. It was not long, however, before we knew all about his hostile activities, and he tacitly admitted his guilt by fleeing to Teheran before we had decided to take action against him.

Among the local gentry we made the acquaintance of Prince Bisharat-es-Sultaneh, a relation of the Sipah-Salar, a charming specimen of the refined Persian gentleman.

Several batches of officers had now arrived from Hamadan, and we were able to begin getting the town into order. Lieut.-Colonel J. Hoskyn had arrived to carry out the duties of General Staff Officer, First Grade (for operations). Lieut.-Colonel Warden, of the Canadian Infantry, was appointed Commandant of the town, and Captain Cockerell took over the arduous duties of Assistant Provost-Marshal. The latter officer was quite the most gifted individual I have ever met in the art of producing law and order from chaos. Two days after his arrival I found him going round the town with the genial Governor, explaining the advantages of sanitation. The Governor was finding it hard to live up to his principle of agreeing with the last-comer, and the perpetual smile on his genial countenance had faded to a hardly perceptible flicker; but he still had sufficient strength to murmur a cheerful assent and to promise great efforts in the near future. For the first time in his life he was going to find some one who would see that he lived up to his promises, and in a few days Kasvin was delighted with the sight of a Persian governor actually engaged in sanitating his town, an event not previously recorded in Persian history.

In spite of our efforts at sanitation, Kasvin was not a healthy town, and our chief Medical Officer, Major Brunskill, soon had his small hospital overflowing. But except for rare isolated cases we escaped the two scourges common to this part of Persia, typhus and cholera.

We must now return to follow the doings of the Rais-i-telefon. We left him hiding in the Governor's palace, with Sovlaiev watching the exits to pounce on him if

A STEP IN ADVANCE

he emerged. But he took very good care not to show his face outside, until at last he received the joyful news that his persecutor had marched down the road to Resht. If he had only known it, this was merely a case of "out of the frying-pan into the fire"; it was only going to result in a change of methods, but the result would be the same.

In a very short time I was shown papers thoroughly implicating the suspected man in every sort of plot and intrigue to "down the British," and the majority of these papers being in his own handwriting there was not much need to ask for corroboration of his guilt. After all, one uses the term "guilty" in a very comparative sense. The term is not really applicable to an inhabitant of a neutral country who displays a preference for one nation as compared with another. But in time of war one has to regard as "guilty" any one who does not side with oneself, and in this sense the documents were most incriminating.

As soon as I saw these papers I determined to arrest the Rais-i-telefon; but not wishing to disgrace the Governor by making a forcible entry into his palace, I sent a request to him that he would come round and see me at Head Quarters on an urgent matter. In a remarkably short time he arrived in his little carriage and pair and entered my room with his usual smile. When I stated the reason of my desiring his presence and gave him the letters to read, the smile, for the first and only time in my experience, left his face, and he literally gasped for breath. I do not think it was the contents of the letters that took away his breath so much as the fact that we had obtained possession of them. At last his indignation (well assumed) found words. "Alas, what treachery! Is there a man in the world one can trust? To think of a former friend of mine sunk to such depths of infamy!" etc.

When he had concluded his long tirade I informed him that I should be under the painful obligation of invading his sacred precincts in order to effect the arrest. This brought back again the accustomed smile to his lips as he retorted with a chuckle, " He isn't with me any more. Since Sovlaiev left, he has gone back to his own house." He now begged, in the polite Persian way, permission to withdraw. But there was a delay in getting hold of Captain Cockerell to give him the orders for arrest, and until he came I could not release the old man, whose anxiety to get away was obviously merely to warn the friend he had so savagely denounced. So we had to keep the conversation going on rather forced subjects, and at every pause the old man bobbed up with his request to depart, and I had to say once more, " Please wait half a minute, I see so little of your Excellency, and I want particularly to ask you if there is any prospect of a fall in the price of grain." At last Cockerell arrived and I was able to give him the necessary orders, and as he would be travelling in a motor-car, I thought he would easily get to the offender's house before the Governor could carry out his obvious intention of warning his " false " friend. I accordingly released the Governor, and it was amusing to note the un-Persian speed with which he rushed to his carriage, hopped in and instructed the coachman to whip up the horses. Cockerell's car vanished down a road to the left, while the Governor's carriage disappeared in a cloud of dust round a corner to the right. And the Governor won the race. Owing to uncertainty as to the exact spot at the Rais-i-telefon's residence the car was slightly delayed, and by the time they reached the house, the offender, evidently warned on the telephone by his friend, had fled.

The failure to arrest him was not very serious. If he had fled the town like the Kar-guzar, it would suit me equally well, and if he remained in the town we should

A STEP IN ADVANCE

get him to-morrow or the next day. I never attached the same importance to these arrests as Sovlaiev did. In the first place, until our arrival, what could be more natural than that the Persians should favour our enemies who were on the spot and prosecuting a most vigorous propaganda ? The fact that the people of Kasvin had favoured the enemy cause was not of any great importance as long as they now agreed to cease their activities against us. To arrest all who were guilty of pro-Turk or pro-Kuchik tendencies would have been to arrest every man of standing in the town. It was not so important therefore to arrest one or two individuals, as to make all of the offenders change their minds. I accordingly issued a proclamation to the effect that we knew the exact measure of every man's guilt up to date, but that all sins of the past were remitted on the condition that no offence was committed after the date of our arrival. Any sign of activity against us from this date would be treated with the greatest severity.

Another advantage in leaving a man at liberty when once we had marked him down as an enemy agent was that, with the requisite knowledge in our possession, we were able to obtain information of the greatest value from his correspondence. We kept a general look-out for the Rais-i-telefon without pressing the matter very much, but the whole situation was brought to a dramatic close by his unlooked-for surrender.

Major Saunders was seated in his office on the day following the failure to carry out the arrest, when the door opened and in walked the Rais-i-telefon. Major Saunders was very much surprised at this sudden entry into his sanctuary of the very man we were supposed to be hunting the town for, and informed him abruptly that he must now consider himself a prisoner. The Rais-i-telefon meekly acquiesced, but begged to be allowed to say a few words, which were to this effect : " I thoroughly admit my former mistaken activities in support of your enemies. I realize that I was entirely wrong, and must plead that I was misled by others. I intend from this date to renounce my former tendencies and to devote the rest of my life to pro-British propaganda."

In the end I decided not to arrest him, and he was set at liberty. It is possible to doubt the genuineness of his conversion, but it is quite certain that during the remainder of our time in Kasvin he entirely severed his enemy connection and was helpful to us in many ways.

A few days later I met the Governor and told him of our surprise at the Rais-i-telefon surrendering himself. The old man chuckled and said: "That was all my advice. I told him to go and walk into the office, and he would find that you would not touch him. I warned him that if you caught him in the town he would be sent to Baghdad for a certainty, but that you would consider it a point of honour not to be hard on him if he gave himself up. He was afraid to risk the plan, but I made him do it."

There were of course many more incidents of this kind, but the above will suffice as typical of them all. Arrests of real importance were as a rule not amusing, and were carried out with a swiftness and secrecy that enhanced their value.

In a conversation with an honest democrat (*rara avis*) in Kasvin we got as usual on to the favourite topic of every one at this time—Kuchik Khan, and I stated that I had quite a genuine admiration for him and a general agreement with his policy. What battle-cry could be more suitable for a Persian than " Persia for the Persians ! " but like all such cries it calls for definition, and it is not easy to define a Persian. In Persia there are large communities of Turks, Turcomans, Jews, and Armenians who have been there for centuries ; are these Persians ? Then as to the second cry of " Out with the Europeans," what desire could be more creditable to the Persians ?

But of course it would entail "Out with the Persians" in other lands where Persians are to be found. And finally it is not enough to give vent to these aspirations; words can never take the place of deeds, and as the Europeans will not go voluntarily, Persia will have to apply force. And that is just the weak point of the whole scheme, there is no force behind it and there never will be.

Persia has no army, and if she started to-day to create one, spending money (which she has not got) lavishly, she would in fifteen years' time be able to put a large number of well-trained soldiers on parade. But putting them on parade would not make brave men of them, and I very much doubt if they would be of any value as fighters. To be good fighters men must have strong beliefs and high ideals. The strongest of all incentives is love of country, and I see no signs of that in Persia.

"What shall we do then?" asked my friend. "What do you propose as a future programme for Persia?"

"Well," I replied, "after my very short acquaintance with Persia, my opinion is of little value, but I would suggest the following. You talk of the glories of your past history; teach it to your children. Talk of it less and live up to it more. You read the works of Sa'adi; quote him less and be guided by him more. As long as every man says in his heart, 'Let Persia sink as long as I swim,' it is no use shouting 'Persia for the Persians.' If you could start to-day to educate all Persian children from six years of age upwards on these lines, they would give you the right kind of soldiers in fifteen years' time, but it will take you fifteen years to get an educational system going; so that you won't get your first soldiers till thirty years from now, and it will take another fifteen years to build them up into armies; so if you start to-day on this simple programme, you will begin trying to turn out the Europeans in 1963. And even then you must remember that you will be only 'trying' to turn them out, which is a very different thing from turning them out."

"Your scheme is rather a hopeless one," said he.

"So is your Kuchik Khan's programme," I replied.

CHAPTER X

THE LAST STAGE TO THE SEA

OUR relations at this time with Bicherakov were becoming rather strained. He was naturally very anxious, and his men even more so, to get on the move.

Kuchik Khan was holding the Menjil bridge, 70 miles from Kasvin and exactly half-way to Enzeli, and although we could not believe that even under their German officers his troops would put up a very serious fight, yet it was clear that he did intend to oppose the Anglo-Russian advance. Every day's delay enabled him to increase the strength of his entrenched position covering the approaches to the bridge, a position naturally very strong even without artificial improvement.

It was impossible for me to agree to a forward move on Bicherakov's part until I could feel sure of some troops to put up behind him, and to hold Kasvin and the various posts on the road to Enzeli as the Russian column marched down to the Caspian; and those troops I had not yet got. The only bond that really held him to us now was the financial one and that was slender, as he had already been offered better terms in the Caucasus if he would throw in his lot with the Bolsheviks. I also impressed upon him the great advantage it would be to him to have the support of aeroplanes and armoured cars, and these I could not give him if he broke away from us. I think he was quite justified in displaying some feeling of exasperation.

At the beginning of June I got the welcome news that troops were on their way in sufficient numbers to meet the demands of the moment. The remainder of the 14th Hussars were marching to Hamadan, eight armoured cars were at Kermanshah, and a mobile column of a thousand rifles of the 1/4 Hants Regiment and the 1/2 Gurkhas with two mountain guns were on their way up with all speed in 500 Ford motor-vans, and would probably arrive in Kasvin by June 12th. The movement of so many cars was rendered difficult by the shortage of petrol, but we just managed to accumulate sufficient to get them all through. But by the time this column reached Kasvin, it no longer merited the designation of "mobile": the rough journey had been very hard on the cars, there was a shortage of spare parts, and less than fifty per cent. of the cars were fit for immediate use.

In addition to these troops, No. 8 Battery Royal Field Artillery was on its way from Baghdad to Kasvin.

We now had before us the final choice of coming to terms with Kuchik Khan or fighting him, though it would be more correct to say that we gave him the choice. There were several interchanges of our respective points of view by means of messengers, but it seemed impossible to hope for any peaceful solution. It was too much to expect of Kuchik Khan that having paraded his brave army, and vaunted its prowess in the most bellicose language, he would now tamely submit to see our troops march unopposed through his entrenchments. Nothing came of these negotiations therefore, and as a last resource I sent down Colonel Stokes with a flag of truce with full powers to speak for me. I was anxious as to what might befall Captain Noel and the other prisoners in the hands of the Jangalis if we declared war on the latter. The number of prisoners had considerably increased, but

THE LAST STAGE TO THE SEA 157

Noel was now the only Englishman among them. Oakshot and Maclaren had escaped; Noel was confined in chains in a dungeon. The other prisoners included one French officer and several Russians.

I authorized Colonel Stokes to make any reasonable agreement with Kuchik, our unconditional points being the immediate release of all prisoners, the opening of the road to Enzeli and a guarantee of non-interference with movements of our troops on the road. In exchange I offered him a free hand as regarded any steps he might take with regard to the internal politics of Persia.

Colonel Stokes remained for two days at Kuchik Khan's Head Quarters near Resht, but was only able to get evasive replies. Finding himself unable to induce the Jangalis to see the folly of their ways, and knowing that according to our programme hostilities would now be commencing he closed the negotiations and left for Enzeli on the same day that the fighting at Menjil began.

On June 5th I agreed to Bicherakov setting his troops in motion, with a view to attacking the Jangalis at Menjil and securing the bridge. Accordingly on that date the combined army set out from Kasvin composed of some thousand Cossacks, including artillery, cavalry and infantry, one squadron of the 14th Hussars under Captain Pope, and two of our armoured cars. It was also arranged that when hostilities commenced, two aeroplanes from the aerodrome at Kasvin should co-operate. To Bicherakov's force I attached Major Newcome, of the Canadian army, as financial adviser and Captain Derbyshire to supervise supplies. Colonel Clutterbuck remained throughout as liaison officer with the Russians, and Major Rowlandson, who also spoke Russian, accompanied the force for general duties.

By June 11, 1918, all was ready for the attack on the Jangali position. On the night of that date Bicherakov had collected his force at Bala Bala, 8 miles from

Menjil, and at dawn on the 12th he moved off to the encounter.

The two aeroplanes sent down from Kasvin to co-operate in the attack had orders to fly over the enemy's trenches, but not to use their machine-guns or to bomb the trenches until the enemy had made his intention of fighting clear by opening fire. I gave this order because I knew that the whole attitude of the Jangalis might well be only another example of the time-honoured Persian custom of fighting a battle by "looks," and if that were to be their line of action, it would only be fair to let them see our "looks" before proceeding to deeds.

The matter was settled at once by the Jangali troops opening a furious but harmless fusillade on the aeroplanes as they flew over the trenches; and thus commenced the Battle of Menjil Bridge.

Meantime Bicherakov was steadily advancing at the head of his troops. This is not the proper place, according to correct ideas of modern warfare, for a General Officer commanding a force about to come into action; in fact it is the very last place where he ought to be; but in Persia the ordinary rules of tactics are reversed, and action that would be fatal in European warfare brings about most successful results.

It is not easy to calculate what strength Kuchik Khan brought into action on this day. He boasted of possessing 5,000 men, and he may have had half that number in the trenches on both sides of the bridge, and on the surrounding hills. He had no artillery, but was well supplied with machine-guns, which were placed in excellent positions to command the approaches to the bridge and the road on the other side of the river.

The road has already been described in Chapter III, but it will make things clearer if I give a more detailed description of the few miles of ground over which the action

THE LAST STAGE TO THE SEA

took place. Approaching Menjil from the east the road runs at the foot of the mountains which lie on the right-hand side while a broad stony river-bed runs parallel to the road on the left. At a point about $2\frac{1}{2}$ miles before the bridge is reached a low spur runs out from the hills, causing the road to take a hairpin bend, on rounding which the plain and village of Menjil come into view. The bridge is not visible from here, in fact it can only be seen from a very short distance, as it lies in a very narrow gap between steep cliffs. At the point of the hairpin bend referred to above is a small tea-shop, whence an uninterrupted view of the whole ground is obtained.

It is obvious from the above description that the enemy should have held this spur to cover the approaches to the field, and to deny so favourable a position to us. But it was held only by an observation picquet, which withdrew without firing on Bicherakov's approach. Standing at the tea-shop and looking west one sees in the near foreground to the left, and left front, the village and the cultivated fields of Menjil, abruptly terminated at a distance of about 2 miles by the river-bed, which here swings round to the right to find its way north to the Caspian Sea through the gap over which the Menjil bridge has been constructed. The country in the distance in this same line of view is fairly open for some 6 miles, consisting of broad river-beds, patches of riverside cultivation and low hills; beyond that the hills rise to considerable altitudes, and close the panorama. The road to the bridge is naturally obliged to follow the lines of the spur, curving beyond it sharply to the right for half a mile till the open ground is reached and then leading due west to the bridge. In the immediate foreground at a distance of 2 miles is a small isolated flat-topped hill about 800 yards in length running at right angles to the line of the road and completely covering the bridge which lies about half a mile north-west of it. On the right the rocky cliffs of the Elburz Mountains rise within a few yards of the road, and render manœuvre in that direction difficult except for well-trained mountain troops.

The German Commander, von Passchen, failed to hold this spur, which was of course the real key of the position, and contented himself with entrenching his troops on the crest-line of the isolated hill, keeping a few small detachments on the lower slopes of the mountains to our right. Without artillery the hill might have been difficult to take, but such a position would be obviously untenable in the face of artillery fire, forming a target which an artilleryman would go far to seek and would seldom find. The crest-line of this small hill is at a slightly lower level than that of the tea-shop spur.

The whole dispositions of the defence were so farcical that I am bound to believe that the Persians never meant to fight, relying upon "looks" to carry the day. But for that class of warfare they found Bicherakov quite the wrong sort of man.

Presumably von Passchen must have known better, but I think the Persians believed that we would argue thus: "The Jangalis hold a hill that lies right across our path, protects the bridge and brings all the road over which we must advance under fire. To turn them out will cost many lives, even if successful. They will not go of their own accord. We must therefore halt here for several days to discuss the situation."

Having omitted to hold the spur, the next most favourable ground for the enemy was the rocky slopes of the mountains on our right and the similar slopes on the far side of the bridge. Troops holding positions on these slopes would be difficult to dislodge, and their machine-gun fire properly directed would have made an attack on the bridge, without first dislodging them, a very costly affair and quite possibly a failure.

THE LAST STAGE TO THE SEA

There were a few troops in these positions, but their opposition was very feeble. They made little use of their machine-guns, and very soon withdrew entirely from the field of battle.

The ball was opened by the arrival of the aeroplanes, which swooped gracefully over the Jangali entrenchments without opening fire, returning to report the details of the enemy's position. They were heavily fired at, but were undamaged.

At the same moment Bicherakov at the head of his army came round the corner of the spur by the tea-shop, where he encountered a small body of the enemy's troops, who had the appearance of intending to resist his advance. Having been badly wounded in the legs early in the war Bicherakov is obliged to walk with a stick, which he now carried as his only weapon, and with which he walked boldly up to the leader and asked him what he was doing there and why his men assumed so threatening an attitude. To this the picquet commander replied, "We are here to hold this post with the last drop of our blood!"

"Get out of it, at once!" shouted Bicherakov, waving his crooked stick at them, and his fierce and threatening gestures so alarmed the Jangalis that they turned and fled as one man down the road, leaving the spur in the hands of the Cossacks. This completed the second phase of the battle.

The third phase was commenced by the arrival of the German officer, von Passchen, with a Persian escort carrying a flag of truce and demanding a parley. The German was dressed in his national uniform and had quite the air of a commander-in-chief, evidently much impressing his Persian associates, but only making the Cossacks smile. Bicherakov advanced to meet him and inquired what his errand might be. Von Passchen replied that he came to treat on behalf of Kuchik Khan and proceeded to express himself in these terms:

"The Jangalis are, as you see, very strongly entrenched, and the troops at your disposal will not suffice to move them from their position. Any attack you may therefore see fit to undertake is foredoomed to failure and will only result in needless loss of life. Mirza Kuchik Khan therefore empowers me to make the following offer to you. If you will dissociate yourself from the English, he will gladly allow you a free road to Enzeli. He has always regarded the Russians as friends and still continues to do so; his quarrel is only with the English. Your men may pass down the road, without disarming, in batches of two hundred daily and the Jangalis will not molest your parties, but no English will be allowed to pass."

Bicherakov was quite overcome with the impertinence of this proposition, but retained some control over his temper and his tongue. His reply was something to the following effect:

"I do not recognize a German officer as a representative of Kuchik Khan, and I consider your appearing before me in German uniform as a piece of insolence. I want no terms from the Jangalis, and intend to open fire as soon as you get out of the way."

The Cossack mountain artillery had meanwhile been taking up an excellent position on the tea-shop spur, and as soon as von Passchen was clear of the field of fire the order was given to open on the isolated hill entrenchments. The Cossack cavalry and the Hussars then moved out into the open towards the enemy's right, and the armoured cars came into action on the road against the enemy's left, while the Cossack infantry extended over the plain.

In a very short time the Jangalis were seen to be evacuating their trenches and making in confusion for the bridge, the cavalry and armoured cars followed up in pursuit and gained the bridge without a check, cutting off a large number of stragglers who were taken prisoners.

THE LAST STAGE TO THE SEA. 163

The bridge should have been untenable at this early stage of the proceedings, as the machine-guns which were sited on the other side of the river to cover it and all the approaches were still in position and had not even come under our fire. But the spirit of panic was in the air, and the machine-gunners fled almost without firing a shot. The mounted troops crossed the bridge, the infantry were reformed and the whole force marched 10 miles down the road to Rudbar without any further molestation. This seems incredible when you consider the nature of this terrible defile which I have already described. Had only one machine-gun remained in action on this road the whole advance would have been stopped. The Jangalis left a large number of killed and wounded on the ground, making no effort to remove them, and so ended the Battle of Menjil Bridge. The casualties on our side were trivial.

Very determined opposition had not been expected, but no one had contemplated quite such an easy victory. The Jangalis are not altogether cowards, as they proved later, and Kuchik Khan explained their flight on this occasion as being due to the fact that he had no intention of fighting and was quite taken by surprise. He had expected the Russians to be overawed by the mere sight of his troops, and had felt certain that they would agree to his terms. He was painfully surprised at the rough treatment they had received at the hands of Bicherakov's force.

The squadron of the 14th Hussars remained at Menjil under Captain Pope to hold the bridge, and were shortly afterwards strengthened by the addition of an infantry detachment from the mobile column.

As our troops were not yet quite ready to take up the various posts that it would be necessary to hold to keep open the road to Enzeli, I had still to use all the tact and gifts of persuasion I possessed to restrain the impatience of Bicherakov. In the end he decided to push on to Enzeli with his main body, leaving small detachments at Rudbar, Rustamabad and Resht to be relieved by our troops as soon as possible and to rejoin him at Enzeli. We were able to carry out these reliefs within the next week and to separate ourselves finally from Bicherakov's force.

Kuchik Khan now inspired his followers by announcing that the Russians having withdrawn, the British were left by themselves and, as they notably were poor fighters, they would soon fall an easy prey to his gallant troops, whom he ordered to attack and harass the British detachments on the road and to exterminate them. The result of these efforts was very similar to the result of a similar order given at the commencement of the war by the Kaiser with reference to a certain "contemptible little army."

On June 18th a detachment of the 1/4 Hants was attacked on the road, Captain Durnford was killed and six men wounded, but the enemy were driven off with considerable loss. At the same time the enemy displayed considerable activity in the neighbourhood of the other posts, especially near Imamzadeh Hashim, 10 miles from Resht, where the road leaves the hills and enters the dense forest and rice-fields of the flat country, and also at Resht itself. The town of Resht is large and straggling and entirely surrounded by alternate tracts of impenetrable forest and rice-fields. It is of considerable commercial importance, and has an even more ugly Europeanized appearance than Kasvin, with theatres, cinemas and many hotels. In the centre of the town are public gardens with a bandstand, and close to these gardens is the humble dwelling that is occupied by the British Consul. This is obviously a very bad site for such a residence. The Russians, more wisely, have built a splendid Consulate standing in its own grounds, just on the southern outskirt of the town and on the

RESHT, CLOSE TO THE CONSULATE

THE LAST STAGE TO THE SEA

main road. Our troops were billeted alongside of the Russian Consulate outside the town, in a position that gave them considerable tactical advantages.

The greatest number of troops we ever had at Resht was 450 rifles and two armoured cars, and with this number it was quite impossible to defend the town against the Jangalis, who were concentrating in the surrounding forest and were never more than a mile away from the outskirts of the town. Only one road led through the forest and that was the direct road to Kasma, 25 miles to the west, where Kuchik Khan had his Head Quarters. Our force was too small to risk an offensive against the Jangalis, of whom there were over 2,000 in the immediate neighbourhood, and even had we possessed sufficient strength it would have been putting men into a death-trap to move them along the Kasma road, while off the road movement in any formation was almost impossible. There was nothing therefore to prevent the Jangalis from taking the actual town, the perimeter of which would be about 7 miles, a distance far beyond the capacity of 450 rifles to defend. The town lies open on every side and the dense undergrowth comes right up to the walls of the outer houses. The troops were therefore kept concentrated on the outskirts, where they could hold their own against a large force of the enemy and whence they could deliver a counter-attack at any favourable moment.

The situation of this detachment would have been precarious but for the aeroplanes, which produced a great effect by bombing and machine-gunning any concentration of the enemy; but this task was also rendered difficult by the density of the forest, which gave the enemy cover from view. The casualties inflicted were therefore slight, but the moral effect was great.

These operations on the Menjil–Resht road were conducted by Lieut.-Colonel Matthews, of the 1/4 Hants, who commanded the mobile column of 800 rifles and two mountain artillery guns, which was a small force to cover the 50 miles of mountain road and forest from Menjil to Resht! There was a good deal of hard fighting and the men acquitted themselves well, both Gurkhas and Hampshire men vieing with one another in showing the Jangalis of what stuff our troops were made. The armoured cars also helped much to impress the enemy, although the country was of the very worst description for their action, it being quite impossible for them to manœuvre off the roads. The one thing an armoured car cannot negotiate is a rice-field.

On June 26th I left for Enzeli with a view of fixing up plans with Bicherakov before he embarked for Baku, and also of ascertaining the present attitude of the Bolshevik Committee. We stayed the night at Resht in the British Consulate, and I noticed the extreme danger of its position in the heart of the town. It was defended by a guard of one N.C.O. and twelve men, but a determined attack could not be beaten off by so small a detachment, and Colonel Matthews could not spare more men from his small force. Mr. Maclaren, who had been a long time a prisoner in the hands of the Jangalis, was now re-occupying the Consulate, but it was intended to replace him by Mr. Moir, and arrangements were made to install the new Consul with due ceremony on our return journey.

We reached Enzeli early on June 27th and took up our quarters as before in the Fishery Depot. The whole of the 27th and part of the 28th were spent in discussing plans with Bicherakov and interviewing Comrade Cheliapin.

Bicherakov had decided to turn Bolshevik, as he saw no other way of getting a footing in the Caucasus. He had written and wired to the Bolshevik Committee announcing his conversion and stating his belief that only by means of the Sovietski Vlast (the power of councils—

THE LAST STAGE TO THE SEA 167

a new name for the Bolshevik authorities) could Russia find redemption. His conversion was loudly acclaimed in the Bolshevik newspapers of Baku, and he was offered the command of the Bolshevik troops or the so-called "Red Army," which he accepted. He was ready to embark at once, and I decided to send with him the staff of British officers who had accompanied him from Kasvin and "A" Squadron No. 2 Battery Armoured Cars (Locker-Lampson's unit). Disembarking at Baku would put his force rather too much in the hands of the Bolsheviks, who might turn round on him at any moment; he therefore decided to land at Alyat, a small port 50 miles south of Baku, where the railway turns at a right angle due west towards Tiflis. This would keep his force separate from the Bolsheviks and would at the same time bring it into the best position for co-operating with that portion of the Red Army which was actually in the field.

The strength of the Red Field Army was calculated at about 10,000 men, and if they really had been soldiers and had had any fight in them the plan evolved by Bicherakov should have been successful. But as usual, revolutionary troops are only troops on paper, and in the field, where each man is out only to avoid being killed, they count for nothing.

The situation in the South-East Caucasus at this time was as follows: The Turkish Caucasus–Islam Army, about 12,000 strong, composed of about one-half regular Turkish troops and one-half levies from the local Mahomedan races in the South Caucasus, was advancing from the Tiflis direction along the railway line with a view of capturing Baku. They were much hampered by the bad state of the railway and rolling-stock and shortage of fuel for the engines. The Germans in Tiflis also were doing their best to prevent the Turks getting to Baku at all, as they had a private arrangement with Lenin, and through him with the Baku Government, that the town should be peacefully handed over to them. To see the Turks in Baku would be almost as bad as to see the British there.

This peculiar situation resulted in a most extraordinary state of affairs. In their anxiety to prevent the Germans obtaining possession of Baku, and also in their eagerness to take any chance of fighting the Bolsheviks, many Russian officers joined this Turkish force, and when we were later fighting against them in Baku we had Russian officers on our side, while the enemy had as many on his.

On July 1st the Turkish Army had not yet crossed the Kura River, over which there is only one bridge, at Yeldakh, 150 miles from Alyat. This river drains the south-eastern half of the Caucasus Mountains from a point just north of Tiflis, and joins the Aras River 100 miles from the point where the latter flows into the Caspian Sea, 50 miles south of Alyat.

The possession of this bridge was therefore all important. The advance guard of the Red Army was approaching the bridge from the east, and Bicherakov hoped to make a dash and capture it before the Turks, advancing from the west, could succeed in doing so. If he could seize and hold the bridge there would be no possibility of any further advance of the Turks on Baku for a very long time. Even should he fail to secure the bridge, his troops might still defeat the enemy in the fighting that would ensue, or at any rate delay their advance long enough to enable the Baku commander to choose a defensive line in the mountainous country west of Baku that should be impregnable.

With these objects in view Bicherakov commenced the embarkation of his force, on July 1st.

My other task at Enzeli was to interview Cheliapin and ascertain his frame of mind. A short précis of our conversation will be given later on.

THE LAST STAGE TO THE SEA

The first thing that struck me at Enzeli was the entire change of atmosphere since our unfortunate visit here in the winter. Then the Committee with some 2,000 men behind them were able to dictate; now with only 200 Red Guards, faced by 100 men of the 1/4 Hants, the air of dictator had vanished. The numerous committee had dwindled to three, of whom we already knew Cheliapin; the second member was Lazarev, a young shopkeeper about thirty years of age, and the third was Babookh, a youth of nineteen years of age, who had served as a trumpeter in a cavalry regiment. The ignorance of this latter member was astounding; he was probably only just qualified as "literate," but he had the courage of ignorance and the conceit of youth, and he undertook to speak severely to me on several subjects of which he knew nothing, such as our Colonial policy and our rule in India. He was a nice enthusiastic lad and really did intend to set all the wrongs in the world right, but the lines on which he hoped to work were not such as were likely to lead to success.

Connected with the Committee was Lieutenant Alkhavi, an officer of Arab descent in Bicherakov's service. He was military governor of the town and representative of the Baku Soviets. As a member of Bicherakov's force he was naturally inclined to help us, but he liked his position as King of Kazian, and seemed a little afraid that in the end we might supplant him.

Our detachment at Enzeli was very much objected to both by him and Cheliapin, but I pointed out that we were preparing a landing-ground for aeroplanes here and I must have a guard to look after the planes. They very kindly offered to undertake the guarding of the planes for us, but I had to insist that this was a duty that could only be performed by our own men.

Another change in the atmosphere was that instead of summoning me to attend a meeting in the revolutionary

Head Quarters, the Committee very kindly came to see me, at my request, in my quarters.

The most important matter to settle with Cheliapin was the supply of petrol. This was entirely in the hands of our enemies the Bolsheviks, and it was not easy to get them to part with the one indispensable product, the lack of which would paralyse all our movements. Of course they should have absolutely refused to part with a single drop of petrol, in which case my force in Persia would have entirely lost its mobility, and we would have found ourselves in an extremely serious situation.

But revolutionaries are short-sighted and not inclined to look very far ahead in their transactions. They wanted motor-cars, with which I alone could supply them. Money they had no need of as long as there was a printing-press handy, but motor-cars were not so easily called into existence as currency notes. So we arranged an exchange of motor-cars for petrol, at the rate of £300 worth of petrol for every £100 worth of cars. They wanted cars badly, but cars were far from being indispensable to them, whereas petrol was absolutely indispensable to me. Had they had the sense to see that they were gaining a very slight advantage and giving away a very valuable one, they might have refused the deal, and my force would have had to cease all movement in Persia. Baghdad objected very much to being asked to find the cars to enable me to carry out this deal, but in the end the demand was never a very large one. I received petrol from the Baku Soviets to a value of about £50,000, and when I had sent over ten Ford cars in part payment the Government was thrown out and I was unable to complete a transaction with a Government that had ceased to exist. These petrol transactions had the additional advantage of enabling me to strengthen our position in Enzeli by sending some officers down to reside there to superintend the unloading and dispatch of the consignments. By

THE LAST STAGE TO THE SEA. 171

means of these officers and the aeroplane guard we had now secured a firm foothold in Enzeli, which was the first step towards gaining control of the Caspian.

Altogether I regarded our visit to Enzeli as extremely satisfactory, we had arranged our future plans with Bicherakov, we had secured an unlimited petrol supply and we had established ourselves in the port. Compared with these solid advantages I made light of having had to listen to a lecture on the iniquities of British Imperialism from the lips of young Comrade Babookh, aged nineteen.

On June 28th we left Enzeli and returned to Resht, staying again in the British Consulate. Some fighting had taken place in our absence, and the Gurkhas at Imamzadeh Hashim had had a very successful encounter with a party of Jangalis near their post, in which the latter were quite wiped out, and the fame of the Gurkha *kukri* spread consternation in the country-side. Two officers driving in a motor-car and not very well acquainted with their surroundings, mistook the Kasma road for the Enzeli one, and headed straight into the enemy's cordon. Within a mile from the town the car was fired on, one officer was killed, and the other managed by a good use of his legs to get back to the town.

The ceremony of reinstatement of the British Consul was arranged for June 29th, and we went carefully into the details of the programme beforehand with the new Governor, Sirdar-i-Kul, so that there should be no hitch in the proceedings. And there were none, except that the Governor absented himself, sending an excuse at the last moment complaining of the usual Persian attack of sickness that arises when an unpleasant duty has to be performed. His share in the proceedings was to have been to make a public apology on behalf of the Persian Government for the insult offered to the flag, and to promise better behaviour in the future—quite enough to bring on a severe attack of giddiness and indigestion.

At the appointed hour a British guard of honour was drawn up in the street opposite the entrance to the Consulate, and an armoured car stood by to keep order. The British Consul, Mr. Maclaren, attended with his confrères of Russia and France in full uniform, and the whole of the Persian town police were formed up in a body under the chief police officer. I opened the ceremony by making a brief speech explaining the nature of the occasion and trusting that this day would see the final settlement of all unpleasantness between the Persians and ourselves, due solely to misunderstanding, and inaugurate an era of peace, friendliness and mutual respect. This was followed by speeches in a similar strain by each of the Consuls present. The flag was hoisted and saluted by the guard of honour. The Persian Head of Police came forward, and made an humble apology for the behaviour of the police in the recent troubles and promised on their behalf better conduct for the future. The entire body of police then marched past and saluted the flag, thus bringing the ceremony to a very picturesque and satisfactory conclusion. Mr. Maclaren then handed over his duties to Mr. Moir, who had been appointed Consul in his place, and with whom I parted with great regret.

On the next day we left for Kasvin, reaching our destination without being fired at on the road, which showed that our system of piquets was a very efficient one. At Kasvin I was able to take stock of events up to date and consider our further movements. With regard to the former we had good cause for satisfaction, and with regard to the latter good grounds for hope.

It may be as well to say a few words here as to our achievements up to date, and to consider what would have happened had the Dunsterforce not been in position on the Kermanshah–Hamadan–Kasvin road in February and March 1918 to thwart the Turks in these parts. It

A BRANCH OF THE SEFID-RUD AT RESHT

THE LAST STAGE TO THE SEA 173

is obvious that in such a case enemy detachments would have occupied Bijar and Zinjan, bringing them into direct touch with the Jangalis, and enormously strengthening the position of the latter. In April, May and June, had we not been on the spot to co-operate with Bicherakov against the Jangalis, the latter would have offered no opposition to the passage of the Cossacks through their country, and there would have been no inducement for Bicherakov to go out of his way to fight people who were not intending to molest him. His interest in Persia had entirely ceased, and his only desire was to get his troops out of the country and into the Caucasus, a desire which accorded in every way with the feelings of Kuchik Khan, who would be only too glad to facilitate his departure. The Jangali Army, under its German and Austrian leaders, with supplies of arms and munitions from the Turks would therefore have encountered no opposition in their advance on Kasvin and Teheran, and the armed population of Hamadan and other towns under their democratic leaders would have raised the Jangali banner and joined the revolution. The whole of North Persia would have been overrun with Bolshevism (into which Kuchikism would soon have degenerated); the British Legation in Teheran, the staff of the Imperial Bank and Indo-European telegraph, the Consuls and the missionaries would have had to flee the country and would have been lucky to escape with their lives. It may seem going rather far afield to build all these surmises on the prospects of success of such an army as Kuchik Khan's, but I do not consider the lurid picture which I have drawn of possible contingencies to be in the least exaggerated.

Finally, with North Persia in a state of Bolshevism, the remainder of Persia following suit and linking up with Turkestan, and whole of Central Asia and Afghanistan would be thrown into chaos. This is exactly what the

Germans were playing for in these parts, and it makes one's blood run cold to think how near they were to a gigantic success. It may fairly be claimed that the action of our force was the sole cause of complete failure of this far-reaching effort of German diplomacy.

CHAPTER XI

TURKS, INFIDELS AND HERETICS

GETTING back to Kasvin had quite a sort of home feeling about it.

What a different Kasvin to the one that had made faces at us in February! Now there was nothing but smiles and polite attentions. The Governor called to inquire after my health, the Rais-i-telefon beamed gratefully as I passed him in my car in the High Street and the inhabitants generally looked cheerful and friendly. We had by this time given English names to all the streets in these Persian towns to facilitate the giving of directions to drivers. Thus Oxford Street, Piccadilly and the Strand greeted one in each town with a cheery reminiscence of the Homeland.

The imposing of such a nomenclature on the streets of these historic towns may savour somewhat of vandalism, and we had many kind suggestions as to a more suitable series of names commemorating the heroes of ancient history. These suggestions made a strong appeal to our artistic sense, but in war time the artistic must give way to the purely utilitarian. Names were chosen which the lorry drivers would remember and which would cheer them up. Memories of Rustam the valorous, and other Persian heroes of the glorious past, would have been quite beyond their powers of appreciation or of memory.

It is quite probable that these names made Cyrus,

Darius, Xerxes and Alexander the Great turn in their graves; if so I regret it. In spite of our historic surroundings we had to be ultra-modern; and I am sure that the names of the streets cannot have been half so distressing to the spirits of the ancient heroes as my "Daylight Saving Bill."

As we approached the period of long summer days, it seemed a pity to be letting all that daylight run to waste, so I ordered all clocks to be put forward two hours. Great consternation reigned for forty-eight hours, and after that the new time seemed no more remarkable than the old. The scheme was a great success from my point of view, but a dead failure from every one else's. It certainly resulted in my getting two more hours a day work out of every one, which constituted the success I aimed at, though just how it achieved this happy result it is difficult to explain. At first sight it looks as if the account would balance itself. You commence the day two hours earlier and you end it two hours earlier. But in practice those two extra hours do come into the work-time somehow, and one still has plenty of time for exercise and recreation. And it is remarkable how one's mind is deceived by one's watch. If I had ordered convoys to start at 4 a.m. the drivers and travellers would have felt aggrieved, but when they looked at their watches and saw the hands pointing to 6 a.m. (although they still knew it was 4 a.m. by real time) they were quite cheerful about it.

The drivers had on the whole a rather worried time of it in these days. Not only were their watches put forward two hours, but from Hamadan northwards they had to have a new rule of the road to meet the Russian or Persian traffic rule, "Keep to the right." If, in addition to fictitious time and a new rule of the road they had also been confronted with streets named after Persian heroes, they would have gone mad. It was only just the cheery sign of Piccadilly and Leicester Square that prevented them from feeling that they were living in Wonderland with the March Hare and Alice.

If we had been isolated, both the new time and the change in the rule of the road would have worked quite simply, but as we had now through connection with Baghdad and there was a constant stream of traffic up and down the road, the sudden change on entering and leaving my area was too much to impose on the men, and eventually I had to give up the daylight scheme. The rule of the road had to be enforced, but it was very hard on drivers to have to remember " Keep to the left " as far as Hamadan, and from there on " Keep to the right," and after a month in my area, having become accustomed to " Keep to the right," to pass down the road again and get run in for not keeping to the left.

About this time Hamadan began to misbehave, and it was necessary for the Governor (the same man who had been Assistant Governor on our first arrival here) and Ferid-ud-Dowleh, the leader of the Extreme Democrats, to be removed elsewhere. From the date of their departure all troubles in Hamadan ceased. The Hamadan levies, under Colonel Donnan, were beginning to look quite smart and soldierlike, and were already doing useful work. The supply question was no longer acute. But another fresh trouble occurred in the shape of a money famine.

The actual currency in Persia is not very extensive and our demands were now very large. The problem was how, after being drained of all their coin to meet our requirements, the Bank was to attract the cash back to their vaults (through the medium of depositors and in payment of bills of exchange on London) with sufficient rapidity to meet our next cheque. As our requirements increased daily, it was necessary that the krans paid out to us at one door, and disbursed by us to our creditors, should immediately enter the Bank by another door to be in time to meet our further demands. Thanks to the ingenuity and skill of Mr. McMurray, the manager of the Imperial Bank of Persia at Hamadan, the circulation was maintained at the high speed necessary to cover these transactions. How he did it no one knows; but the miraculous feat was accomplished, and though the horror of a possible financial crisis was added to that of all the other crises, the crash was always averted. Our paymaster, Major Whitmarsh, lived through very anxious times, and his task was not one to be envied.

In view of the probable advent of troops, huts for their accommodation had to be run up at Hamadan and Kasvin, and the staff of engineers under Major Haslam, R.E., was kept very busy.

We now received an addition to our strength in the advent of a party of the Royal Navy under Commodore Norris, R.N., and several four-inch guns were on their way up from Baghdad to enable us to "rule the waves," once we could get a chance of arming merchantmen on the Caspian.

Colonel Battine also arrived and was selected, owing to his knowledge of the Russian language, to take a party to Krasnovodsk, the port on the Turkestan side of the Caspian immediately opposite to Baku. The Krasnovodsk situation was a very favourable one, the strategical importance of that port being only second to that of Baku as, in the event of the latter being taken by the Turks, we could hold the former and still keep the gate to Central Asia closed to the enemy. The Government of Krasnovodsk, under a most able railway engineer of the name of Kuhn, was strongly anti-Bolshevik and pro-British.

From Krasnovodsk the railway runs to Askhabad and Merv, and a strong Bolshevik force was operating in the neighbourhood of Merv, against which a mission under General Malleson had been sent which was moving north from Meshed on to this railway. Colonel Battine at

TURKS, INFIDELS AND HERETICS

Krasnovodsk would be able to work in with Kuhn and assist the operations of General Malleson's mission.

Lieut.-Colonel Rawlinson, R.F.A., also reported his arrival and was at once placed on special duty as an expert in camouflage and extemporized motor machine-gun work, in which he excelled.

With our eyes fixed on the Caucasus we had none the less to keep a very sharp look-out on our left and left rear aganist the activities of the Turks from the direction of Tabriz and Urumiah. The situation at the latter place must be described.

The town and district of Urumiah lying on the west of Lake Urumiah, the southern shore of which is distant about 220 miles from Hamadan, contain a population estimated at about 80,000, the majority of whom belong to the two Christian communities of the Armenian Church and the Assyrian Church, the latter possessing the tribal name of Jilus. The district had for the past year been entirely surrounded by the 5th and 6th Turkish Divisions, against whom the Christian inhabitants had so far put up a very good fight; in fact in a recent sortie they had signally defeated the Turks, taking a large number of officers and men prisoners and capturing considerable war material. The Jilus were trained and led by a body of Russian officers, who had been sent to them for the purpose, under the command of Colonel Kuzmin. Latterly there appeared to have been some misunderstanding between the Jilus and their Russian staff, several officers of the latter having been killed by their men. The rights and wrongs of this trouble I was never able to ascertain, but it seems that the Assyrians suspected treachery on the part of the Russians. Aga Petros, the spiritual and temporal leader of the Jilus appears to have been a man of considerable character and had the reputation of bravery and skill in action.

At this time our party under Major Starnes in Bijar

was within 120 miles of the Jilu territory, but the Turkish Army intervened at Sauj-Bulaq. The two Turkish divisions were very weak, being certainly well under half strength, and the portion south of the lake was quite insignificant.

The Jilus had got a messenger through to us some time before this, asking for help in the matter of arms, ammunition and money. This help we were quite ready to render and a reply was sent by aeroplane directing them to fight their way through the Turkish cordon south of the lake and meet us at Sain-Kaleh on a certain date, when a party of ours would hand over to them the arms and ammunition asked for.

The weakness of the Turks in this neighbourhood suggested the consideration of a plan for permanently ousting them from this area, and for securing the line from Bijar to Urumiah by our own troops. It appeared that only in this way could the Jilus be finally saved from the Turks, as the pressure of the latter would eventually compel surrender in the ordinary course of events. We had, however, too many irons in the fire to permit of this scheme being entertained, and in any case before it could have been brought into operation the Jilus solved the problem for themselves in another way.

According to the pre-arranged scheme they broke through the Turkish troops south of the lake and met our party who had gone up to take the arms and ammunition to them. But there was some delay in their return; wild rumours were spread in Urumiah to the effect that they had all been slaughtered; and the whole population, men, women and children, with all their cattle and belongings came flying down the road to Bijar in appalling confusion, with the Turks and Kurds on their heels massacring and plundering the unfortunate refugees. As soon as they came into contact with our troops the latter formed a rear-guard, and the remainder of the population, probably some 50,000, were rescued and sent down to Baghdad. These events took place at a much later date than this portion of the general narrative, but the whole incident will be more intelligible to the reader if I conclude it here. The refugees were cared for by the British authorities—rationed and encamped in various localities, the strong men being formed into levies and labour corps and the others, together with the women and the cattle, settled in an encampment in Mesopotamia. They are now being repatriated.

So many questions required discussion and explanation that I thought it would be best to make a hurried trip to General Head Quarters, Baghdad; but before doing so I should have to visit Teheran to get the Minister's opinion on several matters.

I accordingly left for Teheran on July 4th, arriving the same day. I found Sir Charles Marling installed in his summer residence at Gulahek, about 17 miles outside Teheran. The Legation grounds at Gulahek are even more striking than those in Teheran. The house stands on the slopes of the foot-hills of the main Elburz chain in a beautiful English-looking wood, with rippling streams of clear water running through the grounds in channels lined with turquoise-blue tiles. My stay in this delightful spot was necessarily short, and on July 7th I was back in Kasvin arranging for my further trip to Baghdad.

I was particularly sorry to have to leave Teheran at this time, as the capital was in the throes of a "Cabinet Crisis," and it would have been interesting to watch the progress of this political upheaval, which excited only very mild comment in this land of topsy-turvydom and which finally proved abortive.

I could ill afford the time for a trip to Baghdad, and it seemed best therefore to endeavour to carry out the journey by aeroplane. I begged for a two-seater plane to be sent up to fetch me down; an endeavour was made to comply with my request, but with the hot-weather conditions in the Mesopotamian plains it proved impossible to get the plane up to me, and I was informed that it would only be possible to convey my by plane the last 80 miles from Mirjana : even in such a short distance the saving in time would be considerable.

No news had yet been received from Bicherakov's force, and I was naturally very anxious to hear how his adventure was progressing. The possibility of our getting to Baku either through the medium of his assistance or on our own, appeared to be daily becoming more hopeful ; I was now in touch with Baku by almost daily messengers, and our friends the Social Revolutionaries seemed likely to be able to bring off shortly the *coup-d'état* which was to throw out the Bolsheviks, establish a new form of government and invite British assistance. To enable me to seize this opportunity, which might occur at any moment, I still lacked troops ; but I had the welcome news that the 39th Infantry Brigade, composed of new army regiments, was being dispatched to me with all speed in motor-lorries under the command of Lieut.-Colonel Faviell. This brigade was composed of the following regiments from the midlands of England, the 7th Service Battalions of the Gloucesters and North Staffords and the 9th Service Battalions of the Worcesters and Warwicks.

The following extracts from a letter written by me from Kasvin on July 13, 1918, will serve to focus events up to date :

" Since last writing to you many changes have taken place, and these changes have in a general way been favourable to us.

" The various situations are rather perplexing, but they are obviously interdependent, and success on any one of the lines reacts favourably on all the others. Omitting the kaleidoscopic changes of the Russian revolution which affect us very nearly, but are impossible to deal with in the scope of an ordinary letter, there are :

1. The local Persian situation.
2. The Baku situation.
3. The Krasnovodsk-Turkestan situation.
4. The Tabriz Turkish invasion situation.
5. The Lake Urumiah situation.
6. The Jangali situation.
7. The raising of levies and irregulars.

" 1. *The Persian Situation.*—From a military point of view everything in this part of Persia is satisfactory ; troops sufficient for safety are already on their way, and there seems a good prospect of my getting in the end sufficient troops to enable me to deal successfully with all the above situations—all of which are at the present moment favourable.

" The bad morale of the Turkish troops, and the quarrel between the Turks and Germans in the Caucasus, suggests a bold policy on our part. One division, exclusive of line of communication troops, would do all the work.

" As regards the morale of the Turks, they probably have 2,000 men in Tabriz. I have a small party of some 60 officers and N.C.O.'s on the Kasvin–Mianeh road, of which the advanced portion, consisting of one L.A.M. car and a few officers under Captain Osborne, was recently within a few miles of Tabriz on the Shabli Pass. The Turks are probably not aware of my extreme weakness here, but they must know that we are not in force ; yet the above party was not molested and men desert from them to us frequently.

" From a political point of view it is difficult in a short space to convey a correct idea of things. From intercepted correspondence it is obvious that a very large number of officials are pro-Turk : the people of the country certainly are not. A great deal of propaganda work is carried on from the Turkish Legation in Teheran, and the Persian Government make no sign of resisting or even protesting against the Turkish invasion.

"I do very little propaganda work, except that I occasionally yield to the temptation of issuing a proclamation putting facts before the people, which may do some good. But our real propaganda lies in our presence here, the appearance and behaviour of our officers and men and the good cash we pay for our requirements. The towns are now all behaving well; all begin with furious anti-British agitation and end soon after with most active assistance and gratitude for security and order. Taking the towns in turn: Enzeli is still run by the Baku Red Army, who object to our presence there, but I think they are getting accustomed to it, and I gradually increase the strength of the detachment there until I shortly hope to be able to ignore the revolutionaries. Resht, which was in the hands of the Jangalis until a few weeks ago, is a large town with hotels and cinemas, filled with a heterogeneous collection of Persians, Greeks and Armenians. It is distinctly pro-British, but I have not had time to clean it up properly yet. Captain Cockerell, my A.P.M., is the last word in A.P.M.'s, and has the worst conspirators either eating out of his hand or locked up in less than no time. When I can get him down to Resht the town won't know itself.

"Kasvin has ceased anti-British agitation. The religious leaders drink tea with me; the leading democrats, Turkish agents and others are either in prison or have fled. By the excellent Intelligence system run by Saunders I can produce a list of principal inhabitants showing their exact degree of guilt.

"Hamadan, since the arrest of the Governor and of the chief firebrand Ferid-ud-Dowleh, is quite quiet and has not forgotten to be grateful for famine relief, which in the early days when I had no troops was of more value than many machine-guns. Bijar, Mianeh and Zinjan are all quiet and contented. With all this I do not allow myself to be lulled into a false sense of security, and I am prepared to meet an outbreak at any time in any of these towns. With all the enemy activity around us and the weakness of my small isolated parties in distant areas the risk is considerable, and the marvel is that nothing has so far happened. Zinjan is held to be fanatical, pro-Turk and anti-British. On the entry of my party into the town two of their servants were murdered in the streets by day for serving the British, yet the total strength of my party there had to be at one time as low as twenty officers and N.C.O.'s. But we grow stronger every day and the risks are less.

"The capital is quite unlike the rest of Persia. It still keeps up real neutrality, and the first sight on entering the town is the flags of the German and Turkish Embassies. An Austrian officer, whom I rode up to to have a good look at, startled me by taking off his hat and bowing. The Parliament does not sit, and the Cabinet is quite useless and any work it does is against our interests. I have just returned from Teheran, where I stayed three days with the Minister. A Cabinet crisis was in progress, but showed no signs of becoming serious. Teheran is the centre of all enemy propaganda, as it not only contains the enemy Legations, but is a harbour of refuge for all the firebrands in the provincial towns whom I fail to arrest.

"As regards the general military situation, the time is ripe for bold action on our part. The Armenians are not yet finished, and continue to hold their own bravely in isolated localities such as Alexandropol and Urumiah. The Turks are sick of the war and sick of the Germans and have no money. The Germans are quarrelling with the Turks and finding it harder to put up troops than we do. The Turks want to take Baku, the Germans want to stop them from doing so.

"2. *The Baku Situation.*—The power is still in the hands of the Sovietski Vlast (let us call them S.V.'s), another name for the Bolsheviks. They are in touch with the Central Committee at Moscow, but are daily losing power. It seems probable that the Social Revolutionary party (called S.R.'s for short) may oust them at any time. But as Baku depends on Astrakhan for food and ammunition it will not pay the S.R.'s to turn the S.V.'s out until similar action has been successful in Astrakhan. I interviewed Cheliapin at Enzeli a few days ago and attach a short précis of our conversation, from which it will be seen how uncompromising is the attitude of the S.V.'s.

"I have had several talks with the S.R.'s, whose programme is far more suitable for our purposes and is constructive instead of being, like that of the S.V.'s, purely destructive. They want our aid, especially financially. I keep on friendly terms with the S.R.'s, and they know they could rely on us for a great deal if they got the power into their hands.

"Bicherakov sailed for Alyat at the beginning of the month, taking with him five of my officers and four armoured cars. I went to see him off at Enzeli and we mutually agreed on plans which give great hope of success, but which I will not repeat here. He has caused great consternation among the other Russians by throwing in his lot with the Bolsheviks, but I am sure he is right. It was the only way to get a footing, and once he is established it will be a case of the tail wagging the dog.

"None but myself, Russian or English, believes in him, but I do so sincerely. In any case I should have to compel myself to believe in him, as he is literally our only hope at the present moment. He is all for Russia, and the plans he intends to carry out are in the interests of Russia in general and the North Caucasus in particular, but they entirely coincide with our interests.

"I have had practically no news of him since he left and I am naturally anxious. His whole scheme may be a failure, the risks are great and the temper of his men a little uncertain. The Russians here all think they will desert when they get near their homes. I do not share this opinion, though I think some may go.

"3. *The Krasnovodsk Situation* from our point of view has not developed. I am sending on a small body of officers and men, to see how they are received. If the cotton there can be saved from the Germans it will be a great thing; at present it is being shipped up the Volga via Astrakhan for their use. Turkestan is hard to understand just at present and the news we get is very conflicting, but there seems no doubt that the people are inclined to put politics on one side and to accept any form of foreign aid that will lead to a restoration of order. Next in importance to the cotton question is the question of the very large number—possibly 30,000—of German and Austrian released prisoners in Turkestan. If my mission is well received it might be possible seriously to hamper German movements towards Afghanistan in the event of their capturing Baku.

"4. *The Tabriz Situation.*—The Turks have established themselves in Tabriz and have probably about 2,000 men there. I do not see that they have much chance of increasing their strength without altering their present plans in the Caucasus. I do not think that they contemplate an invasion of Persia via Zinjan and Kasvin, but if they do I should soon have sufficient troops to secure that line. They would like to draw off my troops in that direction and content themselves with the occupation of just the north corner of Azerbaijan, including Ardebil and the port of Astara on the Caspian. They would then join hands with the Jangalis, and their scheme would, if successful, at the cost of very few troops give them (a) supplies, (b) a port upon the Caspian, (c) the cutting off from the South Caspian of British movements. They have no enterprise, however, or they would long ago have turned my detachment out of Mianeh, whereas they allowed a very small party to remain on the Shabli Pass till quite recently. Owing to the defection of the Persian Cossacks who it was hoped would act with my party, the L.A.M. car was nearly captured, and the Turkish failure to do so shows how little they are worth.

"5. *The Lake Urumiah Situation.*—This is the most interesting of all, and promises most. All the schemes are interdependent, and our success in Urumiah would mean moving the Turks from Tabriz, joining up with the Armenians near Alexandropol, threatening the whole of the Turkish movement in the Caucasus, and helping Baku and the Caspian situation.

"An aeroplane flew on July 9th to Mianeh, where we had prepared a landing-ground and small stock of petrol. On the 10th it flew to Urumiah, returned to Mianeh, picked up petrol and returned here after a most successful flight. Lieutenant Pennington, the aviator, carried a message from me to Aga Petros, the fighting cleric of the Assyrians. On alighting he was received with a most tremendous ovation, having to submit to having his hands and knees kissed by almost the entire population. The town being entirely surrounded by the Turks had had no news for about four months. They were certain that we had no troops in Persia and were equally certain that we had taken Mosul. They were therefore on the point of fighting their way through to us in Mosul—a population of 80,000 with perhaps 10,000 fighting men. The result would have been a terrible massacre of Christians and the needless surrender of Urumiah to the Turks.

"All this Pennington was just in time to prevent. We

TURKS, INFIDELS AND HERETICS

are taking ammunition up to them and have arranged to meet at Sainkaleh on July 22nd, they fighting their way through the Turks at Sauj Bulaq, where there is no great force. The whole of the Turkish division is in the area south-west of the lake, but the division is weak and dispersed and the operation should be successful. If it prove successful and I can follow up with British troops and hold the line Hamadan to Urumiah, we outflank Tabriz and secure rich crops which the Turks are now engaged in reaping.

"6. *The Jangali Situation.*—The Jangali bubble was pricked at last on June 12th, when Bicherakov fought the Battle of Menjil Bridge with his Cossacks and one squadron 14th Hussars. . . . The aeroplanes are especially useful, as troops fighting through the dense jungle would be terribly handicapped and casualties would be high.

"7. *Levies and Irregulars.*—We have now three groups of levies at Hamadan and Kasvin, with a total of 800 men. They have already been useful in holding posts on the roads and passes and in forming escorts. They are good value as a political move, and are quite useful to the above extent; but I never expect to use them against the Turks.

"The irregulars are being raised by Wagstaff from among the Shahsavens and by Starnes from among the Kurds at Bijar. I wish them to be not merely mercenaries but to be actuated in the first place by a dislike of the Turk and a desire to fight him on their own ground. They will only be assembled for short periods to carry out raids. Both the Shahsavens and Kurds ought to work well on these lines.

"The Turks are playing the same game, and I have told my parties that their first efforts should be directed to countering the enemy's schemes.

"In the early days of the war the Germans were badly let down by their levies, to whom they paid vast sums of money, in exchange for which the levies did nothing and deserted when trouble came; I am therefore working on a system of payment by results, which should prove satisfactory. We have not armed either the levies or the irregulars, so they have no temptation to desert.

"In conclusion I should like to repeat what I said earlier in my letter, that a great deal of our success here has been due to the demeanour of the few troops under my command. The general appearance and behaviour of the N.C.O.'s has produced a most favourable impression on the Persians, and they realize that the British soldier is a very different article to any soldier they have met before. From intercepted letters I learn that Kuchik Khan complains that he finds it hard to work up any feeling against us, as we do nothing to arouse the resentment of the populace—he wishes we would."

The following is a note recording the conversation between myself and Cheliapin at Enzeli on June 28th:

"Cheliapin is the same leader who presided at the meetings at Enzeli in February, when the combined committees of Bolsheviks and Jangalis prevented the departure of the first party of Dunsterforce for Baku. Many of the delegates are quite interesting men to meet, but Cheliapin is of the worst type. He is convinced of his own wisdom, but he is thoroughly stupid and has very little education; he is dictatorial in his manner, talks loudly and has no desire to hear the other side of the question. Like many of the peasant class he is cunning and suspicious, and the absolute honesty of my arguments and intentions only intensify his belief in my treachery. His mental attitude is pugnacious and his mouth is filled with all the well-worn tags of revolutionary orators. He can talk for hours in a rasping and unpleasant voice, but is quite incapable of making a single original remark.

MIRZA KUCHIK KHAN : RETURNED TO CIVIL LIFE

TURKS, INFIDELS AND HERETICS

"He suspects Great Britain of having taken advantage of Russia's temporary difficulties to seize North Persia, and he will not believe me when I explain that our occupation of this country was due to (a) the necessity of guarding our right flank in Mesopotamia, (b) the desire to keep a road open from Baghdad to Baku to help the Caucasus.

"I am inclined to believe that Cheliapin is an honest patriot, but I fancy his brother revolutionaries suspect him of feathering his nest

"Like most Russians he sees a deep ulterior motive in any action on the part of Great Britain, and credits Englishmen with a Machiavellian cleverness that is quite the opposite of the English character. My frank statement to him that we took no side in the revolution, and that we came to the Caucasus only to help the people to keep out the Germans and Turks, was the only thing that made him smile during the whole conversation. He certainly believes that we want to capture and hold for all time the Baku oilfields, to obtain various mineral concessions in the Caucasus, and to reinstate the Czar. His only wise remark (which was probably not original) was, 'Whether you like the Bolsheviks or not, you make a great mistake in not recognizing them. The Germans at once wisely recognized the Bolsheviks and then attacked them; you refuse to recognize them and yet you offer them help.'

"The only change his attitude had undergone since our last meeting was that on the former occasion he said, 'We have no quarrel with the Germans now that peace has been declared and we like them better than we do you.' He now says: 'Germany has betrayed us, and we will fight against the Germans to the last drop of our blood.' Of the Jangalis he used to say: 'They are good, honest patriots fighting, like us, against a criminal monarchy for freedom and the rights of man.' He now says: 'The Jangalis are merely highway robbers and should be exterminated.'

"The term 'Sovietski Vlast' is now used instead of 'Bolsheviks.' Sovietski Vlast means the power of councils. It is meant to include the revolutionaries of all parties.

"The Social Revolutionary party (called the S.R.'s for short) are a party of growing strength who will probably oust the Sovietski Vlast in a short time. It is their declared intention to do so. I asked Cheliapin about this and he said, 'The idea is absurd; they work with us on our committees, where they have a proportion of representative commissaries.' This sounds very well, but the Baku S.R.'s told me they refused to accept the offer and had refused to appoint any commissaries or work with the Sovietski Vlast.

"Cheliapin wished England to help Baku with arms and motor-cars in exchange for oil and petrol. All offers of troops or military instructors were out of the question.

"His chief argument against the introduction of British troops into Baku was that the Germans in North Russia would at once retaliate by taking Petrograd and Moscow. Finally he said, 'It is no use you and I talking, we should never agree. It is impossible for one like me who knows what freedom means to talk to one who subjects himself to a King and Crown!'"

To show the sort of anti-British propaganda that was being worked against us at Baku at this time I give this interesting extract from a Baku newspaper dated July 16, 1918.

"THE ENGLISH IN PERSIA.

"When the question of the occupation of North-Western Persia was decided on by the English Imperialists the whole country, the entire people, who are generally passive and quiet, were filled with disgust.

"Their helpless cries of anguish, horror and hate must

have reached the ears of the Russian slaves of English money, but their ears are deaf when convenient.

"The half-wild, famished, powerless people gathered into bands and threw themselves at every car or cart that they suspected to be carrying English.

"There were cases of murder.

"The rebels did not allow cars to pass if Persian silver was found on the passengers in large quantities, as the only source of this silver for Persians was the English Bank, the buying and bribing capacity of which is well known to the Persians.

"The leaders of Persian democrats in vain tried to turn the stream of popular indignation into a channel of fruitless protests.

"When the English delegation arrived at Enzeli with General Dunsterville at its head on their way to Tiflis in order to bring pressure to bear on the Trans-Caucasian Government, the representatives of the Persian Social Democratic Committee held guard at the Russian Military Revolutionary Committee, and were only satisfied when it was settled that General Dunsterville would not be allowed to pass to Tiflis but would 'clear off' to Mesopotamia. For the Persians know that the wheel of an English Ford is more destructive than the hoof of the Hun's horse.

"Between Hamadan and Kasvin, near Ab-i-Garm, the Persians killed the passengers of a Russian lorry and a Ford, in all ten people, suspecting that they were English.

"The hostility of the Jangalis to the Russian troops arose only because they could not convince the latter that they ought not to be the instruments of the Imperialism of the English. Even after his defeat by Bicherakov, with the few remnants of his dispersed force, Kuchik Khan attacked convoys and is still attacking English Fords, braving the armoured cars and machine-guns. (During one of the attacks the English had some men killed and wounded.)

"Arrivals from Enzeli say that Kuchik Khan has again gathered his force, and with new vigour has commenced guerilla warfare against the English. The exploitation of the native populations in the English colonies and occupied territories where they find no resistance is being carried on in the most shameless manner, and the natives are treated like cattle.

"Our soldiers (from Bicherakov's detachment) who were in Mesopotamia fighting in front of the English line realized very well the English tactics 'Making other men pull the chestnuts out of the fire.' If the English get you you become an Indian (native). This is the result of their labours.

"... But as soon as the news of the Russo-German peace arrived and the Russian soldiers voted a return home, the attitude towards them changed and the British annoyed them in all ways.

"The wounded and sick that returned from Baghdad say that the insults became intolerable and the treatment from the doctors was disgusting.

"The hero of R. Kipling's story complains that since India has had self-government, the 'naukar' does not pronounce the word 'Sahib' with sufficient respect. General Dunsterville, Colonels Rowlandson and Clutterbuck, are specialists in trading in live stock obtained from Russian Counter-revolutionaries, and may they be content. The figure of the social 'naukar' is already seen, with its hand to its forehead humbly murmuring 'Salaam'..." This completes the effusion.

The sneer at the Russian Counter-revolutionaries was of course meant to be a hit at my Russian officers. The statements about the feeling of Bicherakov's men towards the British force in Mesopotamia, alongside of whom they were fighting, are entirely untrue, and are inserted solely for reasons of hate propaganda. The real feeling was one of sincere friendship.

CHAPTER XII

IN TOUCH WITH BAKU

ON July 14th I left by motor-car with Captain Bray, and arrived at the Head Quarters of the 14th Division at Mirjana, 400 miles from Kasvin, on the evening of July 17th, continuing my journey by aeroplane on the next day, and arriving at Baghdad just at daybreak on July 18th.

We were glad to note on the way down the enormous improvement in the road. Work is being seriously undertaken on the whole stretch from Kermanshah to Khanikin, and it now bears no resemblance to the snow-covered track and seas of mud over which we pushed our cars in February.

I remained at General Head Quarters, Baghdad, for forty-eight hours, leaving again by aeroplane to Qasr-i-Shirin, 106 miles, on July 20th, and thence by car 160 miles, reaching Kermanshah the same evening, a very good day's work. On July 22nd I inspected Major Macarthy's group of levies near Hamadan, and was extremely pleased with their progress. They were drawn up in line, with the cavalry on the right as at an inspection of regular troops, and a band performed throughout the inspection with remarkable rigour.

On July 23rd, after a good many breakdowns on the road due to bursting of tyres and engine trouble, we arrived at Kasvin, having been absent for nine days, during which much had been taking place. My visit to Baghdad, which was very necessary, had been carried out just in the nick of time, as it was obvious that we were now on the verge of the Baku enterprise.

At Baghdad I had been able to discuss many minor but important points as well as the major points of Urumiah and the question of petrol supply. The authorities at first were horrified at my suggestion to exchange motor-cars for petrol, but petrol was indispensable. The Baku people would give it on no other terms, and the purchasing price was extremely favourable. Mesopotamia required every car they could get, but the small number I required formed a hardly appreciable proportion of the available supply, and my demands were accordingly agreed to.

I received news at last of Bicherakov's movements, which I was sorry to hear had not met with any great measure of success. Disembarking his force at Alyat on July 5th, he had hastened forward to take over the command of the Baku Red Army operating astride of the Tiflis railway towards the bridge at Yeldakh over the Kura River. His own troops were hurried up to stiffen the Red Army, who seemed to be very lacking in enterprise, and who were already being driven back by the Turks. All hope of securing the bridge had gone owing to the pusillanimous behaviour of the Baku troops, who had allowed the Turks to possess themselves of this all-important point without making any great effort to thwart them.

The Caucasus–Islam army might still be beaten in the field, but Bicherakov soon found to his disgust that no reliance at all could be placed on the Red Army troops, who frequently gave ground without firing a shot, and his own men were all that he could count on for any real fighting. Under these circumstances there was nothing to be done but to fall back on Baku, contesting each mile of ground and delaying the enemy sufficiently to enable the Baku people to prepare a proper line of defence covering the town, a precautionary measure which they altogether neglected. As an example of the behaviour of the Red Army troops I will relate an incident that resulted in the loss of one of our armoured cars at this time.

Bicherakov ordered a reconnaissance to be carried out by one of his Cossack squadrons supported by a British armoured car. The party passed over a bridge which was held by a strong detachment of the Red Army, and they impressed on the commander of this detachment the importance of his post, as this bridge carried the road over an impassable nullah on their only line of withdrawal. The reconnoitring party carried out their duties and proceeded to withdraw. On arrival at the bridge they found that it was in the hands of the Turks. The Cossack cavalry put up a very good fight in the endeavour to regain possession, and to cover the withdrawal of the armoured car, but the effort did not succeed ; the cavalry suffered very heavy losses, and the armoured car fell into the hands of the Turks. One cannot help smiling at the idea of troops in action leaving their posts to attend political meetings, but these comic incidents have tragic endings, and in this case the amusing behaviour of the Red Army soldiers meant the lives of many brave men and the loss of the armoured car. When freedom is carried to the extent of permitting men to leave their military duties during the progress of an action, war becomes impossible.

This is the first example of such failure of duty recorded in the history of this campaign, but it will not be the last. We soon learnt that such conduct was the rule and not the exception.

Arising from such behaviour on the part of the Red Army soldiers a feeling of dislike and hostility grew up between the Cossacks and them, which ended in Bicherakov severing his connection with these worthless troops. Throughout July he made every endeavour to stem the Turkish advance, but his efforts, unsupported by the local troops, were in vain.

In the last days of July the Red Army and Bicherakov's force were driven back into Baku, and the Caucasus-Islam army may be said to have practically captured the town; that is to say, they were in full possession of the heights above it and within 3,000 yards of the wharves, with no troops opposing them.

But at this moment one of those miracles occurred which seemed so frequently to intervene to defer the actual fall of Baku. For no reason that can yet be ascertained, the Turks, in the hour of their victory, were seized with an unaccountable panic and turned and fled. It is said that their flight was due to a rumour that their rear was being threatened by a large cavalry force, but whatever the cause may have been, the result was that the entire army turned and ran, hotly pursued by the Armenian troops, who returned to Baku, proudly (but falsely) asserting that it was they who had saved the town.

During the progress of this fighting Bicherakov realized that the Red Army leaders were trying to force him into a position whence retirement would be impossible, and where it was equally certain that in the hour of danger they would afford him no support. They had come to the conclusion that his professions of Bolshevism had only been a pretence to enable him to get a footing in the Caucasus (which was a very right conjecture), and that he was ready to turn round on them at the first opportunity. They therefore decided to forestall this move by rounding on him and pushing him into the arms of the Turks.

The knowledge of this intention on their part caused

Bicherakov to separate his force entirely from the town troops, and to draw off to the north between Baladjari Railway Station and the seacoast. From here he could again join in the fight from a very advantageous point on the left flank of the Turks, if the town did not fall; and if the town fell, he had a good line of retreat up the railway to Derbend, where he would be sure of water and supplies. His position had been rendered extremely critical during the last few days, owing to the failure of the Baku Committee to meet any of his demands for ammunition or supplies; and signs of a Turkish movement towards the railway line on his right eventually led him to decide on severing his connection with Baku and continuing his retreat to Derbend. The Baku people regarded this as a betrayal, and Bicherakov as a traitor; but we ourselves found later what impossible people they were to deal with, and had equally to withdraw our troops to save them from being needlessly sacrificed.

At the same time, this move of his at this juncture was a fatal mistake. In war time a commander has to form rapid decisions and adhere to them. The decision formed may be absolutely right in view of the known factors, but after action has been commenced an unforeseen factor appears that indicates quite another line. Bicherakov was right to consider the town as already in the hands of the Turks, and this would compel his immediate withdrawal, so he accordingly acted in the light of this assumption. But, as I have described above, the town did not fall into the hands of the Turks, and, had the "partisan" detachment remained in position north of Baku and joined hands with us a few days later, Baku would never have fallen. All we required later, and entirely failed to get, was some sort of stiffening for the local troops, some formed body of regular soldiers who could set the right example and help us to force reluctant troops into the firing line.

Another fatal mistake which was also made at this time by the town troops affords an example of the futility of entrusting military operations to men who have not been trained to think on military lines. The strategy of Baku was directed not by the so-called military authorities, but by the tinkers and tailors who formed the governing committee. The lack of forethought on their part, and the lack of cohesion on the part of the troops, robbed Baku of the fruits of the miraculous victory over the Turks. The brave troops returning to town to loll in restaurants and recount to their admiring women-folk the deeds of valour they had accomplished in defeating and pursuing the Turks would have been better employed had they just carried the pursuit a few yards further, driven the Turk off the high ground west of the railway line and dug themselves in. Preferring, however, to return to the ease and comforts of the town, they left this position to the Turks, and thereby rendered any further defence of Baku merely a deferring of the evil moment. The Turks held this position throughout the remainder of the fighting, and, with troops that hardly knew how to march and obeyed no orders, it was impossible to attempt to dislodge them.

In describing Bicherakov's movements in the course of the fighting round Baku up to this point I have got beyond the date of the general narrative, but when we come to the history of our action in Baku, a knowledge of these earlier events will be necessary, and it will make it clearer for the ordinary reader if I finish the story of Bicherakov's troubles straight away, as I have done in the preceding paragraphs, instead of cutting it up into fragments to secure an actual sequence of dates.

We must now get back to Kasvin and follow the moves of our own force until they lead us finally to Baku.

In the middle of July the first detachments of the 39th Brigade began to arrive in Kasvin. They travelled

IN TOUCH WITH BAKU

from Mesopotamia in motor-lorries as far as Hamadan, and thence motored or marched, according to whether vehicles were obtainable or not, to Enzeli. The greater portion did not arrive in the latter port, however, till late in August. The Ford cars were in a terrible state, and at that moment, when every hour was of value, everything seemed to break down, and I was never able to get any of the detachments to any destination within a liberally estimated limit of time.

The Jangalis had decided about this time to test the mettle of the British troops, who, their German instructors informed them, were notoriously cowardly. In the one or two small encounters we had already had the Jangalis had had reason to wonder if the German estimate of the British soldier's fighting powers was quite accurate, but still, on the whole, they felt that it was worth while having at least one grand attack on the British just to see what would happen.

In fighting irregular troops like the Jangalis it is as a rule hard to get them to concentrate and attack, and unless they can be induced to do this it is difficult to bring matters to a conclusion, and these small campaigns drag on and on interminably. We have therefore to thank their German commander, von Passchen, very much for his success in bringing about the great Battle of Resht, which settled the Jangali question once and for all, and enabled us to make a sound treaty of peace with Kuchik Khan, and to secure the release of Captain Noel, who had been a prisoner for over four months in their hands.

At daybreak on July 20th a determined attack on the garrison and town of Resht was launched by the Jangali troops from the west and south-west. The enemy was obviously determined to put matters to the supreme test by attacking the British detachment under Colonel Matthews, which was billeted outside the southern outskirts of the town in the vicinity of the Russian Consulate. In taking this action the Jangalis were guided by the soundest principle of war, namely, to attack and defeat the enemy's main force in the field. Such action is, however, quite contrary to the tactics of irregular troops such as these, and must naturally be attributed to the leadership of von Passchen. The entire town was at their mercy, and the more usual procedure would have been for them to seize and hold the town itself, whence we should have had great difficulty in dislodging them, once they had secured a firm footing. Their present plan was to combine the two operations; and, while their best fighting men attacked and destroyed our detachment (which numbered about 450 rifles of the 1/4 Hants 1/2 Gurkhas, with two mountain guns and two armoured cars), the remaining portion were to attack and loot the town. The troops allotted to the town attack achieved an easy success, the defence of a town with a 7-mile perimeter being, as I have previously pointed out, quite beyond the power of our small detachment; but the defeat of their main attack on our troops outside the town, and the heavy casualties they suffered in the attempt, reacted on the invaders of the town and caused them to put up only a very half-hearted resistance when we had leisure to set to work to clear them out.

While the fighting was going on between our troops and the pick of the Jangali army on the southern outskirts, a large body of the enemy penetrated to the heart of the town and attacked the British Consulate, which was defended by a garrison of about twenty rifles all told. The unfortunate position of this building has already been commented on; it was surrounded by houses which overlooked it and from which the enemy snipers could fire direct into the courtyard, and reinforcements could only reach it directly by passing through a maze of narrow and tortuous streets. The normal method of reaching

"A MAZE OF NARROW AND TORTUOUS STREETS"

the Consulate from the billets of our detachment on the south was to proceed north along the Enzeli road for 2½ miles, then west by the circular road outside the town for 1½ miles till the Pir-i-Bazar road was reached, and then south into the centre of the town, thus compassing three-quarters of the perimeter.

At an early hour in the morning Colonel Matthews was notified of the perilous position of the party in the British Consulate, and determined to effect their rescue by the direct road that lay through the narrow streets of the town. It was fortunate that these streets were just wide enough to admit the passage of an armoured car, if cleverly steered, and the relieving party, accompanied by an armoured car, succeeded after severe street-fighting in reaching the Consulate just in time and bringing off Mr. Moir and the garrison.

The relief was effected just as the enemy had succeeded in setting fire to the outer doors of the courtyard, and in a short time the Consulate would have fallen and its occupants would certainly have been massacred. This highly successful task was carried out under the command of Captain McCleverty, of the 1/2 Gurkhas, who conducted the operation with great skill.

Repeated attacks on our main body were successfully beaten off, and the Jangalis eventually drew off in despair, having found the British garrison to be made of very different stuff from that which von Passchen had described. Kuchik Khan had had about 2,500 men engaged, and when they eventually broke off the engagement they left over 100 dead on the ground, and fifty prisoners in our hands, the latter including several Austrians. Our casualties all told amounted to only fifty, and the fighting resulted in a victory for our troops that would have been even more signal had it been possible to crown it with a pursuit. The small number of our troops, the nature of the surrounding country, and the fact that the Jangalis were still in possession of the town, prohibited any attempt at pursuit, and as the sun set the firing entirely ceased, and the main attack was withdrawn; but the actual town remained in the hands of the enemy.

The operations during the next two days consisted of getting the Jangalis out of the town. This involved a good deal of street-fighting, but success was mainly achieved by aeroplane bombing, which soon rendered their retention of the various hotels and public buildings impracticable.

By the end of the month Resht was finally cleared of all signs of active Jangali opposition, and came under our effective administration. A military governor was appointed in place of the Persian Governor, who had fled from his unpleasant post, and an excellent intelligence office got to work under Captain Searight, of the Queen's Regiment, who vied with Major Saunders in the cleverness and efficiency of his measures. We had thus finally secured the road to the Caspian, five months after our first hazardous passage in the middle of February. Kermanshah, Hamadan, Kasvin, Menjil and Resht were in our hands, and it only remained to secure the actual port of Kazian (Enzeli) itself.

The road picquets were kept out for some time longer as a precautionary measure, but no further fighting took place, and Mirza Kuchik Khan, now reduced to a sensible frame of mind, began to sue for peace.

To return to Kasvin, there was much important work to be attended to in that rather troublesome town, while we awaited the longed-for summons from Baku. Major Browne, of the 44th Indian Infantry, was proving a very capable commander at Enzeli, and was working hard to clear away the Red Army obstruction in the port. He had some rather delicate negotiations in hand at this time bearing on this point, and it was very necessary to get the obnoxious revolutionary Committee out of the way for a time. They were accordingly invited to visit me in Kasvin to discuss some important secret matters connected with the question of exchange of motor-cars for petrol and other kindred subjects.

I am glad to say they accepted the invitation without our having to apply any pressure, and Comrade Cheliapin with his following duly presented themselves at my Head Quarters—a very meek-looking trio compared to the fierce and uncompromising individuals of earlier days. They had an uncomfortable feeling that their reign at Kazian would soon be drawing to a close, and their forebodings were very shortly to be realized.

They stayed two days with me in Kasvin, which was just long enough to enable Major Browne to carry out what was necessary at his end of the line; they lunched with me and we drank each others' healths in very cheerful mood. We had had so much to do with each other since the hazardous days of February that our common reminiscences almost induced a feeling of friendship.

What we were trying to get at was the exact nature of their relations with Kuchik Khan. We knew that at the time of our first visit to Enzeli they were hand-in-glove with him, but they had latterly pretended that that was merely owing to force of circumstances, and Cheliapin had solemnly promised me that they had now broken off all relations with the Jangalis.

To have arrested the Committee merely as Bolsheviks would have been taking a false step, and would have put the whole of Baku against us. It is obvious that to a revolutionary there can be no worse a person than a counter-revolutionary; we were already suspected of the latter tendencies, and if we had adopted any course of action tending to justify the accusation, we should never have been able to acquire any influence in Baku. There was to be only one plank in our platform there, and that was absolute non-interference with the purely internal affairs of the revolutionaries. The only safe grounds, therefore, on which we could attack the Enzeli Committee were on a charge of complicity with our declared enemies, the Jangalis.

On his departure from Kasvin Comrade Cheliapin very naïvely gave himself away by refusing an escort, and saying, " Oh, they won't touch us, I am sure. I shall fly a white flag on the bonnet of the car, and they will let us through all right." This made it quite certain that they were in friendly communication with the Jangalis, and it only remained to procure proof of this to justify us in carrying out the arrest, which we did a few days later in circumstances shortly to be described.

General Baratov was still in Kasvin presiding over a Committee which was making most praiseworthy endeavours to settle the Persian requisition claims, without being in possession of the necessary funds for the purpose—a somewhat difficult task.

He had received an invitation from the British authorities to visit India, at which he was most gratified, and he intended proceeding shortly to Baghdad in order to avail himself of this courtesy. His position in Persia, as a General without an army, was an absurd one, and a return to his own country was impossible, as a price had been put on his head by the revolutionaries. I had taken a great liking to him, and felt that I should miss his genial companionship. He certainly deserves all praise for his assiduity in pressing the rather farfetched claims of Russia on the British Government. I have never met a more "importunate widow." I had frequently to tell him that the only blot in our friendship was his horrible little pocket-book in which he kept notes of the various points for discussion with me. My heart literally sank within me whenever I saw this book produced ; I knew I was in for a discussion on at least six points, with half an hour devoted to each, provided my time and patience were equal to his demands.

I must record here the agreement made between ourselves and the Russian Road Company to take over temporarily all their property and interests in the road from Hamadan to Enzeli and from Teheran to Kasvin. The road had been constructed by a private Russian company, and was worked as a concession under the Persian Government. Post-houses were built at convenient intervals, and tollgates at every 30 miles. A telegraph and telephone line followed the 380 miles of road, the latter having instruments in every tollgate house. The acquisition of this property with the telephone rights was most valuable to us, and the agreement was an excellent one from a financial point of view. The sum we paid monthly was less than it would have cost us to carry out the repairs to the road, and for this sum we not only got a certain amount of indispensable repairs, but the general control of the whole road, buildings and telephones. The company was glad to have the money for payment of salaries, but their real gain was that by our taking over the road the revolutionaries were prevented from "nationalizing" the company, which would spell ruin to the shareholders and the working staff of engineers.

On July 26th, just in the middle of the Caucasus-Baku fighting which I have described, in which Bicherakov was being driven back into the town, the long-expected *coup d'état* took place at Baku, the Bolshevik Government were thrown out, and replaced by a new body calling themselves the Central-Caspian Dictatorship. Shaumian and Petrov, the two leaders of the Bolshevik party, determined to leave the town with their followers and transfer themselves by sea to Astrakhan, which was now the sole remaining stronghold of the Bolsheviks on the Caspian Sea. They accordingly seized thirteen ships, in which they embarked the greater part of the Red Army, and also loaded them up with the entire contents of the arsenal and all the war material on which they could lay their hands. Had the new Government permitted the departure of these ships it would have been impossible to continue the defence of Baku another day, but luckily the little navy was on their side, and the Dictators rather hesitatingly ordered the recall of the ships; the gunboats pursued, and the whole convoy was brought back into harbour and kept at anchor while the usual interminable discussions took place. The recapture of this convoy is the solitary instance in our experience of Baku of direct decisive action being immediately decided on and carried into effect. The moment the great feat was accomplished the new Government were so out of breath at the rapidity and success of their action, that they very nearly spoilt it all by allowing themselves to be drawn into a week's discussion with Shaumian and Petrov that might have ended disastrously, had we not appeared on the scene and given them the heart to proceed with their good work.

The new Government had no sooner taken up the reins than, according to our pre-arranged plan, they sent messengers to us asking for help. Although troops were not even yet immediately available, except in the form of very small detachments, I decided to accept the invitation, and dispatched Colonel Stokes with a small party of the 1/4 Hants to announce our impending arrival. He reached the town on a very critical date, August 4th, on the eve of a determined attack by the Turks. Although the townspeople were bitterly disappointed at the arrival of only one or two officers and a handful of men, where their uncontrolled imaginations had led them to expect ship after ship pouring out British soldiers on to the quay, yet the mere sight of these fine-looking soldiers inspired them to that extent that, when the Turkish attack took

IN TOUCH WITH BAKU

place on the following day, every man in the town seized his rifle and rushed to reinforce the firing line, with the result that the Turks were thrown back in confusion. This evidence of a fine spirit on the part of the townspeople led us to hope for much later on, but it was the solitary instance of such valour, and hopes based on it were doomed to bitter disappointment.

Troops now began to arrive in small detachments as motor-cars could be found available to transport them to Enzeli, and I sent over Colonel R. Keyworth, of the R.F.A., with an improvised staff to command the fighting troops in Baku.

On August 4th I moved my Head Quarters from Kasvin to Kazian, taking up my residence as before in the Fishery Depot. On our way down we stopped the night as usual at the little post-house in Menjil, where we met a very mournful trio coming up from Enzeli to Kasvin in custody. These were no others than Cheliapin, Lazarev and Babookh. They asked to see me, and I at once went to have a talk with them and find out what it was all about. According to their own account it was all a silly mistake ; I informed them that if that were so they would at once be released with apologies when their case had been inquired into. According to the account of the officer in charge of them they were accused of complicity with the Jangalis, and we had documentary evidence of their guilt in the shape of a letter from Babookh to Kuchik Khan congratulating him on his recent efforts to destroy the British detachment at Resht, and urging him to renew his efforts, while promising all support in his future attempts. This letter was actually handed to me on my arrival at Kazian, and left no doubt whatsoever as to their guilt.

As soon as he had ascertained the undounted genuineness of this letter, Major Browne had decided to seize the opportunity of getting rid of the Enzeli Committee, who had now become an anachronism. The three conspirators were arrested (on a charge of having dealings with our enemies) at the hour of their afternoon siesta, and as soon as they had had time to arrange their garments and put their belongings together they were offered seats in a Ford car and started on the road to Kasvin.

They were apparently quite unlamented, their sudden disappearance caused no stir in the town, and even their own followers evinced no interest in their arrest and deportation. Every one seemed to be glad to be rid of them, and Kazian heaved a deep sigh of relief, which shows how sadly one's best efforts often fail to secure genuine appreciation. Kazian port is a Russian concession forming part of the road concession, and the Fisheries were another concession. Both of these bodies were on the point of being "nationalized" by Cheliapin and Company, and our prompt action just saved them from this dismal fate.

The first thing to do at Kazian was to secure permanently sufficient shipping to enable me to withdraw the troops from Baku in case of necessity. For this purpose I selected a fine vessel of over a thousand tons, with the ominous name of the *President Krüger*, while Stokes in Baku managed to secure two good ships, the *Kursk*, and the *Abo*. These ships we managed to hold until the fatal day when their services were required. I need not enter into details as to how we secured three of the best ships on the Caspian; we should never have been allowed to retain them had the Centro-Caspian Dictatorate suspected our intentions as to their ultimate use. As a matter of fact, every now and then a member of the Government did appear to smell a rat, and several attempts were made to persuade us to give them up, but we always succeeded in holding on to them.

I lay particular stress on this acquisition of the ships because it is a point on which there has been the most unaccountable misunderstanding. I read, for instance, in the newspapers at the time of our evacuation from Baku a surmise to the effect that the Russians must have relented and kindly given us ships at the last moment, whereas it will be seen in the last chapter of this book that the exact contrary was the case.

The *Krüger* was a fine ship and as fast as anything on the Caspian, with the exception of the gunboats, and she had accommodation sufficient for my staff, the clerks, and the office, as well as about 300 men normally; at a pinch she could carry 800 men by utilizing all deck space. We rigged up a pack wireless set which had sufficient range to keep me in touch when at sea with either Baku or Enzeli, in both of which ports the Russians had very powerful wireless installations.

Having cleared the atmosphere by the removal of the obstructive Committee, our next step was to acquire control of the port. In each successive step of these transactions I was urged to use military force; but realizing that that would be a fatal error, I managed to secure all that we required by means of peaceful negotiations.

The key to the Caspian problem was the little fleet, who were now acting loyally with us and with the new Government. At the same time it was obvious that they had their suspicions of "perfide Albion," and any overt act of aggression on our part, such as the arrest of the Committee on grounds other than those on which we had fortunately been able to act, or the acquisition of the port by a display of armed force, would have been too flagrant a display of the "mailed fist" which we were not strong enough to live up to, and which would at once have turned the feelings of the fleet and of the Baku people against us. Moreover, although we had a very efficient staff from the Royal Navy, with some 160 naval ratings, we could never have run the port otherwise than by being on friendly terms with the local authorities and staff. For instance, the keeping open of the harbour is entirely dependent on the efforts of a single dredger. If the harbour staff were hostilely inclined to us, there is no doubt that something would have happened to that dredger, and the harbour would have been useless.

I therefore dealt with the matter of the port on a purely business basis. The income had sunk to almost nothing owing to the fact that everything (except, so far, the port itself) had been "nationalized." All shipping on the Caspian had been "nationalized," and consequently paid no dues. This put the port authorities in a very difficult situation. We drew up a very satisfactory agreement, under the guidance of Commodore Norris, by which we guaranteed all salaries and port expenses, and claimed in return any sources of income.

This agreement was never ratified by the Centro-Caspian Government, and the documents connected with it continued to pass to and fro between them and us up to the time of the fall of Baku; but we had got to understand revolutionary procedure, and regarded this delay in ratification as quite unimportant. Revolutionaries revel in writing and talking, all crises are met by passing resolutions, or haranguing uninterested crowds, so it was obvious that if we neither talked nor wrote, but acted, we should probably get all we wanted. Acting on these lines, we proceeded to put the agreement into force on the day the port authorities signified their assent. We installed an embarkation commandant, and in a few days Enzeli was to all intents and purposes an English port, and has since remained so.

By this I must not be understood to mean that the British Government had any desire at all to acquire any sort of permanent rights in this neighbourhood, either with reference to the port or anything else; the agreement was to last only for the duration of hostilities.

We were not allowed to imagine that our reception

in Baku would be entirely friendly. This extract from one of the Baku newspapers will prove interesting as showing the nature of the propaganda that was being worked against us at this time. The mere title of the paper is another indication of the lack of brevity that characterizes revolutionaries.

"THE NEWS OF THE COUNCIL OF WORKMEN, RED ARMY, SAILORS, AND PEASANT DEPUTIES OF THE BAKU AREA.

"Comrades, workmen, sailors, Red Army, and all citizens of Baku! The agents of the English Imperialists are carrying on counter-revolutionary work; they sow discord among you, they intend to put up the sailors against the workmen, the workmen against the revolutionary Government.

"We have news that the English Capitalists have concluded a close agreement with our local counter-revolutionaries. They wish to destroy our power and put up in its place the power of the English and the Bourgeois.

"The Bourgeois and their despicable dependents are in favour of the English. The Workmen and Sailors are in favour of the Russian Revolution.

"The Bourgeois and their dependents are in favour of cutting adrift from Russia. The Workmen and Sailors are in favour of the unity of the Russian Socialist Federalist Republic.

"The Bourgeois, pledged to the English, bartered souls, pitiful cowards, and all counter-revolutionaries, are in favour of cutting adrift from Russia, for English might, for a new war with Germany. They are against the independence of Russia!

"Away with the English Imperialists!
Away with their paid agents!
Away with the Bourgeois Counter-revolutionaries!

Hurrah for the Peoples Committees!
Hurrah for independent Russia!
Hurrah for Russian Social Revolution!
What can the English give you? Nothing!
What can they take from you? Everything!
Away with the English Imperialists!
All to the front! to arms! All to the saving of Baku!"

The days at Kazian were very busy, getting in the small detachments of the 39th Brigade and embarking them for Baku, arranging for supplies for incoming troops, arrangements for their accommodation, councils of debate with emissaries from Baku, negotiations for peace with Kuchik Khan and settling matters connected with the working of the port under our control.

Among the visitors from Baku was Dr. Araratiantz, a representative of the Baku Armenian National Council. This official expressed to me the disappointment of the Baku people at the small number of British troops arriving in the town in response to their appeal for help. They had expected much larger reinforcements, and he tried to tie me down to definite promises of definite numbers, which I refused to give. In order that his mind should be made quite sure on this important subject, and also in order to prevent him from saying later that we had not acted up to our obligations, I put the gist of our conversation into a letter, the contents of which I begged him to communicate to the Baku people. The letter was as follows:

"KAZIAN,
"*August* 7, 1918.

"DEAR DR. ARARATIANTZ,

"In order that there may be no doubt on the subject, I desire to put in writing my views on the questions you put before me yesterday evening.

"The three questions dealt with were —

(1) The defence of Baku.
(2) The position of the Armenians in Erivan.
(3) The position of the Armenians in Julfa.

" As regards (1) the following is my reply :

" The defence of Baku appears to me to be quite feasible, and its capture by the enemy forces extremely unlikely, *provided that the inhabitants of Baku are heart and soul with us in our determination to defeat the enemy.* It is not sufficient that the town should merely be held, but the defence can only be successful when the Baku troops can issue from the town and defeat the enemy on the field of battle. This particularly affects the Armenians, who form a great proportion of the fighting strength. The forces suffer at present from lack of organization, owing to which much of their gallantry in fighting is displayed in vain. I shall shortly have sufficient officers to remedy this defect.

" The entire defence of the town cannot be undertaken solely by the British who, as you know, have to maintain large armies on several different fronts, and the distance from Baghdad to Baku, with no railway, makes the maintenance of our troops a matter of some difficulty.

" I can assure you, however, that every available man will be sent to Baku as soon as possible. If with the help of some British troops your comrades are ready to undertake the defence of the town, victory is assured. But on the other hand, if your men are undecided and half hearted, it would be better for you to say at once that you do not intend to fight to the end, and you would be well advised to make what terms you can with the enemy, after first giving me time to withdraw my men.

" As regards (2), it is a pity that the splendid fighting material available at Erivan cannot at present be utilized by the Allies. I can hold out no hopes of any assistance in their direction in the immediate future.

"The same applies to (3), though in this case the Armenians are much nearer to a possible line of Allied offensive.

"I write thus clearly in order that I may not later be accused of holding out false hopes which in the end I failed to fulfil.

"There can be no doubt whatsoever of the eventual victory of the Allies and the restoration of the Armenian people, and this alone can give you hope in this dark hour of despair.

"Any change in our policy that may affect the situation in the regions concerned I will duly notify to you."

As the events described in this chapter have been numerous and varied, it will be as well to sum up briefly the achievements of the month.

We commenced with the visit to Baghdad to put everything in train for the next move, when our connection with Head Quarters might be entirely severed. It was pretty certain that when the Turks saw us arriving in Baku they would strike the long-threatened blow from Tabriz on our Persian lines of communication, and it would be necessary to be prepared to meet this.

We next noted the course of Bicherakov's operations on the Tiflis railway, in which we lost one of our armoured cars.

Then came the move of the 39th Brigade by motor-lorry from Baghdad. Resht was taken by the Jangalis and retaken by us, and peace negotiations were entered into with Kuchik Khan.

An important agreement was entered into with the Russian Road Company by which we entirely took over the road with its personnel. A similar agreement was entered into with the Kazian port authorities. The Bolshevik Government was thrown out in Baku and its place taken by the Centro-Caspia which demanded our aid, and our first troops were sent to Baku in compliance with this demand. We had arrested and deported the Enzeli Bolshevik Committee, and secured sufficient shipping to enable us to carry out an evacuation from Baku if necessary. A busy month!

CHAPTER XIII

WE MAN THE BAKU LINE

HEAD QUARTERS were transferred on board the *Krüger* on August 10th, and we hauled down the Red flag of the revolution, substituting the orthodox Russian flag. We had no sooner done this than we received a deputation from the local Committee asking as usual for explanations and wanting to know if we were " counter-revolutionary." I was beginning to get sick of the word and replied that I was not, but that also I was not a revolutionary and therefore absolutely objected to flying the Red flag. We effected a compromise permitting us to continue flying the Russian flag, but only on condition that it was upside-down. This I agreed to cheerfully, and we sailed the Caspian Sea thereafter under the Serbian flag, the revolutionaries not being aware of the fact that the Russian flag upside-down constitutes the flag of Serbia.

The *Krüger* proved to be a very comfortable ship, and we soon got on good terms with the crew. The saloon was just large enough to hold us all at meal times with room for one or two official guests. The only adornment consisted of a life-size portrait of Oom Paul, with his inevitable top-hat surmounting his remarkable features. Many of my officers were South Africans who wore the two medals for 1899–1902, and it was amusing to observe their startled expressions when they came into the saloon

WE MAN THE BAKU LINE

to report and were confronted with this striking portrait.

The lightning sears the night landscape on the eyeball. Here is a flash in the blackness through which we were stumbling.

A British General on the Caspian, the only sea unploughed before by British keels, on board a ship named after a South African Dutch president and whilom enemy, sailing from a Persian port, under the Serbian flag, to relieve from the Turks a body of Armenians in a revolutionary Russian town.

Let the reader pick his way through that delirious tangle, and envy us our task who will!

The Captain was a first-rate man, a good seaman and a brave fellow, and the other officers seemed a fairly good lot. It took us some little time to understand the system of command on board a revolutionary ship. The arrangement was that all movements, and the general affairs of the ship, were run by the ship's committee, of which the Captain was an ex-officio member. In theory this was absurd; in practice we found that the crew were very amenable, and after we had weeded out one or two undesirables, we seldom had any trouble. They never actually refused to carry out any order given them through the Captain, though there were occasions when they carried out movements without consulting him. They had a great idea of the value of their own lives, and once or twice at Baku, when the ship was being shelled and I happened not to be on board, they quietly put to sea till they were out of range, returning when all was quiet.

The first undesirable we had to get rid of was a drunkard. This unfortunate specimen was addicted to a vile Caucasian drink with the suggestive name of "Gee-gee"—a kind of arrack. My attention was first called to him by his peculiar performances on the wharf when under its influence. He had not altogether the appearance of being drunk, but behaved rather more as a madman. When I saw him he was dancing a sort of wild hornpipe, at the conclusion of which he drew a long knife and proceeded to run amok, leaping on to the ship and scattering the crew right and left. At last he vented his fury on the only thing that was unable to get out of the way, which was a water-melon, plunging his knife into it until the unfortunate fruit was bleeding from every pore. He then sat down on the deck and quietly allowed himself to be arrested. One of the crew stated that he was often like that, that he never stabbed or wanted to stab anybody. He invariably contented himself with a water-melon or something similar, and always waited to be arrested as soon as his fury had spent itself. It also appears that this extraordinary behaviour is common to all the devotees of " Gee-gee."

Before leaving Enzeli I was anxious if possible to bring our negotiations with Kuchik Khan to a close, and secure the release of Captain Noel, who had several times been reported dead, but whom we now knew to be alive. But in the end I had to sail without having actually concluded the peace.

In the meantime I received a deputation from Lenkoran, a strip of the coast on the south-west of the Caspian where the Russian frontier runs southward from Baku as far as the port of Astara. The province is bounded on the west by the high mountains which are a continuation of the Elburz range, and on the north, where it includes the Mughan Steppe, by the River Aras. The original inhabitants are Mahomedans of mixed Persian and Tartar origin, but the country has, during the last half century, been colonized by the Russians, who now occupy all the settlements on the fertile low-lying lands bordering the sea, while the original inhabitants, who are not very friendly to the colonists, are rele-

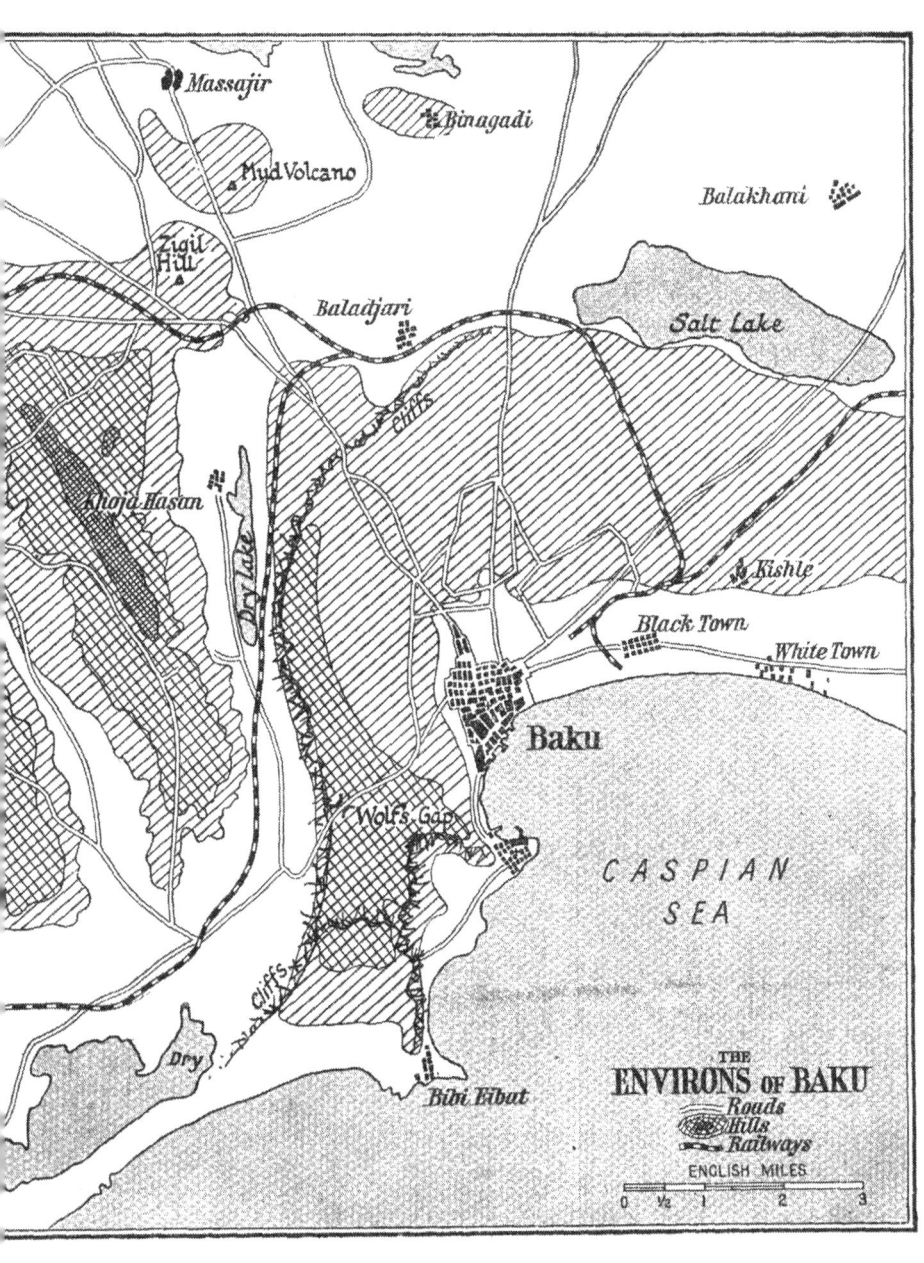

gated to the mountain tracts. The colonists are of pure Russian descent and have all passed through their period of military service. They possess a fairly good armament, including several field guns, and they claim to be able to turn out 5,000 fighting men.

The deputation brought letters from a Russian officer who had been selected by the residents of Lenkoran to guide them in military affairs. Since the revolution the colony had been compelled to run on the lines of inevitable " committees," but the people were apparently quite untouched by the real spirit of the revolution, and paid little heed to the committees, while relying solely on their military commander as a sort of autocratic ruler.

The colony is rich and possessed large supplies of grain, which they were anxious to exchange for cotton fabrics and ammunition. They desired to work with us in any scheme of opposition to the Turks, and might be very helpful to us in Baku, the colony lying on the right flank of the lines of communication of the Caucasus–Islam army. They brought a cargo of flour and other commodities as a present to the force, and desired to enter into some permanent agreement with us, their first demand being for instructors for their troops. They also placed the services of two small steamers at our disposal.

In response to this appeal I sent a small party of officers and N.C.O.'s to visit Lenkoran and make themselves acquainted with the situation there. With this party I sent two Russian officers, who were to remain in Lenkoran, Captains Stepanov and Gurland, the former a distinguished artillery officer who had seen much service in the early stages of the present war, and the latter a specialist in matters of supply. It was very necessary to make the most of these friendly advances; the troops of the colony might be useful to us tactically, and the supplies were very important, in view of the fact that Baku was on the verge of starvation.

On August 15th I received a letter from Colonel Keyworth at Baku, of which the following is an extract:

"You have already received maps showing the present line of defence. It mostly lies along the top of a stony cliff, except on the extreme left and on the right. Rifle pits are badly sited, so that the occupants can only shoot into the air. Even if they were sited on the extreme edge, the fire would be a very plunging one, and the position is equally unsuitable for machine-gun fire.

"The front is not wired; there are no communication trenches. The total length of the present front is 21,000 yards. Rifles available (exclusive of our own men) are some 6,000, organized into twenty-two battalions, which vary in strength between 150 and 500 men.

"I am trying to get the Commander-in-Chief here to dig trenches and wire the front, and they have started this morning after much consultation with our machine-gun officers. The Commander-in-Chief stated yesterday that he had enough wire to cover the whole front. They now seem to think they have no wire at all. It is difficult to find out what stores they have; they do not know themselves. The North Staffords are occupying the extreme left flank and also have about 100 men near the centre of the line, where one of the local battalions had to be withdrawn (or rather withdrew themselves and melted away).

"From our present front line to the enemy is some 2,000 to 3,000 yards. The only possible position for siting trenches is either withdrawn from the crest or at th foot of the cliffs; both have a good field of fire. I prefer the latter, as the moral effect of retiring to the former would not be good. If the former were occupied, machine-guns would have to be placed half-way down the cliff.

The top of the cliff itself is of course a shell trap and the exact edge easily ranged on. So far, wiring has started only on the left flank, where these conditions do not prevail, and to-morrow I am deciding definitely which line to occupy.

"The whole position is absurdly close to the town, and enemy batteries could at any time, with aeroplane observation, bombard the harbour and destroy shipping, especially if they bring up heavy guns. Before Baku can be safely held an advance must be made and a position farther west occupied, and preferably one some 15,000 to 20,000 yards west of the town. This would render the docks and shipping safe from shell-fire. At present we cannot advance, weak as the enemy is. We must first reorganize and hold on where we are.

"Organization of local material for war purposes is also badly needed. They are short of nearly all stores and material. Yet I fancy there is plenty in the town and it only needs requisitioning. Most of the population of the town, both friendly and otherwise, are armed, and there are a quantity of rifles amongst them, but the Government at present feel themselves too weak to take any action. When the Petrov question is settled we may be able to go ahead and disarm the whole lot.

"They are gradually getting a move on, but it takes time. The battalions have not yet been reorganized, there are practically no officers, and men return to the town when they like. There is no supervision over ammunition, and much is wasted. Sanitation is bad. When Colonel Warden and some other officers arrive we can get to work better.

"The one idea of the Baku army is to retire and rest from those parts of the front occupied by us. Hence 100 men of the North Staffords now occupy a front of some 4,000 yards, and their reserve (Baku army) is too far away to be of any use to them—altogether a somewhat impossible situation. Time is precious; yet they dawdle. Of course I know this must be so at first. Political discussions and meetings and speeches occupy far too much valuable time. We have tried our best to make friends of Petrov, but so far he refuses to meet us. Yesterday the Central Committee delivered an ultimatum to him. He replied that he could not possibly fight in alliance with English Imperialism against German Imperialism, and that he would leave the town, but insisted on being allowed to take sufficient ammunition to enable his force to maintain its military efficiency, as he had a possibly enemy country to move through before reaching Moscow. In the meantime he has locked up all his ammunition and guns in an arsenal and has sentries posted everywhere. I told the Central Committee to get a definite statement from Petrov of what he wishes to take away and what he will leave behind. There are the wildest rumours of what he possesses. Some say 500 guns and thousands of rounds of ammunition. Others say five guns with hardly any ammunition. The question should be settled to-day, but you know what these people are—all talk and no action. I have at last got them to agree on a definite line of defence, which runs roughly as shown on enclosed map. The part coloured green has been up to now, and still is, entirely open and not even patrolled, so that Turks have got round into the Tartar villages to our rear which are now full of armed men and machine-guns, and it is this we are trying to clear up now. But these infernal politics hinder one at every turn. Russians will not work with Armenians; Russian officers are said to be with the Turkish troops fighting against us, and therefore Russian officers here decline to go to the front. Most of all this is only talk, but the Armenian seems anxious to work with the Russian if only the Russian will let him.

"We are now living in this hotel, where the food

alone costs £2 10s. a day per head. The food question is becoming acute. It seems Baku has imported nothing for two months and that they have only a week's supply left. The workers in the oilfields are being starved; the price of food augments daily. Lenkoran is giving us nothing at present, as the small railway is not completed, and they lack means of transport, which of course you know. Crawford, now on the Food Control board, is, however, getting a move on, and they are beginning to think, and to-morrow I hope they will begin to act. It is a great pity Petrov will not come in with us, but we have done our best, short of begging on our knees.

" Another difficult problem here is the transport question. Cars cannot go everywhere and animals cannot very well be fed in any numbers; water also has to be carried a long way. The only solution seems to be man-handling from the cars to the front line at night. The heat here is intense and one drips all day and night, making any energetic supervision of this very long front impossible without cars; and even with cars a very large amount of walking has to be done. The army here can give us no cars, instead they expect us to supply them. They either cannot or will not understand the difficulties we have, and insist on looking on us as universal providers."

This letter brought the situation very clearly before us, and it was evident that our departure for Baku could no longer be delayed, in spite of the fact that we had not yet actually signed the peace treaty with Kuchik Khan. Military advisers from Baku were also anxious that I should still further delay my departure; they had an absurd idea that it would be better for me to wait until we had a large body of troops to transport to Baku; when these were ready I should cross over with them and make an imposing entry into the town. They thought that if the British General arrived in the town with only a handful of troops, the effect of the disappointment would be so exasperating to the townspeople as to take all the heart out of them.

But, on the other hand, as I was aware that I should never have a large body of troops with which to make this imposing entry, I thought it best that the people should realize as soon as possible the exact limits of our assistance and get over their disappointment as best they might. Moreover, it seemed to be that there was something peculiar in the reiteration of their remonstrances at my departure. Accordingly on August 16th the *President Krüger* left Enzeli, and arrived at Baku on the afternoon of August 17th (the run is about eighteen hours). As we neared the harbour we caught our first glimpse of an oilfield, passing the Bibi Eibat wells, which come down to the water's edge 2 miles south of the main town. The borings are very close together, and each well is worked by machinery that requires the use of a derrick. A cluster of 1,000 wells means therefore 1,000 derricks. These are built of wood with asbestos and tin sheeting to minimize the risk of fire, and in the distance the fields look like ghostly forests of dried-up trees. Our course lay midway between the Bibi Eibat fields on the west, and Narghin island on the east. Narghin island was, up to the time of the revolution, the main warprisoners' camp in this area, and it was chiefly from here that the Austrian prisoners of war were released who now swell the ranks of the Bolshevik army in Trans-Caspia. Under the shelter of this island lay the thirteen ships of Shaumian's and Petrov's fleet, guarded by two small gunboats.

The view of Baku from the sea is most imposing, the buildings near to the sea-front being in the most florid European style, with a distinct leaning towards German artistic notions. In the centre of the town

OIL WELLS AT BIBI-EIBAT

rises the dome of the Russian Cathedral surmounted with a gold ball and cross. The town, as may be seen from the map, lies in a crater-like cup, the ground on the west and north rising gradually for about 2 miles till it reaches the line of cliffs, whence it falls precipitously to the bottom of the desert valley by which the railway from Tiflis enters Baku. The population is approximately 300,000, chiefly Armenians, Tartars and Russians : there are also a few Georgians and Greeks, and smaller colonies of British, French, Americans and others. The country is entirely barren, except for avenues of trees grown in the town with the aid of the new water supply, and for the surrounding villages, which are really oases in the midst of sandy deserts and partly dried-up salt lakes.

The chief oilfields are at Binagadi, Balakhani and Bibi Eibat. The town as marked in the map shows only the central portion, but the dwellings are really continuous for 9 miles from Bibi Eibat in the south to the White Town in the east. Black Town is the centre of the oil refineries and is a mass of oil and petrol reservoirs, between which are crowded the workmen's dwellings. There are 2 miles of wharves on the sea-front opposite the control town, and there are, as a rule, not less than sixty steamers in the harbour. The streets are paved in the usual Russian style with cobbles, which renders them very durable but unpleasant to ride or drive over. Horse trams run in the main streets, but these had been suspended before our arrival, owing to a shortage in the supply of horses and the excessive cost of forage.

The *Krüger* was berthed at the most western wharf belonging to the Caucasus-Mercury Steam Shipping Company, opposite the centre of the business part of the town. Alongside of us lay the *Kursk* and *Abo*, which I have before mentioned as having been secured with a view to a possible evacuation. Guards were kept on all three steamers with orders to resist any attempt at interference, and the three ships were kept together throughout the whole of our time in the port. As soon as we were tied up Colonel Keyworth came on board to report; all was going well so far, and the Turks were showing no great sign of activity. I also received a message from the Dictators (there were five of them), asking me when it would be convenient to me to receive them. The remainder of the afternoon was spent in inspecting the excellent building we had secured as a hospital, and the officers and men's billets. Every available officer and man was already in the front-line trenches, but there remained in the town the supply and transport staff, the sick and a small detachment to furnish necessary guards.

Colonel Keyworth had selected the enormous empty Hôtel d'Europe as his Head Quarters, and a certain number of billets were engaged in the Hôtel Métropole. Both of these buildings and their appointments were most luxurious, gilt furniture and crimson plush curtains offending the eye at every turn. But the luxury ceased at this point. It was not possible to be luxurious in the matter of food, because there were only the merest necessaries to be got. I noticed from the bill of fare at the Métropole that an ordinary dinner of soup, fish, joint and water-melon, with bread inclusive, cost one hundred roubles—that is at pre-war rates of exchange £10, at present rates of exchange about £2—a large price for a meal and a poor one at that. I will refer to the question of prices later. In the case of the Hôtel d'Europe an arrangement had been made for an inclusive daily rate which was not much more than twice the amount of the allowance that officers received to feed themselves on. On board the *Krüger* I was able to make cheaper arrangements with the caterer, to whom we paid eighty-two roubles a day and supplied our own bread, which brought the daily rate just under £2.

WE MAN THE BAKU LINE

On the next day, August 18th, at daybreak I set out with Colonels Duncan and Hoskyn to inspect the front line. Beginning on the left, where the high ground runs down in a series of rocky spurs to the sea one mile west of Bibi Eibat, the position was a good one, with a fair field of fire and with a naturally guarded flank. The North Staffords had made every use of the folds in the ground and their trenches were already sufficiently deep to afford a certain amount of cover from artillery fire. On their right was an Armenian battalion who, inspired by their activity, had also made some efforts at entrenching. From here the position followed the line of the cliffs due north for about 7 miles from the sea, where they curve round to the west; from this point the line continuing north came gradually down on to the level ground, crossing the railway about 1 mile west of Baladjari junction, and continuing thence to the Mud Volcano, at which point (12 miles from the left) it turned back east for another 2 miles to Binagadi hill. This was of course the weakest point in the whole line which, instead of turning back here, should have continued due north to the sea, thus giving a total length of about 19 miles with both flanks resting on the sea. The right portion of this line between the Mud Volcano and the northern coast required very few men for its defence, as the Masazir salt lake, an impassable obstacle, occupied one-half of the distance. This gap on the right had been originally caused by the withdrawal of Bicherakov's detachment, and the local military authorities attributed all the blame to him; but as they had had three weeks in which to remedy the defect and had done nothing, the fault now evidently lay with them alone.

Various efforts were now being made to fill this gap, but the Turks in the meantime had got well round this flank, and all the villages from north to east of the town (which are nearly owned by Tartars) were full of small Turkish detachments and local Tartar levies. The main Turkish position ran on a slightly higher ground on the opposite side of the railway valley roughly parallel to our line, and 3,000 to 4,000 yards distant. The cliff portion of our line was almost impregnable and could be held by very few reliable troops, but the local troops were not reliable and our small numbers could not be cut up into an indefinite number of weak detachments. We held therefore the left with the North Staffords, with a detachment of theirs at " Wolf's Gap," 3½ miles from the sea, and another at the Mud Volcano, which was the obvious danger point of the line. The Mud Volcano detachment was strongly supported by two complete battalions of local troops in Baladjari railway station, which was all we could do to render the position reasonably safe. As a matter of fact, when trouble came those two battalions were not at Baladjari station, and no support was consequently available.

On the arrival of the Warwicks and the Worcesters both of these battalions were sent up to strengthen this portion of the line. These general dispositions were not materially changed throughout the fighting that ensued. The actual command of the troops in the field devolved on Colonel Keyworth and that of the Infantry Brigade on Colonel Faviell. With so small a number of troops available it was not possible to retain anything in the shape of a general reserve from our own men; this was supplied by the town troops, but was never at hand when required. Supports and local reserves were all we could manage from our small detachments, and they were able on many occasions to save the situation. The actual number of British troops in the position was never more than 900.

This general description will enable the reader to form some idea of the town, the country and the position. As regards the town the greater portion is built in the ordinary continental style. The quays in the neighbourhood of our wharf are beautifully planted with trees and brilliantly lit by electric light at night, when all the people of the town come down to promenade on the boulevards at the water's edge. It must be remembered that the country itself is quite barren; on the west, between us and the Turks, there is not a sign of a single tree, or a blade of grass, and every movement of the troops by daylight can be clearly seen by the opposing sides. As regards the steep cliffs I have mentioned, they are about 500 feet in height and quite precipitous, but a good road leads up the face of them from the enemy's side, debouching on to the upper plain at a point known as the Wolf's Gap : it was here that we had our centre detachment of the North Stafford Regiment.

The local troops, who were for the most part Armenians, dug very little in the way of trenches, and when urged to do so replied, " Why should we dig ourselves in ? We do not want to dig ; cowards do that ; we want to fight ! " They liked to line up in a row just behind the edge of the steep cliff and fire off their rifles at the sky ; they frequently did this when there was no sign of a Turkish attack and when the nearest Turk would be behind cover about 3,000 yards away.

Although we were in full view of the enemy's lines throughout the tour of inspection, the Turks never fired a single shot at my party on this day, which shows that they had more sensible ideas on the subject of controlling ammunition expenditure than our local troops had.

Returning to town I met the Dictators by appointment and spent much time in discussing the situation with them. They expressed to me their deep disappointment at the small number of troops we had sent, to which I replied that I had stated from the first that I could not pledge myself to numbers. I also called on the

Commander-in-Chief, General Dukuchaiev, his Chief of the Staff, Colonel Avetisov (Armenian), and his Adjutant-General, Colonel von der Fless. I invited them to a state banquet on board the *Krüger*, where we exchanged many polite speeches and discussed the various problems connected with the defence of Baku. General Dukuchaiev was not a product of the revolution, but a real Russian General who had originally been with the troops fighting in the neighbourhood of Trebizond. He was an exceptionally refined and pleasant gentleman to deal with, but his character was not suited to the position of Commander-in-Chief of a revolutionary army, for which it may be admitted the qualifications are rare. Only a strong personality could exercise effective command over troops without discipline and who were not liable to any laws, regulations or punishments.

His Chief of the General Staff, Colonel Avetisov, was also a regular officer of the old Russian Army, and a good type of the Armenian soldier. He possessed considerable individuality and was quite fearless in his speech towards the revolutionaries; but he was ill, and I think his work suffered on this account. He eventually went over to help the people in Lenkoran, and his place was taken by Colonel Stokes.

Colonel von der Fless was also a Russian regular officer, young for his rank, and he was one of the very few people we met in Baku who knew what a day's work meant.

On the following day, August 19th, I continued my inspection of the front, and later in the day met the ten members of the Armenian National Council, among whom were some remarkable men of considerable ability. I also paid my respects to the War Minister, General Bogratuni (an Armenian), who was still an invalid, suffering from the after-effects of amputation of his left leg, and I was favourably impressed by him. There were endless

"THE QUAYS IN THE NEIGHBOURHOOD OF OUR WHARF"

WE MAN THE BAKU LINE

official calls to be paid or returned, the details of which I need not record.

The five Dictators were naturally the most interesting of our acquaintances; they were intelligent and zealous, and of the average age of thirty years. The three workers were Lemlin, a former naval officer, Yarmakov, also a naval officer, and Sadovsky, a man of the people. Of these three Lemlin was the most attractive, Sadovsky the most capable, and Yarmakov the strongest character. The idea of five Dictators seemed to me absurd, and I suggested their choosing one of their number as a single Dictator, but all five unanimously declared they were not good enough to run things single-handed. As a matter of fact Yarmakov was a strong enough man, but he was unbalanced and headstrong and quite unfit to steer the ship of state. Throughout our stay in Baku he had his suspicions of our intentions and thwarted us at every turn.

Commodore Norris was naturally impatient to get to work with the arming of merchant steamers, but it was a very delicate matter to handle. I begged for six ships to begin on, and gave the following reasons for requiring them:

1. The Baku fleet had big guns, but no means of replenishing their scanty supply of ammunition. When they came to the end of their supply the guns and ships would be useless.

2. Even while the Russian ammunition lasted our ships would be a great addition of strength. The combined fleets could operate against the railway line, which ran close to the coast south of Baku and which the Turks were using to bring up ammunition and supplies.

3. With my constant movements of troops between Enzeli and Baku it was not safe to run the risk of a Bolshevik ship from Astrakhan attacking one of my

transports. I therefore required my own armed ships for protection.

The above were the principal arguments in favour of my proposal, though there were others.

The navy and the Dictators were dead against the proposal from the very first, and it was only with the greatest difficulty that we eventually secured two ships, the *Ventur* and the *Ignati*. Their armament was not completed when we were compelled to evacuate Baku, but these ships and others that came away with us were eventually armed, and have since taken part in encounters with Bolshevik ships.

The Baku fleet felt that once we possessed armed ships their importance would sink to zero, and they naturally put up a very strong opposition to the proposal. And as the fleet controlled the Government it may be realized that we had considerable difficulty in finally squeezing a very reluctant consent out of the latter. The Caspian sailors admired our bluejackets extremely, but they did not want to see them entering into competition with the Caspian Navy for the ruling of the sea.

The replies of the Dictators to my arguments were:

1. It would be better to let them have our guns and mount them on their gunboats, and so save us all the trouble.
2. The question of our armed ships aiding the existing fleet in its general duties was evaded.
3. They would be glad to convoy our transports for us (though they had no ships to spare for this purpose).

The whole opposition was of course headed by Yarmakov, who never gave in, but remained in a dissentient minority of one, even when permission was finally given.

The situation in Baku was evidently as bad as could

be, and it seemed certain that the most we could hope for would be a passive defence, which obviously entails defeat in the end. We had already set to work to reorganize and train the local units, but it would be a long time before they could be considered mobile. They would be able to sit in their trenches and put up a stout reistance, and we would be grateful enough to them if they would only do this (and they did not). But the saving of Baku could only be effected by mobile troops, who would issue from their trenches and attack the enemy in his position. The only real plan for defending Baku was to secure and hold the heights due west of our lines now occupied by the Turks. If no forward movement on the part of the local troops were possible, the fall of Baku became only a matter of time. Still, even with the certainty of the fall before us, every day that we could delay the entry of the enemy was of value to the cause, and new factors might arise which would alter the balance in our favour.

If the Turkish troops were of any value at all they would have taken the town before now, and there was no hour on any day when they could not have taken it by a determined assault. There was never a day or a night that there was not a gap of one or two miles in our line owing to the intentional failure of local battalions to reach their destinations. The town was full of German and Austrian released prisoners, and the Tartar population of 80,000 might also be regarded as Turkish sympathizers. So the enemy should have been able to obtain most detailed information of our dispositions.

We might reasonably expect another thousand of our own men, which would at once solve all problems by giving us the power of counter-attack without which our situation was hopeless and with which we could ward off any Turkish attack. The Caucasus–Islam army was not made of the stuff that will stand up against counter-attack, for which they gave us great opportunities on each occasion when they carried out an assault.

Should we not receive the hoped-for increase to our numbers, we might get a detachment of Bicherakov's back to the town. If all reinforcements for the town failed we might still hope for a diversion such as the materializing of a contemplated attack by the Erivan Armenians on the Turkish lines of communication in the rear of the troops attacking Baku. Even an indication of this would suffice to produce a panic in the Caucasus–Islam army.

It must be remembered that we had come to Baku under very different conditions from those originally contemplated, the chief difference being the absence of Bicherakov's force, on which we had relied as a nucleus of disciplined troops to set an example to the others. Without Bicherakov we could still carry on, but it meant a greater consumption of time, and this was altogether a time problem.

Had Bicherakov not made that fatal move to the north, but awaited our arrival in Baku, the town would never have fallen. But the future can never be foreseen, and I do not think that he can be blamed for carrying out the move, having due regard to the circumstances in which he was placed. Moreover, up to the last moment, I could not give him any guarantee as to when we should arrive or even if we should arrive at all.

Had we been able to instil the least spirit into the local troops we might even without outside aid have won the day, but cowardice and disobedience of orders were rampant. I am far from wishing to brand Armenians as a whole as being cowardly; my remarks refer only to the Baku Armenians, who are very different from the Armenians of Erivan and other mountainous tracts in Asia Minor, whose bravery has frequently been recorded. And I do not blame the Armenian soldier of Baku for his cowardice, which is at best merely a comparative term. He was not a soldier by instinct or training, but just an ill-fed, undersized factory hand. A rifle was pushed into his hand and he was told to go and fight. He had no equipment, no proper instructors, no decent officers and no regular arrangements for food supply. Meanwhile as he sat in the trenches, with the bullets whistling by and the shells bursting overhead, he knew that most of his mates had skulked back to town and were having tea with the girls, and why shouldn't he go too ? A Baku soldier could hardly be expected to prefer the crash of bursting shells to the delight of ladies tea-parties and the ease and comfort of life in the town.

I hold no brief for the Baku Armenians, but I think it only fit to say that under such circumstances no troops could be expcted to display a high standard of valour. And finally I would add that there were many cases of individual bravery among them.

The following is a translation of a handbill scattered throughout the town at this time in the vain hope of arousing some military enthusiasm:

" DECLARATION.

" We, the ' frontiviki ' (veteran first-line troops) of the 1st and 2nd Model Regiments for the defence of the front, and machine-gunners of the 2nd and 4th Companies, at the present calamitous moment, when the enemy is on three sides of us, when the ring that surrounds us grows tighter and tighter, when shells are bursting in the town, call upon all citizens capable of bearing arms, and appeal to all to whom the Fatherland is dear and in whom the spark of holy fire for the salvation of Russia has not yet been extinguished, to go to the front and defend their interests.

" The present moment is not the time to engage in

election agitations, or to attend meetings. All, as one man, should go to the front for the defence of our native town.

"We must first finish one thing before we start another.

"We protest against the Bolsheviks participating in the elections for the Soviet. That is not the place for the traitors of their country, and against whom we, the defenders of the revolution and proletariat, have been struggling.

"Germans pawns must not be the arbiters of the fate of Russian territory.

"We protest against the fact that many thousands of healthy citizens, armed from head to foot, walk about the town and terrorize the peaceful inhabitants, whereas the place for these heroes of the rear should be at the front.

"We, frontiviki, who in a fateful moment are holding the front and saving the town, and who up to the present have not complained of our fatigue after being in the trenches without relief, protest against the shameful agitation behind the lines, and, expressing our full confidence in the Centro-Caspia only, we demand that the Dictatorship of the Centro-Caspia, with its own power, eliminate unworthy persons holding positions of authority in various organizations, and substitute worthier people.

"(Three signatures.)"

CHAPTER XIV

SHORT OF EVERYTHING

I HAVE omitted to mention a rather curious incident that happened just on the day that Colonel Stokes arrived in Baku. On August 4th the *Kursk* (which had since become one of our ships) had arrived at Baku from Astrakhan with a German mission on board.

As soon as the ship was tied up alongside the wharf the leader of the mission stepped ashore and asked to be directed to the Turkish Head Quarters. His surprise and disappointment were considerable when he was informed that there were no Turkish Head Quarters in Baku, that the Turks had not taken the town and never would. The entire party were taken prisoners, and I know nothing of their eventual fate; they were quite probably released by the town authorities and may have joined the many Germans and Austrians who were wandering all over the Caucasus and Trans-Caucasia at this time. It is probable from their certainty of the town being in possession of the Turks, that positive news of its capture had been sent by the wireless operators at Baku to Astrakhan on July 29th at the moment when the town had appeared, as previously related, to be already in the hands of the Turks.

Questions were now asked officially by the Government as to our reasons for the arrest of the Enzeli Committee. These questions were prompted by the party who were out to discredit us in the eyes of the Baku people by proving that our real aims were counter-revolutionary. I have already described the events that led to the arrest of these officials, and it was lucky that I was able to give an explanation that not only silenced our accusers, but tended to sway popular feeling very much in our favour. The town had no sympathy with renegades who had allied themselves with our enemies in Persia, especially as it must be remembered that the Jangalis had recently done to death several Russian parties on the Kasvin–Enzeli road. The behaviour of Cheliapin and his associates was therefore regarded as being as traitorous to his own folk as to us.

One of the many difficulties that confronted us in Baku was the financial question. I cannot explain this better than by giving extracts from a report written by Major Newcome, of the Canadian Infantry. I was extremely lucky to find in my force this officer of considerable financial skill and experience, and, while I was relieved by his efforts of all anxiety, the British Government was saved very large sums by the protection I gained thereby from local sharks. I had first discovered his talents in Persia and had consequently attached him to Bicherakov's force to supervise the financial arrangements, and he now returned to me in Baku, bringing dispatches from Bicherakov, who, since his entry into the Caucasus, had been promoted to the rank of General.

The report, it will be seen, was not written until immediately after the evacuation, but I insert it here, as a proper knowledge of the exchange question will be necessary for the general understanding of our situation in Baku. I may also note that while Major Newcome gives three rates of exchange, the local Government refused to recognize any difference between the three currencies, and made it a criminal offence to differentiate between them. It was necessary of course for them to issue such an order, otherwise the Baku notes would have been worthless even in Baku, whereas by this means they were compulsorily given a certain value. But in large transactions it was naturally found that if you produced Baku notes the seller regretted extremely he was quite out of stock, whereas the same man had plenty to sell if he saw Nikolai notes in your hand.

The following is the extract:

"I arrived in Baku on the 19th August with dispatches from General Bicherakov, who had just captured Derbend a few days previously. Owing to the uncertainty of normal methods of communication, it had been decided by the General that some one in touch with his plans and situation generally should visit General Head Quarters, Dunsterforce.

"On my arrival here I was placed in charge of financial matters, and on looking into things found that we were confronted with a very serious state of affairs, it being necessary to provide for large expenditure for which no previous provision had been made, and in the entire absence of the usual machinery to facilitate exchange. The banks and larger private business concerns had some time previously been nationalized, the skilled staff done away with, and now ignorant and unscrupulous committees were endeavouring to carry on. As a consequence of the many restrictions, etc., confidence on the part of the public had been entirely destroyed, and the only money in circulation was that required for the daily necessities of life.

"Under these conditions, and also knowing that Persia left only a very limited field, I took immediate steps to persuade the various men at the head of financial matters, that the banks must be reorganized, personal enterprise encouraged and free use made of money deposited in the banks, and other means adopted calculated to restore confidence.

"It was necessary for me to secure some fairly large sums of money almost immediately, and with some little delay an advance of five million roubles was obtained from the Dictators.

"My attention was then turned to the sole remaining means of raising money, namely the selling of either sterling or krans. Transactions in sterling were only available in small amounts, and only from people who wished what money they had hoarded transferred to a safe place, and it would have taken some time to get in touch with these. In fact, only at the time of our leaving had I made arrangements for the first transfer of this nature of any importance, covering some ten million roubles, and delivery was to have taken place the day of the evacuation. The matter of rates took some time to adjust and had finally been settled as follows: Nikolai roubles 57 to the sovereign, Kerensky 71, and Baku bonds 121. These rates were about $5\frac{1}{2}$ points better than the present kran exchange for sterling.

"By these quotations it will be seen that there were three different kinds of money in circulation, all of a different value outside of Russia and also to the initiated in Baku. The Nikolai was the old pre-war currency, the Kerensky was the issue of the early revolution, while the Baku bonds were a purely local issue. When the banks were nationalized all balances were seized, and drawings were restricted to 300 roubles a month. People then naturally began to hoard their money, and normal circulation ceased. In order to keep up some circulation for business purposes these local issues were then made, at first on the town securities with proper legal guarantee, but latterly merely printed as required.

"It is estimated that the total of these local issues amounted to something in the neighbourhood of two

SHORT OF EVERYTHING 243

hundred and fifty million roubles. These different issues all had different values in krans approximately averaging as follows. Nikolai 65 krans per 100 roubles, Kerensky 46–47, Baku bonds 36–40 depending on the trade demands. This rate was also influenced by our heavy and continuous purchases of roubles in Persia for operations in Baku and the north. The first two issues were really current and accepted in other parts of Russia, but the Baku bond outside of Baku was looked on as valueless, and was of no use for the purchase of supplies, etc., at outside points. There was only a very limited supply of the first two currencies. Taking these matters into consideration I immediately decided that for all Baku purchases, expenses, pay, allowances, etc., payments would only be made in Baku bonds.

"I also took steps to sell krans, accepting roubles in exchange at rates varying as above, and from this source obtained some eight million.

"All through my operations it was my intention to establish some means of securing roubles direct for sterling exchange, and in another couple of weeks some of the schemes under way would have borne fruit. This means of obtaining funds had two advantages, firstly easing the situation in Persia, and secondly a much more favourable rate could have been obtained than is at present in force in Persia for the selling of sterling for krans. By obtaining sufficient funds in this way, the selling of krans would be limited to the usual trade requirements only, and thus a double saving effected."

I should explain here that the officer originally entrusted with the financial arrangements for the force, Major Whitmarsh, had had to remain behind in Persia, being quite unable to deal with the two situations. I had foreseen that on moving to Baku I should be handicapped in this way, a large number of my best officers and men being employed in Persia in appointments from which it was impossible to release them. For instance, my position would have been enormously improved if I could have had the services of Major Saunders, Captain Searight and Captain Cockerell, but to withdraw these officers from Persia would have meant a breakdown there. The result was that my Intelligence department in Baku was very weak, and I suffered much from lack of information as regards the enemy; every officer was fully employed—mostly in the firing line—and I had no surplus to draw on to undertake special tasks. Even Colonel Duncan, my able A.Q.M.G., whose services would have been invaluable, was naturally unable to sever his connection with Persia entirely, and was only occasionally able to help me in Baku.

The excitement of the day was now the disarming of Shaumian and Petrov's men, and the unloading of his ships and restoration of their contents to the main arsenal of the town. The Government had nerved themselves to the undertaking, and the Bolshevik leaders submitted after the firing of one or two shots by the gunboats. The disarmament was very methodically carried out, each ship was brought in turn up to the arsenal pier (the arsenal itself being almost on the quay) and the contents of the hold removed and stacked on the wharf. The ships had not been very carefully loaded, and the contents of the hold varied from big-gun ammunition to gramophones, perambulators and stores of every kind, from which it is obvious that the statement of the Bolsheviks as to the necessity of removing a certain amount of ammunition for purely military purposes was only a cloak to cover a general looting of the town.

The process of disarmament lasted several days, at the end of which the thirteen ships were permitted to proceed to Astrakhan with their disarmed troops, a rather weak proceeding. It meant thirteen ships permanently lost to Baku, as the Bolsheviks of Astrakhan naturally retained all they got hold of. On the other hand the Government was not prepared to imprison such a large number of Bolsheviks, and was equally unwilling to have them loose in Baku, so perhaps their departure for Astrakhan was the best solution of the difficulty.

Shaumian and Petrov were imprisoned in the town jail. They were released on the day of the fall of Baku, when they crossed over with a small following to Krasnovodsk. Unfortunately for them, Bolsheviks were at that time very unpopular in this Trans-Caspian port, and the entire party was destroyed.

We were now confronted with the difficulty of food supply. Baku produced nothing itself, and since the revolution very little had been imported from outside. In the days when the seller, and the buyer, and the shipper, each made a profit out of the transaction, the import of the necessary food-stuffs from various Caspian ports was a very simple affair. But under the socialistic plan of nationalization, imports had practically ceased.

The goods in the port of departure were nationalized, and the ships that transported them were nationalized; under such circumstances it was not to any one's interest to import anything whatever. Private enterprise had entirely ceased, and State enterprise was a failure.

If the town was to hold out against the Turks for any length of time, it would be necessary for us to concern ourselves with the question of supplies not only for the troops but for the civil population. I deputed Colonel Crawford, assisted by Mr. Clarke (a Baku resident), to inquire into the matter and report. Colonel Crawford was in command of the Locker-Lampson armoured cars, but as he showed signs of business ability, I added to his normal duties this of the Food Control Board. This is his report :

"Herewith a short report on the various organizations dealing with the purchase and distribution of food in Baku and as to how the food situation is affected by local politics.

"The Commissariat (Food Control Department) is responsible for the purchase of supplies and distribution in the town through its agents in various districts. It is responsible for negotiation with the other departments as regards transport, shipping, etc., as well as with the authorities of neighbouring districts.

"The distributing organizations are:

"(1) The Co-operative Societies and their shops, controlled by a Co-operative Society Federation.

"This organization is at present extremely unpopular owing to its inability to cope with the food shortage or to ensure fair distribution amongst the people. It does not appear to be more corrupt than any other department, but it is composed mainly of small men, only partly educated and without sufficient commercial or industrial knowledge to manage such an organization efficiently. Its recent unpopularity has driven them to ask my assistance to improve this condition. They have very slight political significance, and are at the moment chiefly concerned about preventing their organization from being deprived of its present position.

"(2) The House Committee Organization, composed of:
  "(a) Central House.
  (b) District Committees.
  (c) Sub-District Committees.
  (d) House Committees.

This is the people's own organization. Originally organized for the purpose of giving people protection from robbery and violence, it was looked upon by the Bolsheviks as counter-revolutionary. Later it was made use of by them, and is now a legalized organization. It has latterly obtained a footing in the distribution of food. It is responsible for the statistics, and House Committees draw food for their members from the Co-operative shops.

"This organization represents the householders and more responsible citizens of the town. The head organization, the Central House, is composed of prominent citizens, educated and commercial men. It is composed largely of pure Russians. Its tendencies are anti-socialistic.

"(3) Workmen's Committees.

"These assume on the oilfields the functions of the House Committees. The government is maintained in power by the workmen, whose policy is governed by food. Whichever party can provide food will also have the power.

"The Food Control Department is largely composed of Jews, who are anxious for a firm authority in Russia which will ensure their position. They see no prospect of this in a Russian Russia. Realizing this to be the British policy they are mainly pro-German and in consequence pro-Turk; they are therefore not enthusiastic over improvements suggested by the British.

"It is not possible to devise any social machinery such as would satisfy the collectivist socialism of Russia, and which at the same time could cope with the food situation under existing conditions. The practical methods proposed by me, and which they admit might prove successful, are of such an anti-socialistic nature that to introduce them would defeat their political aims.

"The Food Controller, Roklin, is a social revolutionary and an ardent party man. He has no special qualifications for his present position and no commercial or industrial knowledge. His first thought is his party and not the feeding of the people.

"He is using the food situation purely to further the interests of his particular party, and his proposal is that the British should buy the food and hand it over to him, and he gain thereby power for his party. The Central House have put forward a similar suggestion, with the exception that they would like us to take full control and hand it over when we had got the organization running satisfactorily.

" In my opinion it is not possible to make any definite improvement within two months, and any party attempting to deal with the food situation now will suffer in popularity. I consider it would be unwise for the British to take it over for the same reason. Our interests will be best served by buying from all possible sources and handing over what we obtain to the local authorities, taking steps to make known what we so hand over."

The scarcity in food naturally brought about a rise in the prices of all commodities, of which I will presently give examples. The artificiality of any currency system becomes very apparent in a revolution ; where all security comes to an end the value of money practically ceases to exist. Actual coins of precious metals disappear because the people hoard them, and their circulation entirely stops. Paper money has always played a large part in Russian currency, but there was presumably gold behind the Nikolai rouble, and its fluctuations in exchange before the war were very small. The rouble was then to all intents and purposes the same as an English florin, ten to the sovereign.

As outsiders in Baku it was necessary for us to put down gold or a guarantee of gold to get our roubles, so that every time we spent fifty-seven roubles we put down £1. I mention all rates and prices in Nikolai roubles in order to make the three rates of exchange less confusing to the reader, although as a matter of fact certain commodities were paid for in the ridiculous paper currency of Baku, and for certain others Kerensky notes were accepted.

I cannot recall the price of bread, but the following incident will throw some light on it. I was present at the unloading of Shaumian's ships and found the Tartar coolies working very slackly. I spoke to one through an interpreter and asked what he was paid a day; he replied twenty roubles (£2 old rate of exchange, ten shillings present rate). I said: "What an unheard-of sum of money for the little work you do. In India your wages would be eightpence a day." To which he retorted, "Keep your roubles and give me bread. The twenty roubles do not fill my stomach, whereas eightpence in India probably would."

The price of a water-melon in India is twopence, at Enzeli eightpence, in Baku twenty to twenty-five roubles (ten shillings). A bottle of vodka, normally two roubles, now cost one hundred roubles; a pair of long field boots, a thousand roubles. I have already mentioned that a rather poor dinner in the hotel cost a hundred roubles. Where money has so little value the tendency seemed to be always to run in round figures; the prices of most things seem to be either fifty or a hundred roubles.

As Enzeli is only eighteen hours' steam from Baku the question may be asked why, if water-melons are eightpence in the former port, they should cost ten shillings in the latter. The answer is, because the shipping was nationalized, which means that all private enterprise was dead. The only way in which water-melons reached Baku was the following: Ships, such as my transports, were ordered to Enzeli on duty. Before leaving on the return journey the crew clubbed together and purchased water-melons, stacking them in the hold and on the decks, till nothing was visible but a green mound of melons.

On the arrival of the ship in Baku a queue of intending

purchasers was formed from the ship's side along the pier, out on the quay and up the adjoining streets, so keen was the desire of the Baku inhabitant to possess himself of this uninteresting fruit at the enormous price of ten shillings apiece. The ship's committee deputed salesmen, who dealt with the produce over the ship's side till the stock was exhausted. Baku seemed to live on water-melons, and the only pudding we ever ate during the time we were there was a slice of water-melon, an invariable item in the menu of the hundred-rouble dinner.

It will be seen that the sailors of these ships had quite realized the pleasures of "getting rich quick," and one of my transports from Enzeli, timed to depart on the evening of a certain day, refused to leave till the next evening because there was a shortage of melons on the Enzeli market, and the crew would not sail without. The profits were quite beyond those of an ordinary goldmine; you put down eight pounds, and in twenty-four hours you picked up a hundred and twenty pounds. If the water-melons had been nationalized as well as the ships, the prices would have dropped to normal, but as the nationalization of the fruit would have taken all the profits out of the transaction, nobody would have bothered to bring water-melons over to Baku.

Having given a general idea of the economic conditions in Baku, I can return to the narration of more stirring events.

After having made myself thoroughly acquainted with the situation in Baku, I concluded that the best method of dealing with the main problem, which was the control of the Caspian Sea, would be to visit the various ports whose situations, tactical and economic, linked up with ours.

I intended to run the risks of the Bolshevik pirate ships and get up to Derbend to interview Bicherakov

SHORT OF EVERYTHING 251

and see what he could do to work in with us. From there I would return to Baku in forty-eight hours, then visit Krasnovodsk to examine the harbour (which Commodore Norris was particularly anxious to do); thence to Enzeli to settle up finally with Kuchik Khan, capture everything I could lay hands on in the way of reinforcements, and make arrangements for rice supply from the Gilan country; thence to Lenkoran to cheer up the little army there and arrange a raid north on to the Tiflis line on the Turkish lines of communication, and to fix up a proper supply arrangement. Our supplies from Lenkoran were being much interfered with by the obstructive "committees," who were trying to nationalize the grain, with the natural result that the farmer found that they had none to sell.

I carried out my programme as far as Enzeli was concerned. I failed to reach Derbend, and my plan for co-ordinating all operations on the South Caspian was not approved, so the remainder of the scheme was shelved.

At 9 p.m. on the night of August 20th I sailed from Baku with a view of reaching Derbend (about 180 miles by sea) and rearranging plans with Bicherakov. It was known that Bolshevik ships were about, but I trusted to luck not to run into them. Unfortunately, as Bicherakov had only recently driven the Bolsheviks out of Derbend and had no armed ships to accompany his movements on the coast, there were likely to be a good many of these piratical craft knocking about.

During the morning of August 21st we made good progress against a stiff breeze from the north and at about 4.30 p.m. were approaching Derbend, when we observed a ship lying at anchor off the coast. I was on the bridge at the time with Commodore Norris, and we noticed distinct signs of uneasiness on the part of the Captain, who presently remarked: "I don't like the look of that ship. I think she is the *Usbeg*, and if so she is one of the worst of the Bolshevik craft." "Keep on your course and see what happens," was the Commodore's suggestion, and we continued to steer a course parallel to the *Usbeg* and about 2,000 yards distant, with a view of turning into Derbend, which was now about 4 miles ahead of us. The next thing that happened was a flag signal from the strange steamer, which the Captain read, "Come alongside and report." On this the identity of the ship as an enemy one became a matter of certainty, and two courses were open to us. The first was to steer ahead of the *Usbeg* and reach Derbend, risking the enemy's fire, before she could up-anchor and follow us. This was quite feasible, but if successful the *Usbeg* would only have to cruise outside the port and prevent our getting out, and we should be shut up there for an indefinite length of time, which was a situation not to be contemplated; so that line of action was negatived. The second course and the one we adopted was to steer out into the open sea, turn and get back to Baku.

As soon as our change of course became apparent the *Usbeg* opened fire with fair precision; the shots fell all round but none struck the *Krüger*, and our speed enabled us to escape without pursuit. Thus ingloriously ended our first fight on the Caspian. I determined as soon as I could get back to Baku to use this case as a final argument with the Dictators to compel them to agree to our arming some of the merchant ships, and at last assent was obtained; so we were gainers to that extent by the episode. But it was a great score for the Bolsheviks, having prevented the meeting between Bicherakov and myself, which might have led to important results.

We returned to Baku on August 23rd, and I wasted no time in waiting on the Dictators with my request for the ships we required to arm. The Commodore was getting impatient at the delay and showed no signs of

SHORT OF EVERYTHING

getting accustomed to the dilatoriness and procrastination of revolutionary procedure.

The next step was to get all in order for a possible evacuation, and a general plan was drawn up based on a concentration at the wharf where we now were and which appeared most suitable for the purpose. As a matter of fact there was a more suitable wharf in a position farther east which I had not discovered, but which we found later with the assistance of the Turks. The shelling of my ship became so accurate and constant (though the *Krüger* bore a charmed life and was never once hit) that we were eventually compelled to change our berth, and in searching for another accidentally discovered the wharf near the arsenal, which was in every way ideal and from which the evacuation eventually took place.

Several attempts were now made to get us to release the *Kursk* and the *Abo*. No attempt was made on the *Krüger*, as I intentionally retained it as my Head Quarters, which the Dictators respected. Each ship was permanently guarded, evasive replies in the best revolutionary manner were given, coupled with a stolid refusal to comply with any such requests, and the ships remained in our possession.

The town was rather heavily shelled on the night of the 23rd, terrifying the unfortunate inhabitants, but causing very little loss of life and doing us in a general way much good, by reminding them that the Turk was at the door. Whenever the shelling ceased for a day, the townspeople relaxed their efforts under the impression that the danger was not so imminent; when it recommenced they got spells of great activity, during which the troops made good progress in training.

We were now getting things into excellent order. The Armenian troops were really drilling rather well in the town, though reluctant as ever to take their proper share of duty in the trenches. Colonel Warden had been appointed Inspector of Infantry, his duty being to pass right along the line from flank to flank and see that the town troops were in their proper places (which he never saw), that their demands for food and ammunition supply were promptly met, and to listen to, and remedy if possible, the many just complaints and grievances of the men. This appointment was of very great use and did much to give cohesion to the line.

Major Vandenberg, of the South African contingent, was placed in charge of the machine-gun defence of the whole position and effected great improvements. Before he took over his appointment the machine-gun situation was hopeless, the weapons being placed anyhow: sometimes in trenches with parallel lines of fire, and no field of fire, followed by large gaps with no guns at all. The extraordinary state of affairs that existed may be understood, when I explain that in many cases soldiers regarded their armament as their own property and not the property of the army. On one occasion Major Vandenberg visited the line and sited the machine-guns according to his scheme. On visiting the line shortly afterwards he found one gun missing, thus leaving a gap in the belt of crossfire. He complained of this, and was informed: " Oh, that gun belongs to X.; he's gone off duty and taken his gun with him." This stupid behaviour was put a stop to. A school for instruction in the use of machine-guns was started in the town, which promised to result in a great improvement in general handiness and fire discipline.

Colonel Rawlinson was placed in charge of the main arsenal and soon began to produce order out of chaos. When he took over the arsenal the contents were piled in confusion just as they had lain since the disarming of Shaumian and Petrov's men, when the assorted cargo from the holds of their ships had been thrown in anyhow on top of the already mixed assortment of ammunition. To comply with demands for ammunition on an emer-

SHORT OF EVERYTHING 255

gency was almost impossible, the particular class of shell required having to be sought for anywhere in the heap. The ammunition store was partly occupied also by perambulators, gramophones, sewing-machines and other miscellaneous rubbish off the ships. In the arsenal yard guns of every type and calibre were lying about, sights missing, and breech mechanisms out of order or not to be found. These were soon sorted, put together and sent up to the front, until we had over thirty good Baku guns in action, our own British battery, No. 8 R.F.A., being the only mobile artillery in the defence.

An officer and, where possible, one or more N.C.O.'s were appointed to each local battalion and battery, the latter soon attaining a high degree of proficiency and doing most excellent work.

We now proposed to link up the local troops with our own, so as to bring them under proper discipline. The idea was to attach three local battalions to each of ours: the North Staffords, the Warwicks, the Worcesters, the commander of each British battalion commanding the small brigade thus formed. The idea was an excellent one, but it met with so much stupid opposition and delay that it was never properly introduced before the evacuation. I visited the Minister of War and got him to agree. I saw the Commander-in-Chief and received his assent, and the five Dictators and the Armenian National Council also agreed, after inserting many needless provisions; but from agreement to action was a very long call in Baku, and we only reached the stage of action too late to be of any use.

On the night of August 24th I sailed for Enzeli, reaching there on the afternoon of the 25th. Peace was finally settled with Kuchik Khan, who from this time became our sole contractor for the big rice harvest of Gilan, which was very important to us in Baku. An exchange of prisoners was agreed to and Captain Noel at last released. With reference to this exchange of prisoners a question arose as to whether the restoration of prisoners was compulsory, or dependent on the wish of the individual. The Austrians whom we had taken prisoners at Resht and who had yielded themselves perhaps a little too willingly to us, objected strongly to going back to the Jangalis. But Kuchik Khan had evidently something to say to them, and refused to release Noel until we delivered them, so we had to send them over.

This was to be my last visit to Persia, as we would shortly be reaching the critical stage in Baku and it would be dangerous to absent myself. I took the opportunity therefore of impressing on the commandant and embarkation staff of Enzeli that we wanted all we could get in the way of officers, men and supplies. The command in Kasvin had now been taken over by Brig.-General Bateman-Champain, of the Indian army, and I was no longer responsible for anything on the Persian side.

On August 27th we arrived in Baku, bringing back with us a further consignment of four-inch and twelve-pounder guns and ammunition for the arming of our prospective fleet; it was a good thing we were able to bring these guns with us, as from now on it became extremely difficult to get anything from Enzeli.

Colonel Keyworth came on board to report, and informed me of the Turkish attack on the Mud Volcano on the 26th, in which the Turks had gained their objective and our losses had been considerable. Further details of this action will be given later. It was certain now that the Turks had received the necessary reinforcements and were preparing for their great assault on the town. If we received any considerable reinforcements from Persia we could regard the issue with confidence; if we did not, then it was merely a question of postponing the final fall and making the best arrangements for getting our men away when the crash came.

Major-General Dunsterville and Colonel Aratunov

SHORT OF EVERYTHING

The Turks were of course wise enough to foresee this and, with a view of stopping any further reinforcements for us from Persia, they commenced their advance from Tabriz on Kasvin, hoping that this threat would serve to check any further dispatch of men to me. This move of theirs had been obvious for many months, but there were difficulties in the way of our assembling sufficient troops to meet the attack on the Kuflan Kuh which was the strongest point of our defence on the road. The position was taken by the Turks and the road to Kasvin lay open. They never seriously advanced very far in the Kasvin direction once they had succeeded in their chief design, which was to stop reinforcements reaching me. Even individual officers of my original force, whose services would have been invaluable, were held up on the Persian side owing to the situation there.

While going round the position the following day with Colonel Aratunov (Armenian), I was much struck with the general improvement in the town troops. If we had only had time we would in the end have made quite good stuff out of them. Ammunition, both artillery and small arms, was still being frequently wasted despite the urgent need for economy, and I drew the attention of an Armenian Colonel, who was commanding the right sector, to his artillery which was firing apparently at nothing. He replied, " Yes, they are not firing at anything, but the men in the trenches like to hear the sound of their guns now and then, and if I don't fire them off occasionally they will not stay in the trenches."

The shelling of my ship, the Hôtel d'Europe and the town generally was now becoming so accurate, that I could only believe that the enemy had a telephone line from the town, with an operator within a few hundred yards of myself. I do not think any artillery officer could give any other solution of the accuracy of their fire. They had of course a large-scale map of the town, and without direct observation could easily put their shells within a given area, but the series of shells they fired for ranging purposes progressed with such unerring regularity and precision that it was quite uncanny to watch.

From my ship, lying out in the open, clear of the town, the fall of each shell could be clearly seen, the series coming straight down towards me as down the steps of a ladder. Thus the first shell would land in the upper town, the next half way down, the next alongside, the next between the masts, and then the information of their having got the range would be notified and we would get two rounds battery fire. By some strange chance everything was hit except the gallant *Krüger*. A boat just astern (with no one in it) was destroyed, and a heap of ammunition on the edge of the wharf within three feet of the side of the ship was hit, the shell boxes smashed open and two men on sentry-go slighty wounded, but no explosion took place.

This example of the progressive series of ranging shots was of daily occurrence, and it is not possible to conceive any other means of attaining such unerring accuracy except by means of a telephone, but we were never able to find it.

The Hôtel d'Europe was shelled with equal accuracy, and with equal immunity from loss of life. At the busiest time of the day various rooms were struck by H.E. shells, but never an occupied room. The clerks at their work were peppered with dust, a Russian lady typewriter was knocked over unharmed by the explosion of a shell in the adjoining room, and Major Newcome had a narrow escape. We soon had to give up the upper storey, and in the end evacuated the hotel entirely, removing our Head Quarters to the Métropole, to which the Turk at once transferred his attentions. In the end both hotels were knocked to pieces, people in the street and some of the hotel staff were killed, but of my party not one was touched.

At this time I generally remained on board ship, but occasionally transferred myself to the gorgeous chamber and the plush upholstery of the Hôtel d'Europe. It was extremely inconvenient, but I had to sleep in the hotel for a week, as our traducers had started a rumour in the town that the British General slept on board ship, with a view of deserting the town in case of a serious attack! During the first few days of my stay in the hotel they sent a man daily to see if I was really there.

We were being very closely watched by many parties, and a representative from the Russian Legation in Teheran was also in the town taking notes. I received various deputations every day and occasionally entertained them on board the *Krüger*. Among such deputations was one from the Russian business men, who had much to suggest and propose, but any endeavour to work with or through them would have been damaging to our interest as they were labelled by the town " Bourgeois " and " Counter-revolutionary," so that I could not even afford to be seen talking with them. I also had an interesting meeting with one of the leading Tartars, a very intelligent and highly educated man, but if I were known to be entering into any sort of relations with these excellent people the town would have been in an uproar, so again I could do nothing for the time being. Had we remained in Baku I feel sure we could have eventually settled the Tartar–Armenian quarrel. As it was, in order to meet this gentleman I had to go at dead of night, unaccompanied except by my guide, to a house in the Tartar quarter of the town, where I was ushered, after ascending many flights of stairs, into his rooms.

Steamers were now leaving daily for Krasnovodsk crowded with refugees wisely escaping from the wrath to come. Their departure was an advantage to us, any reduction in the civil population helping very much to simplify the supply question.

Colonel Chardigny, of the French mission to the Caucasus, was also in Baku at this time, and we discussed together the extent to which it would be advisable and possible to destroy the facilities for oil production and refinery before leaving the town to the enemy.

I enlisted a few helpers locally, and among the most useful was Mr. Dana, an American citizen who had been employed in the oil works here and was now at a loose end. I attached him as interpreter and assistant to Colonel Rawlinson, and he did very good work. Ladies of the English colony in Baku were taken on as hospital nurses, and proved a blessing in their care and attention to the sick and wounded.

Captain Noel, just released from the Jangali prison, reported his arrival and at once put up a scheme for a raid on the enemy's lines of communication in a tract of country with which he was previously acquainted. Colonel Rawlinson was also engaged in the preparation of a similar scheme to be undertaken through Lenkoran and across the Mughan Steppe. Schemes of this nature were necessarily extremely hazardous, but their chances of success were considerable; however, the end was too near at hand to enable us to put any of them into execution.

Colonel Battine, who was getting along well with Kuhn, the Dictator of Krasnovodsk, came on August 29th to confer, and returned to his post the same evening. Representations from Lenkoran also arrived, so that we had good co-ordination of work in the surrounding districts. I was particularly anxious to keep on good terms with the Krasnovodsk people, as I hoped that when Baku fell I should be allowed to reform my troops at Enzeli and cross over to Krasnovodsk to recommence operations in the Turkestan direction from there, linking up eventually with General Malleson's mission on the railway north of Meshed.

Major Rowlandson, whom I had sent with Bicherakov's

"Refugees escaping from the wrath to come"

party, had been doing very good and hazardous work and was now on a special mission to join up with Colonel Pike in the North Caucasus. The latter was soon afterwards killed and Rowlandson had a hard time to extricate himself from his Bolshevik surroundings in Vladikavkaz, which he finally succeeded in doing.

Major Haslam, R.E., had been entrusted with the entire scheme for wiring the front. He was engaged on this duty in the neighbourhood of the Mud Volcano when the Turks attacked that position on August 26th. He at once threw in his lot with the defenders and was killed.

The Armenian leaders in the town were really making great efforts to get their men up to the scratch, and it is no fault of theirs that their efforts met with no great success. There were many fine men among them, such as Colonel Amazasp and Colonel Aratunov. The charge of treachery brought against the Baku Armenians cannot be substantiated. Individual Armenians may have had tendencies to betray both us and the town, but I had no evidence to prove even this. It must be remembered that Shaumian, the leader of the Bolsheviks, was himself an Armenian, and he was certainly against us—not as an Armenian, but as a Bolshevik. I may close these remarks on the Baku Armenians by stating that while heroism was rare among the men, there were certainly remarkable instances of bravery, and the Armenian women in the firing line were nothing less than heroines. The lack of fighting spirit on the part of the men as a whole has already been explained ; it was based not purely on cowardice, but also on an utter inability to understand anything about warfare. On one occasion the Turks emerged from their position in broad daylight, moving across the open desert of the railway valley, seemingly with the intention of assaulting a certain portion of our line. One of my officers in charge of an Armenian battalion urged the men to move forward and man the trenches to meet the attack. The troops refused to move, and their spokesman exclaimed, "What, go up there ? Why that's just where the Turks are coming ! "

Commodore Norris now had his first experience of the Baku fleet and revolutionary methods of fighting. He proceeded on board one of the gunboats to shell Turkish trains which were in movement on the line south of Baku. This line was within a thousand yards of the coast, and trains on it offered a splendid target for the naval guns. When within a fair range the guns opened fire, but the shooting was poor and the results were nil. The Commodore suggested to the Captain that he should stand closer in to the shore, so as to shorten the range and make sure of a hit. Orders to this effect were no sooner given than consternation appeared on the faces of the crew, who promptly sent the spokesman of the committee to interview the Captain. "The crew," he began, "wish to know what is the meaning of this change of course ? " The Captain replied, "The English admiral thinks you would make better shooting if we got closer in to the shore." To this the spokesman replied, "The ship is to be put back at once on her former course and no change is to be made till the committee have discussed the matter." The original course was consequently resumed, the committee meeting was held, and decided unanimously that as the enemy were known to have a field battery somewhere on this part of the coast, to stand closer in might be to bring the gunboat under fire from the shore. The order was consequently cancelled and a safer one issued, that the ship should at once return to Baku, which was promptly carried out, and the operations abandoned for the day.

CHAPTER XV

THE ENEMY WITHIN THE GATES

THE accidental discovery of the new wharf was entirely due to the desire of the crew of the *Krüger* to get away from the enemy's shell fire. The occasion which I described when the ammunition dump ought to have been blown up, but was not, showed that the Turks were very accurately aware of the position of my Head Quarters. A move farther east might get us altogether out of the range of their guns, and if it did not it would at least take them some little time to pick up the new range. So when the shelling next began the crew, without waiting for orders (or even holding a committee meeting), took up their position at the new wharf, which they had evidently previously selected. I had not a word to say. It was no more pleasure to me to be shelled than it was to them, and the new wharf offered many facilities for a quiet evacuation that the previous one did not. It was in a less conspicuous part of the town, and in the neighbourhood of the arsenal, and the approaches to it were easy to find by night. The *Krüger* lay on the east side of the wharf, the *Kursk* on the west and the *Abo* tied up on her outer side.

More detailed orders were now issued to units with which each individual man was made acquainted, and each unit was directed to make itself thoroughly acquainted with the nearest route from its position at the front to the embarkation wharf.

In this chapter it will be necessary for me to give several extracts from my correspondence with the local Government. It must not be imagined from these that I had acquired the revolutionary love of writing. I was, as a matter of fact, most unwilling to use my pen, but these statements of opinion had to be put down in black and white to prevent the officials from denying later that they had been informed of certain facts and intentions. The matter contained in the letters was usually the gist of a conversation previously held, and subsequently put in writing for record : nearly all my work was actually done verbally in the first instance. In some cases verbal means were impossible, owing to the difficulty of finding the person to whom one wanted to talk. A luncheon interval of five hours was not unusual for the civil and military officials in Baku, though there were some admirable exceptions to this rule, and it must be admitted that Russians are wonderful night-workers, and they were very probably making speeches and passing resolutions by the score when we were comfortably in bed.

It now remains to describe the fighting that resulted in the capture by the Turks of the Mud Volcano on August 26th. On this day the position of the troops was very much as I have stated in my description of the general position in Chapter XIII. I had visited the spot and spoken with the officer commanding concerning the necessity of keeping in touch with the Armenian support in Baladjari. With this support at hand the danger of the position was not too great to be risked, but if this support failed the position could not be held against a serious attack. The detachment was in telephonic communication with Baladjari station, and if the telephone was cut or failed a mounted messenger would not have far to go to call up the Armenians. As far as I can

THE ENEMY WITHIN THE GATES 265

discover this Armenian support was never there, but Colonel Kazarov, who commanded this sector of the defence, asserts that it was always there except on the day when it was required. On that day there was some misunderstanding as to reliefs, the old troops marched back to town, and the new troops had not reached Baladjari when the attack took place.

The position was assaulted by the best Turkish troops, who were evidently specially selected and attacked with the greatest bravery and determination. Their numbers were not large, and if, when the Armenian support from Baladjari had failed, the local Baku troops right and left of the Mud Volcano had moved out to threaten the flanks of the assaulting column, the attack would have failed. But no movements of any sort took place and the local troops stuck to their usual rôle of interested spectators.

I cannot describe the action better than by quoting in full the report of Colonel Faviell, commanding the 39th Brigade, which is as follows :

"TURKISH ATTACK ON AUGUST 26, 1918.

" The Mud Volcano position was held by D Company, North Staffordshire Regiment, under the command of Captain Sparrow, M.C.

" The attack opened at 10.30 a.m., when the enemy were seen debouching from south-west of Mud Volcano in four lines in extended order, with a body of cavalry operating on their right flank.

" The strength of the enemy forces was estimated about one thousand.

" The attack was launched with great vigour, supported by light and heavy artillery fire on our positions. For some considerable time the enemy were held by our machine-gun and rifle fire. Five separate attacks were launched on No. 1 Post. The fifth succeeded in annihilating the defence in that particular section.

"About 12.30 p.m. the enemy succeeded in working round the northern flank of the Volcano and, bringing up machine-guns, they then opened heavy and accurate fire in reverse on No. 2 and 3 Posts, his attack on the southern flank being at the same time annihilated. By 1.30 p.m. No. 2 and 3 posts were rushed by the enemy; only about half a dozen unwounded men succeeded in getting back from the actual positions attacked.

"All the officers were casualties, and about eighty men of the company are at present missing, including these officers. Reinforcements under Major Ley, D.S.O., consisting of sixty North Staffords, and seventy Royal Warwicks, dispatched in lorries from Baku at 1.30 p.m., arrived too late to save the position. One company 9th Worcester Regiment dispatched as a further reinforcement at 3 p.m., came under Major Ley's orders shortly after 3.30 p.m.

"In conjunction with the above operations the enemy launched an attack on the hill west of Binagadi village from the village of Novkhany. This hill had been held by an Armenian battalion.

"During the attack on the Volcano one company North Staffords at Diga were ordered to move to Binagadi village to support this battalion. Arriving about 2.15 p.m. this company, seeing that the hill was not held by our troops, pushed up the hill, and arriving at the summit found the enemy about 250 strong advancing to occupy it, having already reached the lower slopes on the northern side. The leading men of the North Staffords immediately occupied the trenches below the crest of the hill and poured in a heavy fire with Lewis-guns and rifles at short range, driving back the enemy with severe loss. The company suffered slight casualties, only about ten killed and wounded, including Lieutenant Craig, who was com-

THE ENEMY WITHIN THE GATES

manding the company, and Lieutenant Macbeth, both of whom were wounded. Shortly afterwards the enemy reformed and launched another attack, but this was easily driven off before the enemy reached the lower slopes, and he retired in disorder to a sunken road out of effective range.

" After we were driven off the Volcano, we occupied a new line as follows. From Binagadi hill west of the village to Baladjari railway station with two intermediate posts, one of one company Royal Warwicks among the oil derricks east of the Volcano, and another of one company North Staffords south of them in the low ground between that place and Baladjari station.

" (*Note.*—Two local battalions which had been ordered to Baladjari as reserve for this section of the line had not left Baku when the attack took place. It appears either that they refused to move or that the local staff had failed to transmit the orders of the Commander-in-Chief.) "

The splendid gallantry of this company of the North Staffords saved Baku on this occasion, and once again postponed the inevitable fall. Had the attack fallen on local troops there would have been nothing to check the Turkish advance on to the line of the cliffs and thence into the heart of the town. It now became an urgent question as to whether I could justify myself in allowing more lives to be risked in a cause that seemed beyond all hope.

The rations for troops were a matter of some difficulty. We never suffered from a shortage of good wholesome meat and bread, but all that goes to make food palatable and wholesome such as vegetables, jam, butter and milk were unobtainable. I was lucky getting some splendid honey from Enzeli, and the men were once or twice cheered by an issue of Baku beer which bore some slight resemblance to the real stuff. In Baku, where cheap things were dear, dear things were cheap, and I was able to issue a ration of the greatest delicacy, namely fresh caviare. But caviare requires a trained palate, and the soldiers, who called this rumoured delicacy " herring paste," had no great liking for it.

Another difficulty was the lack of transport. We had with us some of the Ford vans of No. 730 Company, which after nine months of the roughest usage were still doing splendid work, but the number was quite insufficient. The fact that these cars were usable at all was solely due to the great skill and care expended on them by Captain Aldham, who had been with us from the start, and who had nursed the cars as if they were his own children.

The town possessed a good deal of mechanical transport in various stages of disrepair. One of our mechanical transport companies could have got most of the vehicles working in a few days, but these revolutionaries with their committee methods are incapable of accomplishing anything. All matters are referred to committees, and even if the decision of the committee is a favourable one, the deliberations generally last so long that the point under discussion has lost its importance by the time a decision has been reached. Thus every battalion has its committee, and so has each company in the battalion ; and committee meetings are actually held during the progress of an action. One may hazard a guess that the troops allotted for the support of the Mud Volcano failed to arrive because they were holding committee meetings to decide whether they should take action or not.

The futility of these committees is obvious from the fact that when they have reached a decision they have no power to enforce it, and the men do not consider themselves at all bound by the committees unless their decisions are in accordance with their own wishes. They may finally say, " We will not go." The solution is simple —appeal direct to the men. This annoys the committees

THE ENEMY WITHIN THE GATES

very much, but it settles the matter finally one way or another.

There are many brands of revolutionaries in Russia at the present time who disagree on many points, but all unite in asserting the freedom, equality and brotherhood of man. It is this freedom and equality that puts a stop to all enterprise, each man saying, " I'm not going to do it, if the other fellow doesn't "; so nobody does anything. The Bolshevik troops and officials are in just the same frame of mind as the soldier I mentioned in Chapter III, who said, " I am a Bolshevik, but I do not know what Bolshevism means, as I cannot read or write. I just accept what the last speaker says. I want to be left alone and helped home, and as the committee in Kazian is Bolshevik, I am too. If it were anything else I would be that." Lenin and Trotzky from the first have held the money and the arsenals, then obviously if you want a daily wage you must enrol yourself as a Bolshevik, and if you want to fight you must fight as a Bolshevik, because they alone control the supply of arms and ammunition.

In addition to the two leaders, all the Bolshevik committee men are in a minor sense true Bolsheviks, and would not be willing, like the ordinary man in the street, to accept any other form of revolutionary government that could feed and arm them. Men change their minds like weathercocks, and the Bolshevik of to-day is the Menshevik of to-morrow. In Baku most of the previous Bolsheviks were now sincere well-wishers and active supporters of the British Government, simply because we represented cash and armed strength.

But I should imagine that the whole of Russia, to whatever category of revolutionary ideas they may subscribe, are longing, like the people of Baku, for any form of government that will restore some sort of law and order. They are heartily sick of their liberty, equality and fraternity. Revolutionaries are quite the least brotherly people towards each other that the world contains, and constitute a living refutation of their fundamental doctrines.

On my return from Enzeli I took an early opportunity of discussing the events of August 26th with General Dukuchaiev, and received from him many explanations and assurances that such failure to support our troops would never occur again. His intentions were certainly of the best, but we found later that he was unable to give effect to them.

I also addressed the Dictators on the same subject, and took the opportunity of pointing out that I had never seen any of them or the military staff (with the exception of von der Fless) at the front. They contented themselves with studying the position on maps in their offices, and issued orders based on reports that were frequently untrue, and they never attempted to verify these reports by having a personal look round.

During the next three days the Turks kept us pretty busy with minor attacks which were not pressed home, and on August 31st, they again attacked in force, this time on Binagadi hill, which was held by our troops for the reason that it had seemed to be the most likely place of attack. This time every precaution had been taken to secure adequate support, but again the town troops failed to do their duty. I give Colonel Faviell's report in full.

"Report on Turkish Attack on Binagadi Hill on August 31, 1918.

" At dawn rifle fire was heard from the direction of Binagadi hill, occupied by one company 7th North Staffords, strength eighty all ranks, under Lieutenant R. L. Petty, M.C., who reported an encounter with a strong enemy patrol. At 6 a.m. a second report was received to the effect that the enemy, strength about 500 rifles, was massing for an attack at the foot of the western slopes of Binagadi hill. Information received from various sources confirmed the report, and it became obvious that an enemy attack was about to take place.

"I accordingly ordered Head Quarters and one company Royal Warwicks at Diga to move to the centre of Binagadi oil derricks and remain there in reserve. At the same time I asked Colonel Kazarov, commanding Right Section to move the armoured train to Baladjari and there create a diversion against Mud Volcano. At 6 a.m. the attack developed, supported by machine-guns and about twelve field and mountain guns. The machine-guns had been brought under cover of darkness to within 500 yards of our position, and so placed as to enfilade our trenches. These machine-guns were placed in the open behind large shields, without any attempt at concealment. The hill was swept with intense machine-gun fire and the defences considerably weakened by casualties, and the necessity of withdrawal, unless the hill could be reinforced, became probable. The Russian commander was asked for support which was eventually given, but the reinforcing troops only reached the eastern slopes of the position after the evacuation. At about 7.50 a.m. Binagadi hill became untenable. Lieutenant Petty, the company commander, had been killed, and to avoid complete annihilation our troops at 8.30 a.m. were compelled to withdraw, and fell back steadily to the right of Warwick Castle. The Royal Warwick Company from Diga arrived too late to save the position. At 11.5 a.m. an attack against Warwick Castle developed. The loss of Binagadi hill, together with the failure of the Armenian battalions in reserve in Binagadi village to support the right, exposed that flank, and the retirement of an Armenian battalion on the left of Warwick Castle left both flanks of the position in the air, a weakness of which the enemy took full advantage, and he soon began working through the rough ground round the position to within forty yards of it, compelling the withdrawal of the garrison to avoid complete isolation and capture.

"The Royal Warwicks then fell back steadily to the line of Binagadi derricks, thence turning north-east through the western end of the derricks. Our line roughly was then from Baladjari—running north towards the eastern end of Binagadi derricks, and then to Diga, with large gaps at intervals.

"I then ordered the company of the Royal Warwicks in reserve to occupy the line of Binagadi derricks, but they only succeeded in obtaining possession of the southern edge of the line, and considering the line unsatisfactory I withdrew them to a more southerly position about 200 yards clear of the derricks. Having no further reserves at my disposal, I decided that it was impossible to hold the line with the troops then occupying it, and consequently asked permission to withdraw to the line Baladjari village along the forward railway embankment to the western edge of the Darnagul salt lake. Sanction having been obtained, the withdrawal took place after dusk, and the new line established. Two companies of the Royal Warwicks at Diga having been placed under the order of Major Dayrell, remained at Diga, which place was attacked the same evening, for which operations I am submitting a separate report.

"Total casualties: One British officer killed and one British officer died of wounds, thirty-four British other ranks killed, wounded and missing. Reports received as to enemy casualties all agree that they were very considerable. The enemy carried out the attack with vigour and determination. Having no reserves under my hand to assist the garrison at Binagadi hill, complete annihilation was merely a question of time,

THE ENEMY WITHIN THE GATES 273

and further resistance would have produced no other result."

During the progress of the action described above, I came across Major Engledue with one of the town battalions. The moment was one when, without even waiting for orders, every man should have been moving to the front, yet the men of this battalion were rapidly progressing towards the town with their backs towards the enemy. Major Engledue, assisted by two British N.C.O.'s, was vainly endeavouring to stem the tide, but with no great success. He managed at last to get them to line up on the railway embankment, but by this time two-thirds of the men were already well on their way into the town. This officer remained doing splendid work with the local troops till the end, and was very severely wounded in the final action of September 14th.

The result of the day's action was enough to fill one with despair. I returned to the town, spoke with the Commander-in-Chief and with the Dictators, and later embodied my remarks in the following letter :

" *To the Provisional Government of Baku.*

" (Copy forwarded to the Chief of the Staff.)

" SIRS,
    " I feel it my duty to put before you my opinion of the present military situation in Baku.

" To begin at the beginning. You are aware that for six months I was looking out for an opportunity of helping Baku.

" Towards the end of July the Bolshevik Government of Baku was overthrown and I was invited to come to the aid of the town. I had at that time very few troops at my disposal, and of those not many could be spared owing to the necessity of dealing with many situations in Persia, including the movement of Kuchik Khan. I arranged terms of peace with the latter and sent you the few troops I could. I then wired to Baghdad and have forwarded on as fast as possible all troops as they arrived.

"It must be remembered that Baghdad is 900 versts from Enzeli; the road is not good, and even with automobiles reinforcements cannot move quickly.

"I took it that the situation in Baku was that there were perhaps 15,000 fighting men, scarcely trained at all, but armed and inspired with a fierce determination to save their town. I therefore regarded the proposition as quite favourable—with a nucleus of some 2,000 to 3,000 regular troops and some artillery, such citizen soldiers should be able to accomplish a good deal on the pure defensive.

"Unfortunately the Baku authorities apparently expected at least 16,000 British troops, and, lacking military knowledge, had not calculated the great length of time necessary to convey that number of troops with stores, supplies, ammunition, equipment, etc., a distance of 900 versts. They expected that this number of troops would suffice to hold the town with an active defence (as indeed they would), while the Baku citizen army retired entirely from the front line and occupied itself with training in the rear. The result has been, I understand, a deep feeling of disappointment on the part of the inhabitants of the town, and a sense that they have been deceived by their English Allies. It should be understood by all that no exact number of troops was asked for or promised.

"The Turks are not merely attacking Baku, but are threatening my lines of communication in Persia, advancing towards Hamadan and Kasvin from the north-west, and they will also probably succeed in making Kuchik Khan break the peace I have lately concluded with him. Thus my difficulties of reinforcing Baku are very much increased, and troops intended for us have had to be diverted to meet the various Turkish movements towards the Kasvin–Hamadan road.

"At the present moment a great additional reinforcement of British troops is not to be expected, owing to the Turkish advance from the west on my line of communication, and in the end it is possible that the line of communication may be cut and we shall be quite isolated from Baghdad.

"I was present at the front this morning during the Turkish attack on Binagadi hill. When I arrived on the scene, large numbers of Baku soldiers were moving in twos and threes from the direction of the enemy back to Baku. Meanwhile the small British detachment of seventy men held on to the position and asked for a counter-attack by the Baku troops in reserve in the village of Binagadi. To bring off such a counter-attack was not difficult, and it was certain of success, but nothing happened, and my troops had to retire and yield the position to the enemy. I believe a few troops did move forward, but nothing really serious was afforded in the shape of support.

"Under such conditions it will shortly be necessary to withdraw the line of defence to the high ground just south of the railway line. This will shorten the line considerably, but has the disadvantage of being the last stronghold, from which any retirement means the surrender of the town. It also gives the Turks full possession of the whole Baku peninsula north and east of the town, and enables them to shell the town at their pleasure from three directions.

"Still, even in this position the actual town and port can be saved, *but only if the Baku troops develop, what they do not now possess, the spirit to fight and the determination not to yield. If, on the other hand, these retirements are to continue every time your troops come under fire, the further defence of Baku is a waste of time and life.*

"I am willing with my troops to continue the defence to the bitter end, but it is quite hopeless to endeavour to do so with troops who have no intention of fighting.

"BAKU, *August* 31, 1918."

In the afternoon I received an invitation from General Dukuchaiev to be present at 8 p.m. at a Council of War. I replied that I was not in favour of such councils, but if it was decided to hold one I should be glad to be present.

Accordingly at 8 p.m. I presented myself at the Government offices, accompanied by Colonel Clutterbuck and Captain Bray, Colonel Stokes was also present as Chief of the Staff to General Dukuchaiev.

I found the Commander-in-Chief seated at the central table with maps spread before him, and he offered me a seat at his side. The entire room was filled with the members of the various committees. The Armenian National Council was there in full force, the five Dictators, Workmen's Delegates, Soldiers' and Sailors' Delegates, and Peasant Deputies. It did not appear likely that a Council of War held on these lines was going to achieve anything useful.

The proceedings commenced by General Dukuchaiev giving a very clear but lengthy appreciation of the situation, his remarks being punctuated by interpellations of assent or disapproval from the members of the various committees. He was, however, permitted to conclude his address without serious interruption, and he finally summed up his remarks by saying, "The enemy have taken A and B, and will probably next move on to C, which will render D untenable, etc. I therefore propose to alter the whole line as follows . . ."

Before the concluding remarks were out of his mouth, a burly sailor arose and strode up to the table to give his views of the situation. He made use of the General's map, indicating points as required by the use of his broad

THE ENEMY WITHIN THE GATES

thumb, oblivious of the fact that his thumb covered more than a square mile of country, leaving his points rather vague. He spoke for an hour with obvious enjoyment, repeating himself a good deal and wandering off the track every now and then to work in some well-worn tag, or to give vent to some such sentiment as " We will fight to the very last drop of our blood," which produced vociferous applause. He eventually arrived, in the correct manner, at his summing-up, which was the exact contrary of that of the Commander-in-Chief, and he suggested plans of action which were the reverse of those outlined by the Commander-in-Chief, and urged the taking up of a line totally different to that advocated by the Commander-in-Chief.

His final peroration was to the following effect : " The General says the Turks are holding such and such points. That is not so, their line runs thus (describing the enemy's imaginary line with considerable detail). He says we have had to give up B. That is not so. I have just had a telephone message from a friend of mine out there. The General says we must take up such and such a line. He is quite wrong. That is not the line to take up. This is the one (more detail). His counsel is not that of a brave man. We mean to fight to the bitter end, etc."

To my surprise the General in no way resented this amateur interference with his plans, in fact he seemed to think there was a good deal in what the sailor said.

When this speaker had reluctantly resumed his seat, the Armenian National Council had their say, proposing plans neither agreeing with those of the Commander-in-Chief, nor with those of the sailor. After them the Dictators had quite a fresh plan to propose, differing from all the others. The Dictators were followed by other speakers, each with his own views to put forward, and each inspired by a desire to continue talking as long as his breath held out.

So time went on till the clock struck one and my patience was exhausted. How long the meeting continued I do not know, but having decided that it was quite time for my Staff and myself to be in bed, I apologized quietly to the Commander-in-Chief and withdrew, leaving the assembly to continue their futile discussions.

CHAPTER XVI

THE SHADOW OF COMING EVENTS

ON the following day, September 1st, I talked over the situation with General Lewin, who was on tour from Baghdad and was returning that day, and decided that a further continuance of the defence of Baku must be given up and the British Garrison withdrawn.

I accordingly sent a message round to the Dictators and the various committees asking them to meet me in the Hôtel d'Europe at 4 p.m., when I would have a very important communication to make to them.

At the hour named the various committees had assembled and I addressed them as follows:

"What I have to say can be said in a very few words. No power on earth can save Baku from the Turks. To continue the defence means only to defer the evil moment and to cause further needless loss of life. Up till now my men have done all the fighting. In each action, in spite of the bravery of my soldiers, the Turks have succeeded in capturing each position, owing to the lack of support from local troops. I will not allow my men's lives to be thrown away in vain in this manner. We came here to help your men to fight the Turks, not to do all the fighting, with your men as onlookers. In no case have I seen your troops when ordered to attack do anything but retire, and it is hopeless continuing to fight alongside of such men.

"I am about to give orders to withdraw my men from the firing line and I shall move them from Baku to-night. I have invited you here to give you this warning, so that you may be able to fill the gaps in the line caused by the withdrawal of my men. You would be best advised to send out a party at once with a flag of truce to the enemy and see what terms you can make with him. You will have no difficulty in securing terms which will enable you to get your women-folk away, and you will at the worst be able to bring about a better condition of affairs than will be the case if you wait till the Turks and the Tartars take the town at the point of the bayonet. I beg you will forego your usual custom of speech-making and the passing of resolutions; this is a time to act and not to talk. Every man in this town knows and feels the truth of what I have said; what then will be the use of prolonged discussions? I will leave you here, however, to make what decisions you like, and will return in an hour when I hope you will have completed your deliberations."

While I was making this speech I noticed expressions of doubt, horror, despair, and in some cases rage and hatred on the faces of my listeners. They seemed absolutely thunderstruck, as if the idea of the possible fall of Baku was being put before them for the first time. As I spoke of the withdrawal of the British detachment, Yarmakov sprang from his chair and left the room. I begged Major McDonnell to follow him and watch him. He was always a man of action and capable of making a quick decision, and I knew he had gone to the telephone to call up the gunboats to open fire on our ships if we attempted to leave the port.

During the next hour I visited General Bogratuni, the War Minister, and found he had nothing to say against my proposal to withdraw my troops, beyond begging that I would not do so.

THE SHADOW OF COMING EVENTS

When I returned to the hotel I found the various committees all passing resolutions as fast as they could. I begged of them to cease the resolutions and take some action, and again left them. In another hour I returned and found a sailor just putting the fourteenth resolution to the vote. After that it appeared certain that no action would be taken that day. Under such conditions I could not, in fairness to the town, carry out the immediate withdrawal of my troops, and they remained in their position. I sent, however, a warning note to the Dictators, to which I received this reply:

"*September* 1, 1918.   No. 34, BAKU.

" *From the Provisional Dictatorship of the Centro-Caspian.*

" *To Major-General Dunsterville, British Army Staff.*

" We beg to inform you, in reply to your letter of the 1st inst., that the British troops can only be permitted to leave Baku at the same time as our own troops and on the same terms, and only after evacuation of the town by non-combatants.

" Signed by six members of the Prov. Dictatorship of the Centro-Caspian and the Presidium of the Provisional Executive Committee.

" Signed by the Secretary (*illegible*)."

On September 2nd and 3rd, the Turks showed little signs of activity, and our troops remained in their previous position, but from this moment everything was prepared for an immediate evacuation, and only the word " go " was necessary to set the whole scheme working.

On September 3rd I addressed the following letter to the Commander-in-Chief:

"*To General Dukuchaiev.* (Copy to Dictators.)

"I learn with regret that the decision adopted on September 1st by the majority of those interested in the fate of Baku was overridden by some of the young members of the Dictatorship. The members responsible for this decision, in opposition to the more experienced leaders, do not perhaps realize the future tragedy for which they have made themselves responsible.

"The plan I put forward was with a view of saving the large population of women and children from needless massacre, a result it would have achieved. The present course of action will, I fear, end in a *sauve qui peut*.

"So many miracles have so far occurred in our favour that we may have perhaps even more, but nothing less than a miracle can save the town from falling into the hands of the enemy. And when it does fall there will be no further warning. A successful attack from the north-west would bring the Turks into the town before the inhabitants were aware of their proximity.

"The danger point now is the right angle formed north and west of Baladjari Station. It seems to me now clearly indicated that this is where the final Turkish attack will be made, while their cavalry will possibly endeavour to come round our extreme right. No one can foresee military events with certainty, and the attack may come elsewhere, but this is a point where large reserves are necessary.

"As regards my own troops, I am glad to have the honour of accepting your orders tactically, as long as my troops are not cut up into small detachments. But as I understand that your war plans are controlled by the Dictators, young men of no war experience, I must decline to carry out any movements which I consider injudicious.

"With regard to the very curt reply of the Dictators concerning the withdrawal of my troops, I do not consider

THE SHADOW OF COMING EVENTS 283

the command of my troops to be in the hands of the Dictators, nor do I intend further to waste the lives of my men by allowing them to hold on to positions when not supported, and when units on their flanks retire.

"I have therefore instructed my commander at the front to use his own discretion and to withdraw his troops entirely from the fighting line when he thinks fit.

"This is the second time that I have spoken to this effect, and when the time comes it will not be possible to give you any further warning."

On September 4th I received this interesting communication from the Baku Government:

To Major-General Dunsterville, British Army.

"YOUR EXCELLENCY.

"Your letter to the Dictatorship, dated the 31st August, and your own and your assistants' verbal statements that Baku will have to be surrendered, that beyond the number of British troops already forming your army you are unable to give 'a single soldier,' and finally your letter to General Dukuchaiev of the 3rd September, compel the Dictatorship of Baku to inform you in your capacity of Commander of the British Forces and representative of the British Government at Baku as follows:

"When we entered into a military agreement with you WE ASSUMED JOINT RESPONSIBILITY WITH YOU for the preservation of the town and district of Baku, both for the Russian Republic and for the common front of the Allies.

"Our alliance with you led to a rupture with the Bolshevik power in Russia. The supply of fighting men, ammunition and *matériel*, foodstuffs and other commodities to Baku had ceased altogether. You are, we trust, not aware that after the overthrow of the Bolshevik power in Baku, the representatives of Lenin's Government were willing to acknowledge a Coalition Government in Baku, to supply soldiers, ammunition and *matériel*, etc., and to afford us active assistance in the defence of Baku on one condition, viz. THE WITHDRAWAL OF BRITISH TROOPS FROM BAKU AND DISTRICT.

" We were unable to accept this condition. We believed that in order to save Baku, to secure a democratic peace in Europe, to bring about the annulling of the degrading peace of Brest, and to upset the plans of conquest formed by Germany and her Allies, concerted action with you was necessary.

" We considered therefore (and in this respect we based our conclusions on our negotiations with you and on your own and your Government's declarations and announcements), that you would bring to Baku a sufficient force, not only to relieve the town from siege, but even to clear the enemy out of Trans-Caucasia which has been torn from the Russian Republic.

" Unhappily we were mistaken. During a period of more than a month to the 3rd September you have transferred to Baku LITTLE MORE THAN ONE THOUSAND MEN, with six guns and some other technical items.

" Leaving on one side the question of the force required to drive the enemy out of Trans-Caucasia, the assistance supplied by you is TOTALLY INADEQUATE even for the purpose of compelling the enemy to raise the siege of Baku.

" Whatever explanation may be forthcoming of the inadequacy of the support you have rendered, however excellent the military behaviour and technical equipment of your Baku detachment, we consider it necessary to inform you (and we request you to communicate our views to your Government) THAT YOU HAVE NOT RENDERED THE AID WHICH WE WERE ENTITLED TO EXPECT OF YOU, on the grounds of your own pronouncements and declarations and those of the representatives of your Government.

THE SHADOW OF COMING EVENTS

"Moreover, having in view the terms as offered to us by Lenin's Government, we assert that your forces have not only failed to augment but have actually reduced the defensive strength of Baku, on which we might have relied had we accepted the terms of the Bolshevik party.

"In view of the foregoing we insist THAT YOU IMMEDIATELY TRANSFER SUFFICIENT REAL FORCES FROM PERSIA OR BAGHDAD. We consider this assistance INDISPENSABLE FOR US AND OBLIGATORY ON YOU. In the expectation of this assistance (we also expect reinforcements from Bicherakov in Petrovsk and the North Caucasus) we consider it imperative to sustain the attacks of the Turkish Army for the next few days.

"We trust that in this we shall be successful. We reject the suggestion to surrender the town to the enemy, and are surprised at your insistence in urging such a course. We are imbued with the sense of the imperative necessity to fight to the end, to the last possibility. We are convinced that your small, but in every respect admirable, detachment will do its duty and share our common fate. United by the bond of a common purpose, WE MUST AND SHALL BE TOGETHER. Either we win, or if history decides we perish together.

"Your letter to General Dukuchaiev was based on a misconception. You suggest the surrender of the town. We value your experience very highly, but we hold that the suggestion of surrender is inadmissible and that all possible means have not yet been exhausted. Such being the case, your detachment must operate in contact with the whole of the Baku army, of which it constitutes part. The commander of your forces must act under the general operative control of the commander of the Baku army. In no case can he be permitted to 'act on his own initiative and to withdraw his troops from the firing line,' as you say in your letter of the 3rd September, 'whenever he may consider it necessary.' There is a fundamental principle of military wisdom ; UNITY OF ACTION—UNITY OF CONTROL.

"We trust that your military experience and the excellent organization of the British Army will not only enable us in these difficult days to realize such unity of action, but will furthermore create such conditions in our army, feebly organized as it is and deficient in training and officers, yet prepared to lay down its life, as will enable it to offer effective resistance to the enemy's attempts to take the town.

"In conclusion we beg to point out that the Dictatorship has no intention whatever 'to command your detachment' or to influence military operations. The Dictatorship of the Centro-Caspian and Ispolkom (Executive Committee) represents the supreme power in Baku, pending the assembling of the Baku Council of Workmen, Soldiers' and Sailors' Deputies, and has appointed suitable and trained specialists (the Commander of the Force and the Chief of the Staff at the front and the Military and Naval Commissary at the rear) to the office of directing the fighting forces, to whom is entrusted the control of the military operations of the army and who, we trust, with your direct co-operation, will carry out firmly and energetically, the only military demand of the Dictatorship, viz. the defence of the town at all costs from the Turks, until such time as the necessary reinforcements are forthcoming, whether from your side or other parts of Russia, and thus strengthen the common fighting front of the Allies against the armies of the Turko-German coalition.

"(Signed) PRESIDENT OF THE DICTATORSHIP :
    H. TUSHOFF,
     Vice-President, Members and Secretary.
      (*Signatures illegible.*) "

Judged purely on its merits as a literary effort this letter could hardly be improved on, but judged from the standpoint of facts its merits are entirely lacking.

The narrative up to this point will enable the reader to see for himself the fallacies on which most of the arguments are based, but I will single out the most important ones.

The statement of their basing their expectation of more substantial aid on the grounds of my pronouncements is entirely refuted by my letter to Dr. Araratiantz in Chapter XII.

As to the Dictators not desiring to command my troops, the truth of the matter is that although they had appointed a Commander-in-Chief, they interfered in all military matters, even going to the length of issuing orders direct to the town troops and sending indents for ammunition required at certain points direct to the arsenal.

Finally, the statement to the effect that the Baku army was prepared to lay down its life was as far from the truth as any statement is capable of being. Had the Baku army been inspired by any such feeling, the defence of the town would have been easy, and we could have driven the Turks back to Tiflis. But I have already given a few examples, out of the many that occurred daily, showing that to "lay down its life" was just exactly what the Baku army was unanimously determined not to do.

Before receiving this letter, I had already sent the following communication to the Dictators:

"DICTATORS.

"As it is essential to any form of success that allies should work together in friendly harmony (and I regret to state that since my arrival here the Government have never ceased to regard the whole of my work in a most unfriendly way), I think it advisable to forward for perusal copies of certain dispatches, the originals of which may be seen in my office on application to me.

"My contemplated withdrawal of my troops in the last extremity has been also regarded as a dishonourable act. I wish to point out for the benefit of those who have not studied war and who do not know the rules of war that it is the first duty of every commander to avoid needless sacrifice of lives when a situation is hopeless, to avoid surrendering his troops to the enemy and to place them in a fresh position whence they may be able to continue their general operations against the enemy.

"It is said that by failing to send a larger detachment here the British have betrayed the town of Baku. This cannot for a moment be admitted. In the face of immense difficulties, and at the sacrifice of their plans elsewhere, the British responded to your appeal for help, and sent to you every man they could spare. For three weeks the British troops have borne the brunt of attacks by overwhelming numbers, and it cannot be denied that they have fought with courage, and have freely given their lives for you. Their presence here has at least postponed the evil day of the fall of Baku, and in the last event I am confident that it will enable you to make better terms with the enemy than you could otherwise have done.

"With this explanation, together with my letter of August 31st, I trust the whole matter may be made quite clear and that we may avoid misunderstanding in future. The enemy has agents among you even of your own nationality, whose one task is to sow discord between us. Do not let them succeed."

The whole correspondence was closed by the following letter, which I dispatched on September 5, 1918:

THE SHADOW OF COMING EVENTS

" *To the Dictators of the Centro-Caspian Government.*

" GENTLEMEN,
"I have received your letter of the 4th September, the contents of which I have transmitted to the High Command in Baghdad.

" Since writing, you will have received my letter of the same date, with extracts from telegrams which I trust will completely remove any misconception as to what my attitude has been.

" I am fully in agreement with all that you say as to the importance of saving Baku, and I have never ceased to impress this view on my Government. I am bound to point out, however, that your view of the conduct of the British Government in failing to provide a sufficient force to raise the seige of Baku is based on a fallacy. Neither I nor my Government have ever declared that we could bring to Baku a sufficient force to save Baku unaided. On the contrary, we were led to believe that Baku already possessed a fighting force of at least 10,000 men, who only required organization and a backing of a small British force to render them capable of defeating the enemy. I have no desire to belittle the bravery of the men of Baku, still less to enter into a controversy with you on the subject; and in saying that neither in discipline nor in steadiness under fire have they come up to my expectations, I refer to this matter for the last time.

" It now remains for us to face the situation together, and to do our best to meet it with the means at our disposal. I have submitted to your Minister of War a proposal for the organization of the Baku forces in brigades, which I am confident will lead to good results. If you see any objections to the proposal, I trust that you will tell me frankly what they are.

" The promise of reinforcements from Petrovsk,

together with a thorough reorganization and the infusion of a new spirit into the Baku troops, may temporarily put a new complexion on the situation. But it is still my duty to warn you that the chance of saving Baku by military force is very remote. I have reliable information that the Turks and Germans are sending very large reinforcements, including aeroplanes and heavy guns, to their army before Baku ; and I put it to you in terms of the strongest recommendation that you should urge on the evacuation of your women and children by every means in your power.

"Baku,
"September 5, 1918."

The foregoing extracts from the correspondence which passed between myself and the Baku Government will give a very clear idea of the situation in that town in the first week of September 1918.

Before I finally quit this subject of the Baku Government, the military command and the peculiarities of revolutionaries in general, I wish to make it quite clear that I have no intention of belittling their laudable efforts or of making fun of their troubles. The ridiculous situations I have described would presumably take place to a greater or less degree in any revolution in any country.

It is extremely easy to break down an existing form of government, but to build up anything substantial in its place is a matter of considerable difficulty ; and a long period of disorder must ensue during which the best efforts of the best men will not suffice to prevent ridiculous situations from arising. The military staff could not be expected to accomplish much more than they did with untrained troops and with no powers of enforcing discipline. The young men who composed the Dictatorate were keen, intelligent and enthusiastic. In many ways they achieved remarkable successes.

THE SHADOW OF COMING EVENTS

While all previously existing laws were in abeyance, the maintenance of order among the citizens of Baku was remarkable, and the difficult task of rationing the population was dealt with courageously.

On September 6th a shell intended for our Head Quarters fell a hundred yards short and set fire to a house in the adjoining street. In five minutes the fire engines were at work, the firemen being smartly turned out and as efficient as in any town in Europe. The fire was quickly got under, and by that time the fire brigade received an urgent summons to another quarter of the town, to which they responded with equal alacrity. This episode struck me as showing a very marked advance towards the restoration of general order in the town.

During the week from September 5th to September 12th good progress was made in training of troops, but discipline still remained weak, and troops dispatched to take up certain positions in the line often failed to reach their destination. The enemy contented himself with minor operations carried out with a view of discovering our weak points, and with very frequent shelling of the town.

We had now two Russian hydroplanes and two of our own aeroplanes at work, and as the enemy possessed no aircraft this should have given us a great advantage over him. But September is the month of hot winds and dust-storms in Baku, and the advantages we might have gained from aerial observation were nullified by the bad weather conditions.

We had six armoured cars in action, three of our own, and three Russian under Captain the Marquis d'Albizzi, all of which did extremely good work.

On September 12th an Arab deserted to us from the Turks, and from the information we obtained from him we gathered that the enemy were preparing for a great assault on September 14th. This information was extremely useful, as it enabled us to have all our troops on the ground, whereas on ordinary occasions a certain proportion were always employed on various detached duties. But our informant was unwilling or unable to give any exact information as to where the attack would fall, and we had therefore to make dispositions with our very small number of troops to meet an attack on a large scale on any part of a 14-mile front. The Arab certainly made suggestions about our left being the point of attack, and that flank was accordingly strengthened; but it was impossible to rely on his rather vague assertions, nor was it likely that he would be in possession of such information which would certainly be kept secret by the enemy Head Quarters till the last moment.

The warning as to the probability of an attack on the following day came just in time to enable me to keep back Colonel Rawlinson, who was to have left on September 13th for Lenkoran, whence he was to carry out a raid in Ford cars on the enemy's lines of communications north of the Mughan Steppe. The intention was to destroy a bridge on the Tiflis line and so cut the railway in the rear of the Caucasus–Islam Army. Colonel Rawlinson had made very careful preparation for this task, and I am convinced that it would have met with success had time allowed of its being undertaken.

A slight increase to our garrison had recently been received in the shape of 500 men with ten machine-guns sent by Bicherakov, with a promise of more as soon as he could arrange for dispatch. These men were not of his best troops, in fact they were mostly composed of Baku men whom he had taken north with him in August, and who were now merely returning to their homes, but their training and discipline was superior to that of the local forces, and they were a welcome addition to the garrison.

It was certain that during the ensuing fight and possible

THE SHADOW OF COMING EVENTS 293

withdrawal telephones would play a large part. We were well equipped with these, and Major Pulverman, who had been in charge of our signalling arrangements for the last six months, was busy throughout the day and during the next day's fighting in keeping the lines in working order. Both he and Captain Foxlee were experts at their work, and the success of the final evacuation is due in a great measure to their being able to keep communication going up to the last moment.

Our aeroplanes had during the last week been able, in the occasional lulls in the dust-storms, to observe the enemy's movements, and their reports were to the effect that a large number of troop trains were constantly arriving from the west, from which it became increasingly clear that considerable Turkish reinforcements were arriving. In spite of this the Dictators persisted in clinging to the fanciful idea that the Turks were evacuating!

Up to the very last moment the question of the Brigade organization to which I have referred was still under discussion, furnishing our last example of the dilatoriness of revolutionary procedure. The Dictators demanded that in all cases the Brigade Commander should be a Russian or Armenian officer. To this I replied that I had no objection to my troops serving under a Russian or Armenian commander, provided that he were not only of the proper seniority, but also an officer of considerable experience in the present war. They had no officers of the necessary war experience, but I would have eventually agreed to anything to get the movement started, and would have relied on getting things into order later. In any case I knew that the British battalion commander would see things through on the right lines, whether he were in command or not.

At the same time the army, the fleet and the town generally were daily becoming more impatient at the ineffectiveness of the Dictators, and a strong movement was on foot to remove the present Government and to hand over the entire control, civil and military, to the British.

This was a question I had already considered. It had sometimes appeared to me that the only solution of the difficulty would be forcibly to remove the Dictators and set up an allied government, with full power of civil and military administration in my own hands.

I was very much tempted to take this line of action, but I had to abandon the idea in view of the paucity of officers available for the various tasks that would become necessary. The great majority of my officers had been left in Persia, and not one of those now in Baku could be spared from the firing line or from the various administrative appointments we were already holding.

I had therefore to rest content with the limited control we had already secured by having a British officer as Chief of the Staff and others in charge of the arsenal, the machine-guns and the combined infantry of the defensive line.

On the night of September 13, 1914, the general disposition of the Baku troops and our own was as follows :

The high ground on the extreme left of the line, covering the Bibi Eibat oilfields, was held by A Company of the 7th North Staffords, about 60 rifles, under Captain Bollington. A battalion of Armenians (probably not much over 100 strong) was in local reserve in rear of this flank. At Wolf's Gap was a detachment of Russians with two machine-guns. A hundred rifles of the North Staffords, which were the only British troops in general reserve, were sent at dusk to occupy the crest of the hill in rear of A Company, the intention being to guard that particular point, which dominated the whole of the left flank from a night attack, and to withdraw the reserve at daybreak by motor transport to Baku.

On the northern slopes of this hill were a battery of three-inch field guns and two howitzers.

To the north of Wolf's Gap about 800 yards of the line were held by B Company of the North Staffords under Captain Turkington. The line was prolonged to the right by Armenian troops to a point opposite the village of Khoja Hasan. One battery of howitzers and one of three-inch field guns were posted north of the Wolf's Gap road. A reserve of two Armenian battalions was posted at White House, 1½ miles on the road to Baku, where was also the Head Quarters of the left section, commanded by Colonel Beg Surab, with Major Dayrell as liaison officer.

The right section of the defences, commanded by Colonel Kazarov, with Major Engledue as liaison officer commenced from opposite the village of Khoja Hasan. From that point to the apex of the Baladjari salient the line was held by Bicherakov's brigade, about 600 strong.

Baladjari was held by two companies of the 9th Worcesters, and the line from Baladjari to Darnagul by the 9th Royal Warwicks. The south bank of the Darnagul salt lake (which was almost dry) was held by an Armenian battalion, and the defile immediately east of it by four machine-guns of the Armoured Car Machine Gun Squadron. One company of the North Staffords, about 50 strong, was in local reserve at the point where the Baladjari road crosses the ridge; and a company of the Warwicks, 100 strong, was in local reserve at the 39th Brigade Head Quarters, about 2 miles east of that point on the Baku–Binagadi road. Four field batteries, including the 8th Battery R.F.A. and one battery of howitzers, were with the right section. Two of the British armoured cars were stationed at Baladjari, the third was in reserve at Baku. A force of about 500 Armenians with a battery of three-inch guns, three Russian armoured cars and the cavalry squadron, was operating in the vicinity of Surakhani on the extreme right, in order to check a Turkish mounted force which was threatening that flank. This threat was never of a serious nature, and General Dukuchaiev was urged to withdraw the greater portion of this force to reinforce his left, but he was unaccountably nervous about his right flank and refused to weaken it. The command of the combined troops was of course in the hands of the Russian Commander-in-Chief, but the executive commands for the movements and dispositions of the British troops on September 14th were actually given by Colonel Keyworth, who was throughout in communication with Colonel Stokes, Chief of the Staff to General Dukuchaiev, and by Colonel Faviell, commanding the 39th Brigade, on the right, and by Major Ley, commanding the 7th North Staffords, on the left. I was myself in close touch with General Dukuchaiev, as well as with the Dictators, and General Bogratuni, the Minister of War.

This statement takes no account of most of the Baku troops, whose dispositions were never known to us. We received copies of the orders issued by General Dukuchaiev, but the troops never moved in accordance with these orders.

CHAPTER XVII

THE WITHDRAWAL

BEFORE dawn on this fateful day, September 14th, the information given by the Arab deserter had been proved to be entirely accurate.

At 4 a.m., from my Head Quarters on board the S.S. *President Krüger* alongside the Caucasus-Mercury wharf, the sound of very heavy firing all along the line announced that the great attack had begun. Now for the supreme test of the Baku troops! If they would only hold firm, all would be well. Their training and morale had latterly much improved, the position had great natural strength, and if the Turks gained a footing on the heights above the town they could only do so after suffering heavy loss. Should this happen a counter-attack would give us the victory, and before another attack on a large scale could be brought off reinforcements from Bicherakov in the north and from our own people in the south would render the town practically impregnable.

So it was with high hopes that we realized that the issue was now to be put to the test, hopes that were to be dashed to the ground on the receipt of the first telephone message. This despairing message was to the effect that the battle was over, and the victorious Turks were advancing at a run, without opposition, on the town. This was no great exaggeration of the actual facts, which were as follows. Attacking at 4 a.m. due east across the Railway valley on to the Wolf's Gap, the Turks had stormed this strongest part of the line, where the road leads directly up the steep cliffs, and having broken right through the Baku battalion supposed to be holding this line, were now actually in possession of the heights immediately above the town, within some hundreds of yards of its outskirts and 3,000 yards from the wharves. It was incredible that this strongest portion of the whole line should so easily have fallen to the enemy, especially when all troops had been warned of the impending attack, but though incredible it was true. With troops who suffered immediate defeat with every factor in their favour, truly there was nothing more to be hoped for from Baku, and the problem now became one of how to save a rout and hold up the enemy long enough to enable an orderly evacuation of our troops to be effected.

If the enemy already had his cavalry and infantry on the high ground, his guns should be there shortly, and once they were there the harbour lay at his mercy.

But at this moment the Caucasus–Islam Army was seized with its usual hesitation, giving us time to make such dispositions as almost enabled us to turn defeat into victory; in fact, victory would even now have been assured if the town troops would only have made the smallest effort.

The 900 rifles of the 39th Brigade—which with some of Bicherakov's men and the town artillery were all that could be relied on—were disposed with the Warwicks and the Worcesters on the right, facing north opposite the Baladjari Railway Station, and the North Staffordshire on the left, with their left on the sea.

The pressure being now entirely on the left centre and left, and the Turks being in actual possession of the centre, it became necessary to withdraw the North Staffords to a second position, thus saving them from being outflanked and shortening their line, while still retaining hold of the higher ground. This shortening of the line enabled Major Ley, who handled his battalion throughout the day with great skill and bravery, to send one company to engage the Turks holding the plateau, while Colonel Keyworth dispatched further reinforcements to strengthen this part of the line and endeavour to render the enemy's position on the plateau untenable.

These dispositions, which were effected by 8 a.m., entirely stopped the Turkish advance, but owing to the security afforded to the enemy by the folds in the ground, and the small number of British troops available rendering counter-attack impossible, our efforts did not succeed in driving him from the position, which he held throughout the day.

However, the enemy's advance was now checked, and all hope was not lost. To use a considerable portion of the 39th Brigade for counter-attack, which one was much tempted to do, would have resulted in the usual melting away of the portion of the line from which they would have to be withdrawn, and was consequently not to be thought of. Was it too much to still hope for some form of counter-attack from the town troops? This was the hope we clung to throughout the day, and which more than once seemed on the verge of realization. Counter-attacks ordered by General Dukuchaiev seldom even got as far as the assembly of the necessary troops, those detailed for the task mysteriously failing to reach the rendezvous. But there are exceptions to every rule, and among unheroic people one does get remarkable instances of heroism.

Twice a counter-attack was got on the move and advanced bravely, but bravery without skill is unavailing. The leading was bad and failure was the result. In most cases the Baku battalions had fine commanders, but company and platoon commanders, who are all-important in counter-attack, were miserable.

However, at 8 a.m. the situation was not so bad. The left was fairly secure, the centre had been reformed, and the Turks on the plateau were now unable to pursue the victorious advance that they could so easily have maintained earlier in the day but for their initial hesitation. The Warwicks and Worcesters, under Colonel Faviell, were holding their own on the right, but were threatened by a Turkish attack from the north. This attack materialized later, but was successfully beaten off. The line was being reinforced and strengthened everywhere; two aeroplanes were busy with machine-guns and bombs, and the six armoured-cars—three British and three Russian—were doing fine work on the plateau.

But as the enemy was now holding the heights right and left of Wolf's Gap, he was enabled to bring up his reinforcements almost unimpeded, and, unless a successful counter-attack could be brought off, it would soon be impossible to prevent him from completing his capture of the town. Any further advance on his part would drive a wedge in between the two portions of the 39th Brigade and compel their withdrawal.

All this time the town was being shelled at intervals. The shells did little harm, but the Turk knew well the moral effect of shell fire in a town. He calculated on maintaining a state of panic, and the town fully justified his calculations.

About 9 a.m. came the joyful news that two ships had arrived bringing reinforcements from Bicherakov. As his troops could certainly be relied on, it seemed that now indeed the situation might be saved. The news went round the town and up to the fighting troops with extraordinary rapidity, and the fighting value of the local army increased by fifty per cent. There were the ships slowly coming into harbour, crowded from bow to stern. But alas, our field glasses showed us only too plainly that whatever they were they had not much the appearance of troops. In a short time it transpired that the ships contained not Bicherakov's heroes, but the unheroic elements of Baku itself, who had boarded two steamers and put to sea in ignominious flight and had been recaptured by one of the gunboats and brought back. But the false news had been helpful, and the reaction on discovery of the disappointment could not make things any worse than they were before.

The principal targets in the town for the enemy's artillery were the two hotels, the Europe and the Métropole, which had been alternately used as Colonel Keyworth's Head Quarters. These were soon rendered untenable.

Throughout the morning I was very loth to interfere with General Dukuchaiev, the Commander-in-Chief, as I was quite aware of the need for his being able to work out his plans without disturbance, and with Colonel Stokes as his Chief Staff Officer I felt quite confident of the liaison between the 39th Brigade and the local troops being maintained and of sound measures being undertaken. When I did determine to visit him in his Head Quarters I found that I had been needlessly diffident.

I was admitted to his office at 11 a.m., and a worse state of confusion I have never beheld. This indeed made me lose all hope. I am not blaming the General himself; it is hard to play the part of Commander-in-Chief in a revolutionary army when all are equal and all have an equal right to make and discuss plans, but the adoption of any consistent line of action amid such turmoil becomes impossible.

True enough the General's room was in a sort of inner sanctuary, reached after passing through several other rooms containing an unnecessary number of soldier-clerks and officials, but on opening the door I soon found that though in a remote corner, it was by no means a sanctuary. In fact it is hardly an exaggeration to say that the sound of the shells bursting in the street outside was drowned by the din within. The first sight that met my gaze was the General himself, not seated quietly with his Staff pondering the problem before him, but standing in the middle of the room with a tall Cossack Lieutenant towering over him and gesticulating with such fury that I really thought he was about to strike him. There is no advantage in mentioning this officer's name, but he was well known to us all as a man of most excitable temperament, and he will doubtless recognize himself if this book ever comes his way.

When the Lieutenant was removed, the General, instead of ordering his arrest, merely said, "Yes, he's a hot-tempered fellow, isn't he?" Truly the Russian temperament is a wonderful mixture of extremes. Frantic excitement instantaneously replaced by placid calm.

Other less furious advisers stood ready to take the Lieutenant's place, the telephone bell rang incessantly, and the General answered most of the calls himself, while on the balcony were gathered Colonel Stokes and other British officers, who found the turmoil of the street noises less disturbing than the clamour of the office.

The object of my visit was firstly to find out how things were going at Russian Head Quarters, and secondly to impress on the General that only by determined counter-attack could the situation be saved. The latter point had naturally been already considered, and after short discussion it appeared that the orders the Chief was about to issue should bring about the desired result, But judging from the half conversations that I overheard as the General spoke on the telephone to some Staff Officer, I entertained small hope of the attack being brought off. The following are examples of the telephonic fragments I overheard. "Why isn't his battalion there?" "I gave the orders two days ago and have since repeated them three times." "Don't you know where that battalion is?" "If he doesn't obey orders he'll have to be placed under arrest."

The result of this visit was to convince me that unless a fresh miracle were added to the already long list, Baku could not be saved, and it was time to consider the preliminary steps for evacuation. I therefore returned to the ships and gave instructions to commence precautionary measures. Commodore Norris, R.N., thereupon took all necessary measures for the preparation of the ships. The *Kursk* and *Abo* were made ready for the sick and wounded, while the *Krüger* was to carry the guns and the greater portion of the fighting men. The latter would number about 1,300, as in addition to the 900 in the firing line, some 400 were employed on town duties, guards, supplies, etc. This last reserve was also to find, in case of a *sauve qui peut* with which we were always threatened, a rallying point and general support amidst the confusion of a fighting retirement. Cotton bales from the wharf were hauled on board and disposed so as to protect the bridge and the more vulnerable parts of the ship against rifle fire. This was all we could do in the way of protection, as no strengthening could help us against the fire of the larger guns from the Baku fleet if, as seemed probable, it turned against us at the last moment.

It was a great boon that so far the telephone lines had not been cut, in spite of the fact that the town was full of enemy agents, and as a matter of fact they remained intact up to the last moment, thereby greatly facilitating movements covering the evacuation.

Detailed orders had been previously issued on the subject of the withdrawal and made known to every man in the force. The final order would now merely require to state the hour at which the withdrawal should commence, and the flank from which it should begin. But even with every possible contingency foreseen, the operation would be attended with very great risks, and the chances of success were not great. To endeavour to extricate troops from the fight is in itself a risky proceeding, and is likely, with an active enemy, to result in disaster. Luckily one might safely say that our enemy was not a very active one. Then, when the news of our intended withdrawal spread round the town, the entire population would regard us as enemies, and my troops would have to fight their way through the streets to the ships. And finally I was convinced that the Government would order their fleet to open fire on us as we left the harbour.

Up till 4 p.m. I considered that a faint ray of hope still remained. It would take so little to defeat an enemy who had been kept at bay for twelve hours after having gained the key of the position. But by that hour the last flicker of hope was extinguished by the news that once more the endeavour to mass troops for the counter-attack had completely failed. So off went the final order to the troops. The retirement to commence from the right at 8 p.m., covered by the left, where the North Staffords would have to hold on for another hour, till 9 p.m.

The sick and wounded from the shore hospital were brought on board the *Kursk* and the *Abo*, and arrangements made for future cases to be run straight on board from the dressing stations. Guards were placed as unostentatiously as possible at important street corners to help the withdrawing troops through in case of pursuit by a mob, and all entrances to the pier were strongly held.

Now remained only a matter of honour and conscience. I had previously notified the Dictators that when I should judge the moment right for departure, I would remove my troops without giving any further warning. I was quite within my rights, therefore, if I acted up to this and slipped away without any notification. But nothing is ever certain in war, and miracles might happen after our departure that would still enable the inhabitants to hold the town if given a fair chance of doing so; and a secret withdrawal, leaving gaps in the most important parts of the line, would not be giving them a fair chance. The Turks were not yet actually in the town; they had once before been seized by panic and fled in the moment of victory, under circumstances very similar to the present, and this might happen again.

On the other hand, it was a foregone conclusion that if I warned the Dictators of my intentions they would turn their own troops and the guns of the fleet on to us. The problem of how to save both my honour and my men was not an easy one to solve.

I finally decided to inform the Dictators of my intentions and to take the chances, rather than leave them with a feeling (unjust but natural) that they had been betrayed by the British. I accordingly dispatched Captain Bray, my Russian A.D.C., with a written communication to the Dictators informing them briefly that I was about to remove my troops. When Captain Bray reached the Government Head Quarters the building was being heavily shelled, and those of the Dictators who were there together with the various Commissaries and Deputies were in such a state of bewilderment that they merely replied verbally, "Do what you please." This was satisfactory so far, but the mood was not to be relied on, and I relaxed none of the precautions.

Up till sunset the battle raged very fiercely, and the whole safety of the withdrawal depended on whether the North Staffords could hold on to the southern ridges till dark.

Nothing could exceed the gallantry of this battalion, which accomplished its mission to the last letter. The whole Brigade worked with unexampled steadiness and precision, and many stories could be told of the heroic lives laid down on this last day of the Baku fighting. Among others a very fine soldier, Major Beresford Havelock, of the North Staffords, grandson of the famous Sir Henry

Havelock of Lucknow, was mortally wounded while leading his men, and continued issuing calm and collected orders with his last breath.

As the sun set the fighting died down, both sides feeling the strain of fourteen hours' unbroken effort. The great advantage of this was that it made the extrication of troops easier, and secondly casualties almost entirely ceased about this hour. The problem of the removal of wounded men in the dark under all these difficulties was a nightmare to me, and I was grateful that the problem thus solved itself.

Soon after dark all the sick and wounded were safely on board the *Kursk* and *Abo*, and the two steamers got under way for Enzeli. Their instructions were to offer no resistance to any serious opposition, to comply with all orders in case of a meeting with the fleet, and to explain that the steamers held the sick and wounded, to the evacuation of whom no objection was likely to be raised. It was fortunate that we were able to get both of these ships away before the suspicions of the town had been aroused. That was not likely to be our case.

By 10 p.m. all troops and guns were on board the *Krüger*. The artillery horses we had been able to hand over to a portion of Bicherakov's detachment, who had room for them in a steamer, in which they were evacuating north to rejoin their Head Quarters at Petrovsk. Nothing now remained but to get on board as much ammunition as possible, and to see that Colonel Rawlinson was ready to follow with his small steamer.

The Arsenal, of which Colonel Rawlinson had been in charge, was within 500 yards of our wharf and had a small pier of its own. During the day he had been engaged in transferring the contents of the Arsenal to barges moored in the harbour, which could be sunk at a moment's notice if necessary. But it was obviously advantageous to take away with us such munitions and

THE WITHDRAWAL

stores as might be likely to be of use to us in a renewal of operations. For this purpose Colonel Rawlinson had commandeered a small steamer, the *Armenian*, of only 200 tons, and had completely filled her with arms, ammunition and explosives. The crew of this ship were mutinous and determined not to sail. It was obvious therefore that if compelled to sail by force they would steer a wrong course, so it was arranged that when I was ready to get the *Krüger* under way I should haul down my three lights from the masts (which had been the guiding signal for any individual soldier who might have got lost in the town), and Colonel Rawlinson, on seeing this, would get his steamer on the move and follow immediately in our wake. This sounds fairly easy, but in the event proved so difficult that it is a wonder that the *Armenian* ever found her way out at all. How it worked out will be told later in Colonel Rawlinson's own words.

Now that all was ready for the start, with the exception of some ammunition which we were still loading on to the *Krüger*, came the event which I had foreseen.

The spirits of the Dictators and the town rose and fell, not as the news from the fighting troops was good or bad, but as the number of shells bursting close to them in the town decreased or increased. The only shells that did not matter were of course those that fell in the town, but it is the habit of towns to think otherwise.

In Baku, when the town was heavily shelled but with trifling casualties, the people wailed, "All is lost"; when the shell fire was concentrated on to the fighting troops, and all might well be truly lost, they cried, "We are saved!"

Now with the cessation of shell fire on the town the spirits of the Dictators rose, and the fighting spirit that had hitherto been so well concealed became rampant. Once more was raised the cry that only came with the lulls in the firing, "We will fight to the death!" Then came the anxious queries, "What are the British doing?" "Why are they deserting us?" and so on, resulting in the dispatch of emissaries to convey orders to me on board the *Krüger*.

Meantime the town also was beginning to take alarm, and had the wharf not been carefully guarded the trouble might have begun. A mounted soldier of the Baku force galloped up to the entrance of the wharf, where he was confronted by the stolid sentry, to whom he shouted out, "What's all this going on here?" "Why are the British deserting us?" "Stop these movements at once," and then galloped off to alarm the town. The gist of his remarks were quite lost on the sentry, to whom I did not think it necessary to translate them.

At this moment the expected delegation from the Government put in its appearance. Two Dictators, Lemlin and Sadovsky, arrived on the wharf and demanded to see the British General on an urgent matter. I took them on board the *Krüger*, seated them in the saloon and inquired their business. The spokesman Sadovsky replied: "I bring you written instructions from the Baku Government to the effect that any attempt at withdrawal on your part will be regarded as treachery and treated as such. If you have removed any of your troops from the firing line you are at once to send them back to their original positions. The Turks are not yet in the town and we mean to continue the fight."

In reply to this demand I stated briefly my point of view in the following words: "Please inform the Baku Government that my present withdrawal is not in any sense a betrayal, as you have had full and ample warning of my intentions. My troops have sustained the fight throughout the day for sixteen hours without relief or any real support from your troops, who have done little of the fighting. Under such circumstances I refuse to sacrifice any more of their lives in a vain cause. As to their returning to their original positions in the firing line, they are physically incapable, after their sixteen hours' fighting, of carrying out that order, and I will give no such order. I sail at once."

On this Sadovsky assumed a fierce and truculent air and said, " Then the fleet will open fire on you and sink your ships," to which I replied, " I hope not," and bowed them off the ship.

A Staff Officer whispered in my ear, " Why not arrest them and take them along ? " a useful suggestion, but I felt we could accomplish what we wanted without introducing any complications, and so I decided against it.

I should be able to sail by 11 p.m.; the gunboats were some distance away. It would take the Dictators some time to get their orders decided on and transmitted to the fleet, and revolutionary fleets do not obey orders with any alacrity. The fleet also did not care much for any Government and were rather friends of ours ; at the last moment they might, and probably would, hesitate to fire on the only troops who had done anything to try and save Baku from the Turks. Moreover, we would leave with all lights out, and the gunboats had no searchlights, as we had borrowed them for use on the front ; we could risk a good deal of fire under such circumstances. The only real danger was the Guardship stationed at the exit of the harbour to check all arrivals and departures. It would be necessary to pass within 500 yards of her, but we would be going dead slow and the night was fortunately dark. If she opened fire she had no large guns on board—certainly nothing larger than a field gun—and the probability of her sinking us was quite small, so the risk was not an undue one.

It was an anxious moment when the clock struck eleven and Commodore Norris gave the order to cast off. The three lights were hauled down from the masts, giving the signal to Colonel Rawlinson that we were off, and the ship silently slipped away from the wharf. Quietly we glided through the calm waters of the harbour, the Captain steering cleverly so as to keep some anchored ship or barge between us and the Guardship.

It is always at such moments of tension that the ridiculous intervenes and brings tragedy very close. The silence of the night was suddenly rent by an excited Russian voice. A sailor rushed on deck exclaiming in accents of despair, " My wife ! My wife ! I've left my wife behind ! Oh, save my wife ! " an appeal that to the sentimental crew was far more urgent than any orders from the Captain of the ship. The engines stopped, down went the anchor with a clang and a rattle, the ship slowly swung round, up came the anchor again and we retraced our course to the wharf where, after some clever manœuvring, the *Krüger* was brought alongside and the lady rescued. All such incidents have just to be put up with when dealing with revolutionary crews. The crew rule the ship, and any interference with them only turns them sulky and defeats its own object.

No particular alarm appeared to have been caused by the rattle of the anchor chains, and the only thing I regretted was the delay and the knowledge that I was making things rather difficult for Colonel Rawlinson, whose orders to " follow the *Krüger* " would become rather difficult to carry out.

On a second attempt to leave the wharf another female voice was raised in supplication, and further delay occurred in getting this second forlorn person on board, and when at last we got away again it was well past midnight.

All went well now till the critical moment when we were dead opposite the Guardship, creeping along behind a row of barges at anchor. At this crisis some clever ill-wisher among the crew turned all the electric lights full on. Now indeed matters would be put to the test!

With the first flash of lights came a signal from the Guardship, "Who are you? Anchor at once." To which we responded with alacrity signifying acquiescence, and went full speed ahead.

It did not take long for the Guardship to realize that we were disobeying orders, and she immediately opened fire with a gun of small calibre. The first shot whizzed over in close proximity to the bridge, where Commodore Norris and Colonel Hoskyn were standing by the Captain. This was too much for the man at the wheel, who incontinently fled, leaving the ship to look after herself. In half a second the Captain, Alexander Ivanovitch Feodorov, had hold of the wheel and kept her on her course. Our speed soon took us into safety, and no shots struck the ship, but from the continuation of the fire I judged that the little *Armenian* had been discovered and was getting the full benefit of the Guardship's attentions. Colonel Rawlinson's predicament in his vessel loaded with explosives under so heavy a fire was as bad as it could be, and I momentarily expected to hear the sound of an explosion, which would mean the fatal termination of his enterprise. No such sound, however, reached our ears as long as we were within hearing distance of the harbour, but there still remained the great risk of so slow-steaming a vessel with a sulky crew falling into the hands of a pursuer, and the chances of his escape seemed very small indeed.

As regards the *Krüger* her risks seemed now at an end. Pursuit was improbable and her speed was only about one knot less than that of the gunboats. When dawn broke on the morning of Sunday, 15th, we were making good way over the smooth surface of the Caspian, and the Baku happenings were already beginning to seem unreal. The ship was crowded and uncomfortable with seventy officers and 800 men on board, but the shortage of food was all there was to worry about.

This was not due to lack of precaution. Dry rations had been kept on board from the beginning, sufficient to feed the largest possible number of troops that the ship could accommodate, but tinned provisions such as bully beef, etc., were not to be procured in Baku, and the provision of fresh meat at the last moment, under the circumstances in which we left, was obviously not possible. But it was sad to see the heroes of yesterday's hard fighting having nothing to regale themselves on but bread, biscuit and tea. If ever men deserved a Lord Mayor's banquet they did. This Brigade, composed entirely of New Army Battalions, had covered itself with glory second to none in the annals of our best fighting regiments. The eight or nine hundred men who had composed the firing line had been in the position for six weeks, and had kept at bay for that period a Turkish army ten times their strength.

It would be idle boasting to pretend that they alone had held the 20 miles of front that constituted the defensive position of Baku; many of the Baku detachments who held the line with them did on occasions very well, and the Baku artillery was quite good. But no one in Baku would argue that anything but those brave lads of the English Midland Brigade kept the Turks out of the town.

The total casualties of this small force in this last fight were 180 killed, wounded and missing of all ranks, or about twenty per cent. of the numbers engaged. The casualties of the Turks opposed to them were certainly very much greater. The result of the day's battle was that the Turks were fought to a standstill, and it was owing to this that the extrication of our troops was so successfully accomplished. It was impossible for any sane person to hope any longer for counter-attack on the part of the Baku troops. Had such an attack been

THE WITHDRAWAL

possible in the early hours of the 15th, the Turk would probably have been finally driven off, but in the certain absence of such effort further delay in evacuation would merely have meant that evacuation would have become impossible, the Turks would still take Baku, and more of these good British lives would have been needlessly sacrificed.

The loss in *matériel* was not great. The two aeroplanes that had taken such an active part in the fight were riddled and had to be destroyed. The armoured cars that had throughout the six weeks' fighting so nobly maintained their reputation for gallant action, and also the thirty Ford cars which had worked like Trojans on transport duties, were left to the Turks, but not in such a condition as to be of much use to them.

As we steamed away from the wharf the only thing left there was the skeleton of the brave little Ford touring car that had carried me through so many difficulties and dangers since we left Baghdad in January.

Towards sunset we caught sight of the familiar outline of the Elburz range as we approached the Persian shore. It was good to know that so large a portion of the force as the *Krüger* contained had been safely brought back to Persia, but my mind was filled with anxious surmises as to the fate of the *Kursk* and the *Abo*, who had preceded us. The first news we got on anchoring in Enzeli harbour was that they had long been in and all the sick and wounded were comfortably housed in the shore hospital. The only remaining anxiety now was the *Armenian*, and as the hours slipped by with no signs of her, I despaired of her ever being seen again. But to our great delight, just twelve hours after our arrival, the brave little vessel steamed into port and came to anchor, reporting "All's well." She had had six direct hits from shells, but none below the water-line. The following is an extract from Colonel Rawlinson's report :

"... I made certain preparations on the night of September 14th to endeavour to get the *Armenian* away from the Arsenal quay with such munitions as might be of service to the enemy and would be of use to Dunsterforce, in the event of its becoming necessary to evacuate the town.

"I received notice that this decision had been taken at 4 p.m.

"On proceeding on board the ship there was at once apparent a hostile attitude amongst the crew numbering twenty-six, who refused to work and generally obstructed the proceedings. The pier was becoming congested with nervous townspeople and runaway soldiers from the firing line spreading rumours of disaster. Under these circumstances I got my two A.S.C. drivers and my batman and Captain Jackson under arms, and was able with fixed bayonets to clear the pier and posted them to hold the shore end, whilst I reported to the *Krüger* and asked for a picket. This was duly sent, and consisted of four men of the Hampshire Regiment.

"On my return I found a Commissar, who stated that he came by order of the Government to prevent the ship leaving and to give notice that we should be fired on by the gunboats if we attempted to pass. He likewise trumped up a demand for one of the guns on board (reported to me as unserviceable) to be sent to the front. I took him into the cabin, from which he at once attempted to bolt, with the obvious intention of communicating with the shore. I therefore placed a sentry at the door and made him prisoner, and proceeded with my preparations with all speed. In the meanwhile the picquet was holding the shore end successfully.

"Soon after dusk arrived a second Commissar (whom I know personally) with the same orders as the other, and he assured me it would be impossible to pass the gunboats, but that he would get me a pass to do so and

AFTER THE EVACUATION THE 39th INFANTRY BRIGADE AT ENZELI

THE WITHDRAWAL

that he would send for his wife and family and come also. I agreed at once, and having passed a quantity of his relations on to the ship, I proceeded to the *Krüger* to report, returning with the instructions that as soon as she lowered her three lights I was to get out at once, as she would then be coming out herself.

" On return to the Arsenal pier I found things very nasty-looking, and at once withdrew the picquet and swept all those who were crowding round the gangway on to the ship at the point of the bayonet, at the same time giving instructions to cast off and to draw out to anchor.

" Driver Norris and Private Parsons, by their courageous attitude in the face of large numbers, were of the greatest assistance in the operations of clearing the pier and gangway, and all attempts on the part of many people to leave the ship and give notice of our departure to the town were resisted at the point of the bayonet, and we left the pier at 11.30 p.m.

" It was my intention to anchor close by and to await the *Krüger*, but there had been foul play with the cable, and on letting go it snapped, and the anchor was lost. Owing to the necessity of keeping steerage way in the crowded anchorage, the boat was a long way out before I could get her turned, and the *Krüger's* three lights had been hauled down. The *Kursk* passed me, going in a direction opposite to where I conceived the entrance to be, and I concluded she was proceeding to a prearranged anchorage to await the *Krüger*, and I held on to the *Krüger's* pier, where I found her and spoke her and was then told she was coming out and that I should follow as closely as possible.

" In spite of this she rapidly left us, and it was evident we were not getting steam. However, I stood by the Captain on the bridge with my revolver drawn and repeatedly impressed upon him the danger of any underhand work on his part. So that when the Guardship signalled us to stop and he replied that " he was turning to starboard," I was successful in prevailing upon him to hold his course and to ignore the fire to which we were at this time subjected. It was at this juncture that Mr. Dana repaired to the engine-room with his revolver, with immediate and marked success and speed increased.

"The Guardship now opened fire with her small gun, and on several shots striking the bridge in the proximity of the explosives, it proved too much for the Captain, who deliberately tried to pass me and leave his post, and was only retained by force, from which time onwards my pistol was always in his view, and I called our four men on to the bridge with their arms, and we proceeded on our course. The next incident was the arrival of the spokesman of the Ship's Committee to announce that the crew would not allow the ship to be taken out. He was promptly made prisoner on the bridge, and we proceeded.

"I subsequently intimated to the crew that I would give them a reward on arrival at Enzeli, and that if they would not accept that offer we would fight them at once.

"As the spokesman of the crew was in my hands and would have been the first to take part in the proposed fight from a very bad starting position, he placed the proposal before them in such an inviting manner that it was at once accepted and we had no further trouble."

The final scene in this drama was the arrival of a deputation from the revolutionary sailors of the *Kursk*, who presented a written petition in the following terms:

"We, the Committee and the crew of the S.S. *Kursk* have witnessed with intense admiration the heroic conduct of your brave British soldiers in the defence of Baku.

We have seen them suffering wounds and death bravely in defence of our town, which our own people were too feeble to defend. It is wonderful to us that these fine fellows from that distant island in the North Sea should have come all this way to the Caspian and have given up their lives there in the cause of honour and glory.

"We are so much impressed by their bearing and valour and by the whole episode of the British endeavours to save Baku from the Turks, that we wish to be at once taken over as a body and granted British nationality."

A finer testimony than this it would be hard to conceive, and a New Army Brigade that could evoke a feeling of that sort in the minds of the Baku sailors has indeed something to be proud of.

The only task now left was to call the roll, and assure myself that not a single man had been left behind in Baku.

I felt certain that all had been brought away, and was therefore dismayed to find that Major Suttor and Sergeant Buller, of the Australian Contingent, were missing, and also the infantry guard of one N.C.O. and six men posted at the aerodrome. In neither of these cases did I feel that the careful arrangements made by my Staff were at fault, but it was not easy entirely to exonerate oneself, and it was therefore very gratifying to hear shortly of the safety of both these parties. Major Suttor and Sergeant Buller escaped with the town refugees to Krasnovodsk, and the guard joined up with Bicherakov's men and sailed with them to Petrovsk.

Orders were now received for the dispersal of the Force, and their place has since been taken by regular troops from the 14th Division.

So ends the story of the adventures of Dunsterforce.

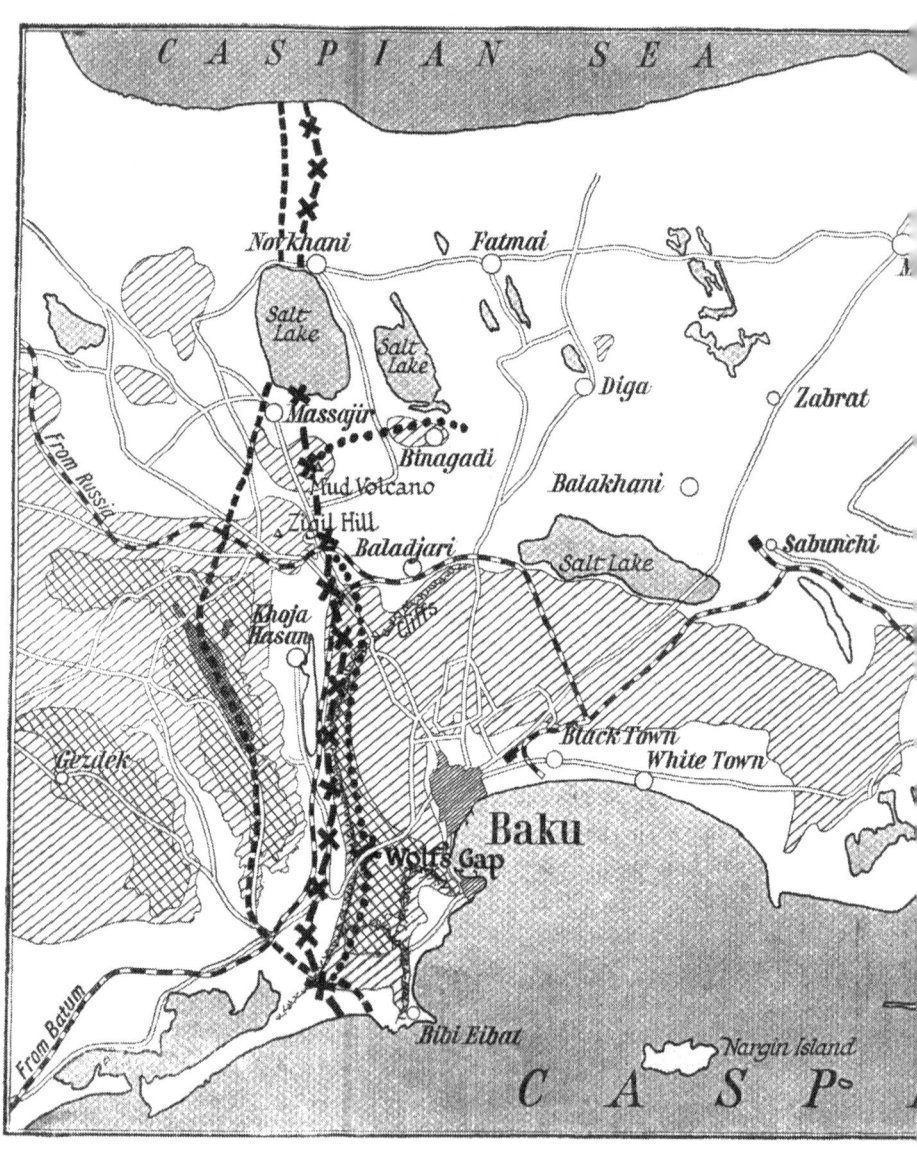

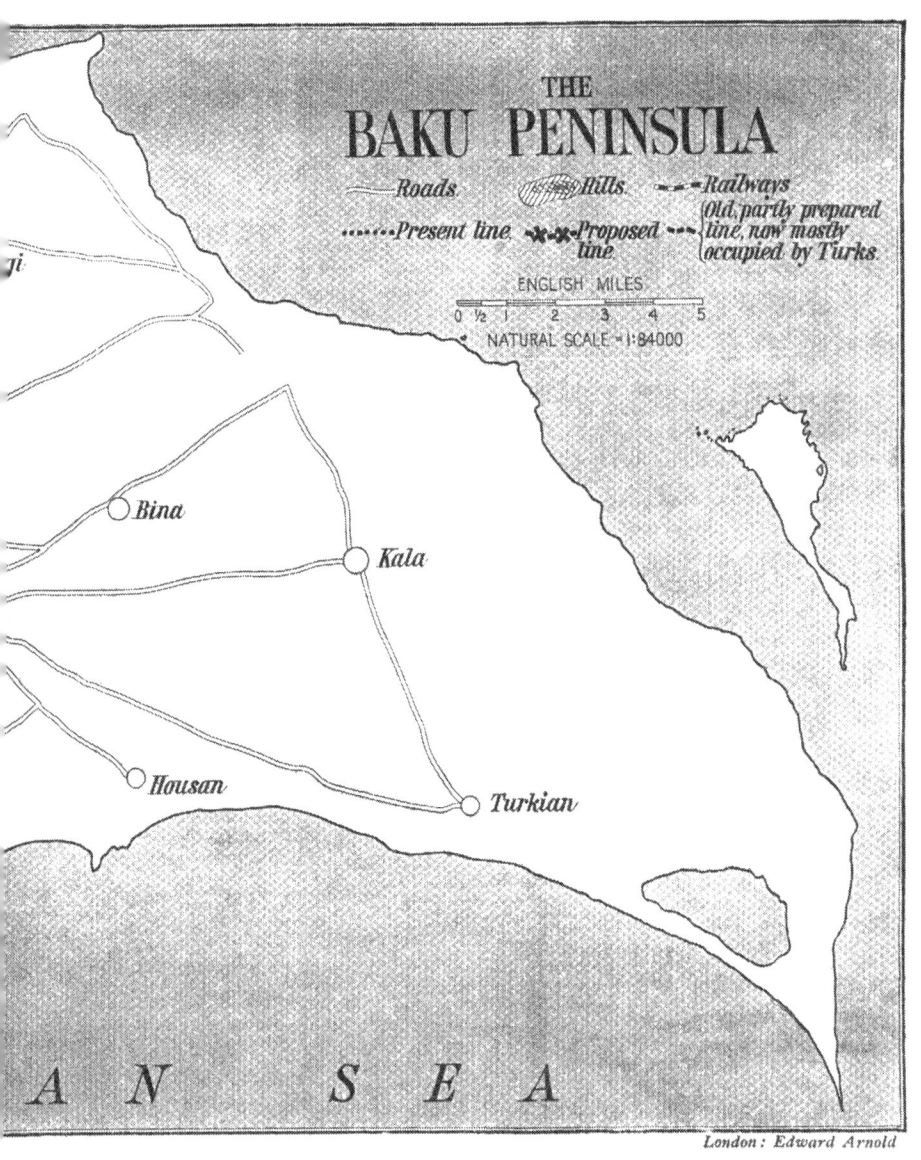

INDEX

Abo, s.s., 210, 227, 253, 263, 303, 304, 313
Aerodromes, 142
Aeroplane observations, 293
Aeroplanes, 142
Aga Petros, 179, 188
Akbar, Lieutenant, 82
d'Albizzi, Marquis, 291
Aldham, Captain, 16
Alexandropol, 188
Alkhavi, Lieutenant, 169
Alyat, 167, 186, 196
Amazasp, Colonel, 261
American Mission, Karind, 20; Kermanshah, 21; Hamadan, 26, 55, 63, 103, 137; Kasvin, 141
Amir Afgham, 89, 90
Amir Afshar, 131
Annett, Captain, 16
Araratiantz, Dr., 214
Aras River, 168, 220
Aratunov, Colonel, 257, 261
Ardebil, 187
Armenian, s.s., 307, 311, 313
Armenian National Council, 115, 214, 232, 255, 276, 277
Armenian soldiers, fighting value of, 236, 261
Armenian troops, 2, 3, 4
Armenians, political complexion, 118
Armoured car, M.G. Squadron, 295
Armoured cars, 156, 291
Arsenal, 306
Artillery, 8th Battery, R.F.A., 156
Asadabad, 23
Asadabad Pass, 58
A.S.C. (M.T.), No. 730 Co., 268
Askhabad, 178

Assembling of mission, 9
Assyrians, 179
Astara, 187, 220
Astrakhan, 7, 8, 208, 233
Austrian instructors, 29
Austrian officers, 79
Austrian prisoners, 134, 140, 187
Aveh, 26, 55
Avetisof, Colonel, 232
Azerbaijan, 187

Babookh, "Comrade," 169, 171, 209
Baghdad, capture of, 1, 2
Baku, importance to enemy, 140
Baladjari, 199, 229, 264, 265, 267, 295, 298
Balakhani, 227
Baratov, General, 25, 61, 63, 70, 71, 72, 73, 81, 206
Barttelot, Major Sir Walter, 12, 15
Basra, 11
Bateman-Champain, Brig.-General, 256
Battine, Colonel, 178, 260
Beg Surab, Colonel, 295
Berlin-Baghdad railway, 1
Bibi Eibat, 226, 227, 229, 294
Bicherakov, Colonel, C.B., D.S.O., 21, 61, 79, 83, 121, 122, 143, 155, 196 *seq.*, 250
Bijar, 116, 120, 127, 130, 185
Bikandi, 51
Binagadi, 227, 229, 266, 267, 272
Bisharat-es-Sultaneh, 148
Bisitun, 22
Black Town, 227
Bogratuni, General, 232, 280, 296
Bokhara, 1
Bollington, Captain, 294

INDEX

Bray, Captain, 145, 195, 276, 305
Browne, Major, 204, 209
Brunskill, Major, 16, 148
Buinak, 31
Buller, Sergeant, 317
Byron, Brig.-General, 62, 81, 109, 137, 141

Campbell, Captain, 16, 113
Cannibalism, 124
Caspian fleet, 233, 234
Caspian Sea, commercial importance of, 2, 8; Russian fleet on, 8
Caucasus, North, political complexion, 123; Southern, 1, 2; political complexion of, 4, 123
Centro-Caspia, *see* Dictators, *passim*, 210, 212, 216
Chardigny, Colonel, 83, 126, 260
Cheliapin, "Comrade," 39, 42, 47, 48, 49, 50, 54, 166, 168, 169, 170, 186, 190, 205, 206, 209, 240
Clarke, Mr., 245
Clutterbuck, Lieut.-Colonel, 22, 157, 276
Cockerell, Captain, 148, 150, 184, 244
Cossacks, first meeting with, 21; political complexion, 118
Cost of living, 144
Counter-proclamations, 65
Craig, Lieutenant, 266
Crawford, Colonel, 225, 245
Currency, 241

Daghestan, political complexion, 118
Dana, Mr., 260, 316
Darnagul salt lake, 295
Daylight saving, 176
Dayrell, Major, 272, 295
Derbend, 250, 251, 252
Derbyshire, Captain, 157
Dictators, *see* Centro-Caspia, *passim*
Dictators, 231, 233, 234, 252, 255, 273, 277, 279, 293, 296, 304
Diga, 266, 272
Donnan, Colonel, 177
Donohoe, Captain, 81
Dukuchaiev, General, 232, 276, 282, 296, 299

Duncan, Lieut.-Colonel, A.Q.M.G., 16, 24, 106, 229, 244
Dunning, Captain, A.D.C., 16, 87
Dunsterforce, official name, 65
Durnford, Captain, 164

Elburz Range, 8, 27, 134, 220
Engledue, Major, 128, 129, 273, 295
Enzeli, 7; held by Bolsheviks, 14, 15, 28
Evacuation of Russian troops, 31, 32, 70, 75, 85
Evacuation of sick, 303, 304
Eve, Captain, 81

Famine, signs of, 20, 62; causes of, 102
Famine relief, 80, 104 *seq.*; apathy of notables, 107; success of, 108, 113
Faviell, Lieut.-Colonel, 182, 230, 296, 300
Feodorov, Alexander Ivanovitch, 311
Ferid-ud-Dowleh, 97, 177, 184
Firman-Firma, 135
Fleet, Caspian, 233, 234
Fleet, Russian, on Caspian Sea, 8
Foxlee, Captain, 293
French officers, 83
Funk, Mrs., 137

Garmakov, "Comrade," 280
Geldakh, 168, 196
Georgian troops, 3, 4
Georgians, political complexion, 118
Georgiev, Lieutenant, 23
German agents, 57, 59, 60, 66, 122, 125
Gilanis, hostility of, 13, 14
Gloucestershire Regiment, 7th Service Battalion, 182
Goldsmith, Captain G., 12, 15, 25, 47, 61, 126
Goodwin, Mr., 26, 53
Grigorievitch, Mr., 36
Gulistan of Sa'adi, 91
Gurkhas, 1/2nd, 155, 166, 171, 202
Gurland, Captain, 221

INDEX

Hamadan, 13, 15, 24; ancient Ecbatana, situation, 55; commercial importance, 57; political complexion, 60; change of feeling, 65
Hampshire Regt., 1/4th, 17, 18, 82, 119, 156, 164, 166, 202, 208
Harris, Sergeant, 58
Harunabad, 17, 20
Haslam, Major, 178, 261
Havelock, Major Beresford, 305
Hay, Major, 116, 133
Henderson, Captain, 128
Hooper, Captain, 16, 114, 115, 135
Hoskyn, Lieut.-Colonel J., 148, 229, 311
Hôtel d'Europe, 228, 257, 258, 259, 279
Hôtel Métropole, 228, 258
Hunin, M., 37
Hush-Hush Army, 66
Hussars, 14th, 113, 116, 156, 157, 163

Ignati, s.s., 234
Ihtidar-ul-Mulk, 147
Imamzadeh, Hashim, 35, 164, 171
Imperial Bank of Persia, Hamadan, 25, 103, 178; Kasvin, 26, 78; Kermanshah, 21; Resht, 36, 78
Infantry Brigade, 39th, 182, 200, 214, 216, 296
Intercepted correspondence, 99
Irregulars, Persian, 79, 127; Kurdish, 127; native, 189

Jackson, Captain, 16, 314
Jangali movement, 27, 28, 59; opposition, 67; attack on Resht, 201
Jangalis, 76, 121, 137
Jilus, 125, 179, 180
John, Captain, 16, 105
Julfa, 58

Kangavar, 23
Kar-guzar, 62, 89, 147
Karind, 20

Kasma, 165, 171
Kasvin, 133; description of, 142
Kasvin, importance of, 26; unfriendly attitude of, 27, 52; intended attack by Jangalis, 76, 78
Kazarov, Colonel, 265, 295
Kazian, 28; arrival at, 36
Kazian Soviet, 39; meeting with, 42
Kennion, Colonel, 22, 124
Kennion, Mrs., 22
Kermanshah, 15, 21, 195; American Mission, 21; Russian wireless station, 22
Keyworth, Colonel, 138, 209, 222, 228, 230, 256, 296, 299
Khanikin, 13, 16, 195
Khoja Hasan, 295
Kifri, 125
Kirkuk, 125
Krasnovodsk, 178, 179, 187, 251, 260
Kuchik Khan, 14, 251; hostility of, 27, 28; parleys with, 156; sues for peace, 204
Kuflan Kuh, 257
Kuhn, Mr., 178, 179
Kura River, 168, 196
Kurds, hostility of, 13; road guards, 19
Kursk, s.s., 210, 218, 227, 239, 253, 263, 303, 304, 313
Kuzmin, Colonel, 179

Lake Urumiah, 117, 125
Landing grounds, 142
Lastochkin, General, 61
Lazarev, "Comrade," 168, 209
Lemlin, "Dictator," 233, 308
Lenkoran, 221, 225, 232, 251, 260, 292
Levies, Persian, 79, 116; Kurdish, 124; Persian, 124, 126, 189, 195
Lewin, Brig.-General, 279
Lewis gun, 16
Ley, Major, D.S.O., 266, 296, 299
Locker-Lampson's armoured cars 167

Macarthy, Major, 129, 195
Macbeth, Lieutenant, 267
MacDonnell, Mr., 115
Mahi-Dasht, 21
Malleson, General, 178, 179, 260
Marling, Sir Charles, 26, 181
Masazir salt lake, 229
Matthews, Lieut.-Colonel, 165, 166, 201, 203
McCleverty, Captain, 203
McDonnell, Major, 280
McDowell, Mr., 25, 86
McLaren, Mr., 36, 137, 157, 172; a prisoner, 78
McMurray, Mr., 25, 72, 93, 113, 178
Medem, Colonel Baron, 71
Menjil, 7, 31, 33, 51; fortified by Jangalis, 78; Battle of, 158 *seq.*
Merv, 178
Meshed, 178, 260
Mianeh-Zinjan road threatened, 116
Mianeh, 185, 188
Midhat-es-Sultaneh, 147
Moir, Mr., 97, 172, 203
Mosul, 188
Mud Volcano, 229, 256, 261, 264, 265, 266, 268
Mughan Steppe, 220, 260

Nagober, 35
Narghin island, 226
Naval ratings, 211
Newcome, Major, 157, 240, 258
Nizam-es-Sultan, 86, 87, 89
Noel, Captain, 78, 137, 156, 157, 201, 220, 255, 256, 260
Novkhany, 266
Norris, Commodore, 212, 233, 251, 303, 309, 311
Norris, Driver, R.F.A., 315
North Staffordshire Regiment, 7th Service Battalion, 182, 222, 223, 229, 230, 231, 255, 265 *seq.*, 294, 295, 296, 298, 305

Oakshot, Mr., 36, 78, 137, 157
Offley-Shore, General, 25
Osborne, Captain, 183

Pai-Taq, 17
"Partisans," 21, 22
Pennington, Lieutenant, 188
Petrol, supply of, 49, 63, 170
Petrov, "Comrade," 207, 223, 224, 225, 226, 244, 245, 254
Pike, Colonel, 26, 47, 61, 126, 261
Pike, Private, A.S.C., 37
Poidebard, Lieutenant, 83
Pope, Captain, 113, 157, 163
Parsons, Private, 315
President Krüger, s.s., 210, 226, 227, 232, 252, 253, 263, 297, 303, 307
Proclamations, 64
Profiteering, 249
Pulverman, Major, 293

Qasr-i-Shirin, 195

Rais-i-Telefon, 145, 146, 148, 150, 151, 152
Rawlinson, Lieut.-Colonel, R.F.A., 179, 254, 260, 292, 306
Red Guards, 54
Resht, capital of Gilan, 28, 164; political complexion, 184; Battle of, 201 *seq.*
R.F.A., 8th Battery, 255
Road Company, 207
Road-guards, Kurdish, 124
Rouble notes, 241
Routledge, Sergeant, 16
Rowlandson, Major, 25, 157, 260
Royal Navy, 211
Royal Warwickshire Regt., 9th Service Battalion, 182, 230, 255, 267, 272, 295, 298, 300
Rule of the road, 176
Russian battle-line, 2, 5, 6
Russian fleet on Caspian Sea, 8
Russian officers in Turkish army, 168
Russian officers with mission, 10
Russo-British Volunteer Corps, 71
Ruz, Dunsterforce camp at, 65

Saad-es-Sultaneh, 62, 87, 111
Sadovsky, "Dictator," 233, 308
Sahneh Pass, 23
Sain Kaleh, 189

INDEX

Sakiz, 130
Salt lake, Masazir, 229
Sauj-Bulaq, 117, 180, 189
Saunders, Captain, G.S.O., 16, 42, 43, 45, 48, 60, 87, 93, 97, 117, 147, 151, 244
Searight, Captain, 204, 244
Sefid Rud, 33
Shabli Pass, 182, 188
Shahsavens, 131, 189
Shaumian, Bolshevik leader, 115; "Comrade," 207, 226, 244, 245, 254
Sheverin, 61, 75
Singer, Lieutenant, 15, 27, 35
Sinjabis, 125
Sinneh, Turkish Consul at, 98, 120, 131
Sipah-Salar, 133, 135
Snowstorms, 13, 18, 24, 52, 57
Sovlaief, Lieutenant, 143, 145, 146, 148
Sparrow, Captain, 265
Starnes, Major, 116, 127, 130, 131, 179, 189
Stepanov, Captain, 221
Stokes, Lieut.-Colonel, 122, 126, 156, 157, 208, 232, 276, 296
Stork, Captain, 16
Sultanabad, 116
Sultan Bulaq Pass, 26, 31, 55, 82, 135
Supplies, 61, 62, 76, 94, 114
Surakhani, 295
Surkh-a-Disa, 18, 19, 20
Suttor, Major, 317

Tabriz, 58, 117; attack on, 125
Taq-i-Giri Pass, 7, 17
Teheran, visit to, 117, 133
Tiflis, 2, 3; political complexion of, 4
Topham, Captain, 117
Trebizond, 232

Urumiah, 179, 180
Usbeg, s.s., 252

Vandenberg, Major, 254
Ventur, s.s., 234
von der Floss, General, 232
von Passchen, 29, 160, 161, 162, 201, 202, 203

Wagstaff, Major, 117, 127, 131, 189
Warden, Lieut.-Colonel, 148, 223, 253
Watson, Sergeant, 16, 58
Wheat, prices of, 124, 144
White House, 295
White Town, 227
Whitmarsh, Major, 178, 243
Wolf's Gap, 231, 294, 295, 300
Worcestershire Regt., 9th Service Battalion, 182, 230, 255, 266, 298, 300

Yarmakov, "Dictator," 233

Zageh, 24
Zemski Soyuz, 74
Zinjan, 117, 127, 131, 185
Zypalov, Lieutenant, 24

Printed in Great Britain by
UNWIN BROTHERS, LIMITED
WOKING AND LONDON

www.ingramcontent.com/pod-product-compliance
Lightning Source LLC
Chambersburg PA
CBHW031131160426
43193CB00008B/107